CENTRAL-LOCAL RELATIONS IN ASIAN CONSTITUTIONAL SYSTEMS

This book examines territorial governance in Asia in the context of central-local relations. In an era of attempts to deal with issues such as decentralisation, conflict involving ethnic and religious enclaves, and demands for regional autonomy, it is timely to examine central-local relations from a pan-Asian perspective, assessing the attempts in a range of different systems, federal and unitary, to re-order constitutional structures for territorial governance, including local government. The book looks at the constitutional systems for organising central-local relations of this kind, and attempts to draw conclusions from contemporary experiences.

Central-local Relations in Asian Constitutional Systems

Andrew Harding and Mark Sidel

·HART·
PUBLISHING
OXFORD AND PORTLAND, OREGON
2018

Hart Publishing
An imprint of Bloomsbury Publishing Plc

Hart Publishing Ltd
Kemp House
Chawley Park
Cumnor Hill
Oxford OX2 9PH
UK

Bloomsbury Publishing Plc
50 Bedford Square
London
WC1B 3DP
UK

www.hartpub.co.uk
www.bloomsbury.com

Published in North America (US and Canada) by
Hart Publishing
c/o International Specialized Book Services
920 NE 58th Avenue, Suite 300
Portland, OR 97213-3786
USA

www.isbs.com

First published in hardback, 2015
Paperback edition, 2018

British Library Cataloguing-in-Publication Data
A catalogue record for this book is available from the British Library.

ISBN: PB: 978-1-50992-107-2
HB: 978-1-84946-640-0

Typeset by Compuscript Ltd, Shannon

Preface

This book examines territorial governance in Asia in the context of central-local relations, and the impact of constitutions, constitution-making, and constitutional practice and politics on those issues of territorial governance within a number of states in North-East and South-East Asia. In their excellent book[1] on constitutionalism in Eastern and Southern Africa, Hatchard, Ndulo and Slinn offer us a perspective on the issue of devolution of power to local communities that is entirely applicable, in our view, to the countries studied in this book:

> In answer to the demands for greater self-determination and influence in decision-making, many countries worldwide are devolving political, fiscal, and administrative powers to sub-national tiers of government. This trend can be seen in countries with a long tradition of centralist government, as well as in federalist systems, and in developing as well as industrialised countries.[2]

They also point out that the independence constitutions of these African states 'did not provide for elected governments accessible to the people at the local level'. Central-local relations have indeed been neglected to a large extent in constitution-making in Asia, as well as in Africa. Therefore, attempts to devolve power and entrench that devolved power constitutionally, to guarantee local autonomy and police the boundaries of power, are fraught with constitutional obstacles. As nations throughout Asia seek to deal with such complex and conflict-laden issues as decentralisation in the interests of efficiency and accountability, the creation of ethnic and religious enclaves, and responding to demands for regional autonomy, it is timely to examine central-local relations from an Asian perspective, assessing the attempts to re-order constitutional structures for effective and accountable territorial governance and local government.

This book will look at the constitutional systems for organising central-local relations, and attempt to draw conclusions from contemporary experiences in Asia. In the introductory essay by the editors, we draw together some of the many strands discussed in the chapters of this book and in the dialogue between the chapter authors and other participants at a workshop organised by the Centre for Asian Legal Studies at the National University

[1] J Hatchard, M Ndulo and P Slinn, *Comparative Constitutionalism and Good Governance in the Commonwealth: An Eastern and Southern African Perspective* (Cambridge, Cambridge University Press, 2004).

[2] Ibid, 184.

of Singapore in Singapore in July 2013.[3] The introductory essay will provide some theoretical structure for the ensuing chapters, and draw some lessons for constitutional theory arising from the Asian examples discussed in this volume.

At the same time, Hatchard, Ndulo and Slinn' s warning, 'What framework the devolution of power takes in individual states depends on the political and economic conditions that prevail',[4] is also borne in mind. Local context is crucial in this theme, as both the introductory essay and the authors' chapters clearly show. One obvious point to note at the outset is that all of the nations discussed here are unitary states. This largely precludes discussion of federalism, except in so far as federalism might come into debates as a possible reform issue, as it has in Myanmar. We therefore necessarily concentrate on central-local relations within the assumption of a unitary state, generally not analysing issues of sovereignty or of international law. A marginal exception here is Malaysia; however, Andrew Harding's chapter on that country (chapter eight) discusses local government as an aspect of the federal system, rather than federalism as such in central-local relations. Having said this, it is of course also true that many of the issues that arise in federal systems are also discussed here, such as constitutional design, division of powers and revenue, and modes of dispute resolution.

We take this opportunity to thank the Centre for Asian Legal Studies for funding, and Regana Mydin for organising, the workshop in Singapore; the various participants in the workshop for their helpful insights; Benjamin L Berger and Gregoire Webber for their highly insightful and helpful comments on the draft manuscript as well as their encouragement; and the staff of Hart Publishing for their careful and highly professional attention to the production of this book.

Andrew Harding and Mark Sidel

[3] Ch 4 on Vietnam, by Bui Ngoc Son, was completed after the workshop.
[4] Hatchard, Ndulo and Slinn, above n 1, 185.

Summary Contents

Contents

List of Contributors

Simon Butt is Associate Professor of Law and Associate Director of the Centre for Asian and Pacific Law at the University of Sydney.

Melissa Crouch is Lecturer of the Law Faculty, University of New South Wales, Australia.

Andrew Harding is Professor of Law and Director of the Centre for Asian Legal Studies and of the Asian Law Institute at the National University of Singapore.

Shigenori Matsui is Professor of Law, Director, Japanese Legal Studies, and Acting Director, Korean Legal Studies, at the Allard School of Law at the University of British Columbia.

Mark Sidel is Doyle-Bascom Professor of Law and Public Affairs at the University of Wisconsin-Madison and Consultant for Asia at the International Center for Not-for-Profit Law (ICNL).

Bui Ngoc Son is a Research Fellow at the Centre for Asian Legal Studies, National University of Singapore Faculty of Law.

Jiunn-rong Yeh is University Chair Professor at the National Taiwan University College of Law and Director of the Policy and Law Center for Environmental Sustainability at the College of Law.

Zhang Qianfan is Professor of Constitutional Law at Peking University and Vice President of the Chinese Constitutional Law Research Association.

Table of Cases

Table of Cases

[illegible] Case (2006) [illegible]

Indonesia

Supreme Court Decision No. [illegible]
Supreme Court Decision No. [illegible]
Supreme Court Decision No. 12 P/HUM/2012 [illegible]
Supreme Court Decision No. [illegible] P/HUM/2007 [illegible]
Supreme Court Decision No. [illegible] P/HUM/2011 [illegible]
Supreme Court Decision No. [illegible] P/HUM/2004 [illegible]

Malaysia

Government of the State of Penang & Another v [illegible]
Government of Malaysia & Anor (2014) [illegible]
[illegible] Journal [illegible]

Taiwan

Judicial Yuan [illegible] (Judicial Legislation Case) [illegible]
Interpretation No. [illegible] (Judicial [illegible] Cases) [illegible]
Interpretation No. 2[illegible] (Constitutional [illegible] Case) [illegible]

United States

Marbury v Madison 5 US 137 (1803) [illegible]

Table of Legislation

China

Japan

Malaysia

Myanmar/Burma

Indonesia

Taiwan

1

Analysing Central-local Relations in Asian Constitutional Systems

Decentralising Power in 21st-Century Asia

ANDREW HARDING AND MARK SIDEL

DECENTRALISATION

DECENTRALISATION IS A development that has been implemented in various places across the globe over some decades, especially since the early 1990s. It is a function of modern states that in the search for national identity and common citizenship, in the attempt to reach all areas and peripheries, and in the increase of state power more generally, they have deprived local communities of the ability to make their own decisions. Indeed for some states, such Supomo's 'integralist' Indonesian state,[1] or Mao's communist/collectivist China or, like China, the single party state of Vietnam, the idea of local self-government would be anathema: the only proper role for local government would be to implement faithfully decisions reached centrally. The Asian developmentalist states of the post-war era did not in general embrace a constitutionalist form of local government in which autonomy could be exercised and local initiative and competitive desire released. Japan may be an exception to this in some respects.[2]

However, since the early 1990s in particular, it has become quite common for states to decentralise both decision-making and service delivery. This trend has not been an isolated one but has gone hand-in-hand with democratisation, good-governance reform, privatisation and the reform of the structures of public administration in the search for more equalised development and cost-effective government.[3] This has occurred even in Asia,

[1] T Lindsey, 'Indonesia: Devaluing Asian values, rewriting the rule of law' in T Lindsey (ed), *Law Reform in Transitional and Developing States* (Abingdon, Routledge, 2007) ch 9.

[2] See ch 7 by Shigenori Matsui.

[3] D Oluwu, 'Democratic decentralization and multi-level governance in developing countries' in A Munsch (ed), *Decentralisation and Legitimacy, Aladin Yearbook, 2001/2* (Leiden, Association for Law and Administration in Developing and Transitional Countries, 2003) ch 1, 9–10.

with its predominance of unitary states and dominant-party or one-party political systems. In Europe, it is worth noting, the dominant paradigm historically is that local government existed before national government and survived its establishment, contributing to the establishment of central government. In Asia, however, a dominant paradigm in recent times has been a deliberate decentralisation of power from a powerful or imperial centre that has strongly asserted control over its peripheries.

States in Asia have decentralised in pursuit of a number of different purposes. One is to galvanise local initiative and encourage policy development, for example to draw foreign investment or to find better ways of achieving environmental sustainability. Decentralisation has also served to resolve tensions between different ethnic, religious or language groups, or between political parties (often parties represent such groups), by giving them some measure of control over their own futures, especially in the case of minority groups. For this reason, within Indonesia for example, Aceh has been given special autonomy in the form of control over its natural resources and its power to implement *shari'a* law.[4] This aspect of decentralisation is discussed in the next section.

At the same time decentralisation has not always been easy to implement.[5] This has been because of its association with democratic development, which can create tensions between the centre and the locality; or because it affords more opportunities for corruption; or because it is simply difficult to develop the new models for central-local relations that are required, and that can also be complex and confusing to administer even when correctly identified. Shigenori Matsui's chapter on Japan (chapter seven) reveals that, even in a state with stable central-local relations such as Japan, confusion and mismanagement can arise when an emergency situation challenges the normal condition of such relations, giving rise in turn to fresh examination of those relations. All this points to a need for intelligence and clarity in the design of central-local relations, and to a need to constitutionalise these relations and the mechanisms that are needed to conduct them. There has to be an effective relationship between the political, fiscal and administrative aspects of central-local relations if the enterprise of local self-government is to work.

From the studies in this book it would appear that all the states in question have decentralised, but at the same time all have problems with central-local relations. Vietnam symbolises one side of this problem, through what Bui Ngoc Son calls its Constitution's 'Delphic provisions, which both stipulate political decentralisation and insist on central control over local

[4] See ch 5 by Simon Butt.

[5] D Rondinelli, 'Government decentralization in comparative perspective' (1981) 47(2) *International Review of Administrative Sciences* 133.

government'.[6] The authors in this volume appear to think that decentralisation, or more decentralisation, is a desirable outcome, or else is a desirable reform for the various states they discuss. One possible outlier here is Shigenori Matsui's discussion of central-local relations in Japan in chapter seven, but his topic is central-local relations in situations of extreme emergency, following the great earthquake and tsunami of 2010 and the Fukushima nuclear incident. In these circumstances he finds that the centre had insufficient power to control and direct the actions of local government. However, he also finds that insufficient autonomy was afforded to local authorities in their engagement with the recovery and rehabilitation process following the emergency. This position is not in fact necessarily inconsistent with advocating more decentralisation in general. Indeed, the author finds that Japan's government system is too centralised. His chapter is, however, a reminder that there must always be reserve powers to deal with some kinds of accident and natural disaster, and this can be extended to insurgency, breakdowns of law and order, and even constitutional breakdown or inability to discharge financial obligations or statutory duties. Central-local relations need to embrace issues of high constitutional import.

Where the policy of decentralisation has been pursued, one might well also ask whether this is simply a result of democratisation, or is rather an attempt to retain control over local decision-making and thereby re-establish central authority in place of power in changed political conditions. It appears from the contributions to this book that, whatever the cause, decentralisation does in general lead to increased local political participation.[7] Nonetheless, the relevant factors in these states in terms of the context of decentralisation could hardly differ more: Myanmar is emerging from half a century of military dictatorship and is threatened by ethnic divisions; China has decentralised but faces problems of legislative conflicts, effective dispute resolution, corruption and democratic deficit; Indonesia presents much the same kind of picture, having decentralised as part of *reformasi* from 1998 in order to by-pass separatism and deepen democratic reforms, but again we find legislative conflicts, confusion and the lack of an effective regulatory mechanism; Vietnam has undertaken some cautious and limited political decentralisation through a recent constitutional revision, following on from earlier forms of fiscal and administrative decentralisation, but that process is just beginning; Taiwan is a stable state with a history of authoritarian government, but it has developed a complex system of local government during the period of multi-party democracy since the mid-1980s: its problems lie in the area of dispute resolution and the role of the judiciary; Malaysia is

[6] Ch 4, 'Introduction'.

[7] R Crook and J Manor, *Democracy and Decentralisation in South Asia and West Africa* (Cambridge, Cambridge University Press, 1998).

the sole federal system considered here, and under authoritarian government since 1970 has, overall, centralised rather than decentralised, so that federalism, as well as local government, searches for a new role and relevant forms of accountability in an emerging two-party system.[8] These problems are examined here via the ongoing debate about local government elections.

One clearly successful example of decentralisation in Asia is the Philippines, which in 1991, under the Local Government Code, embarked on ambitious plan to empower local government, automatically transferring 40 per cent of national revenues to local authorities, giving them extensive discretion as to how to deploy these resources and including civil-society organisations in decision-making, for example by allowing them to occupy a quarter of all seats on the council. As Eaton puts it, the idea was that local councillors should not be dependent on national politicians 'for getting windows fixed in city hall'.[9]

In the ensuing chapters we shall see that central-local relations in Asia are a highly contested space, where the context of local politics and history is crucial for understanding and where the outcomes go to the fundamentals of constitutional ordering.

ETHNIC RIGHTS, POWER AND CONSTITUTIONAL ORDERING

In any discussion of central-local relations examining the ways in which contextualised constitutional systems deal with complex and difficult issues of territorial governance, the questions of ethnic status, ethnic regions, ethnic claims and representation, and regional autonomy stand out. How constitutional systems deal with these difficult and sensitive issues can play an outsized role in the success or failure of constitutional arrangements and legitimacy, national harmony, political stability and democratisation. As Melissa Crouch points out, these issues stand out particularly in the recent and fast-moving context of Myanmar (Burma), where 'the central Government now faces the need to resolve ethnic conflicts and grievances as part of the process of transition to a quasi-civilian democracy under the 2008 Constitution',[10] and a significant part of the population—and an even more significant source of constitutional debate and conflict—is a vibrant community of ethnic peoples.

States can, as Crouch indicates, provide status to or recognition of ethnic and cultural groups and their rights in various ways through constitutional processes. These processes can give rise to significant and interesting

[8] A Harding and J Chin (eds), *50 Years of Malaysia: Federalism Revisited* (Singapore, Marshall Cavendish, 2014).

[9] K Eaton, 'Political obstacles to decentralization: Evidence from Argentina and the Philippines' (2001) 32(1) *Development and Change* 101.

[10] Ch 6, 'Introduction'.

issues, both in federalism and in relation to local government, especially where states or regions are themselves ethnically complex, as is the case in Myanmar. Myanmar has begun to provide such recognition, shifting downwards the administration of local areas while continuing and adapting past methods in which ethnic nationalities are represented in both houses of the national parliament. All of this has been accomplished under a continuing, although since 2010 increasingly more open, militarised regime that now recognises the need to acknowledge cultural and ethnic rights. In Myanmar, as in some other states, these issues could not be more important. As Crouch notes, '[t]he relationship between the national union Government and ethnic nationalities is of crucial significance, because one of the ongoing challenges for the Myanmar Government moving forward is how it deals with the demands of ethnic nationalities'.[11]

For the Government, and in the Myanmar constitutional processes now embracing constitutional revision, these challenges and their ongoing treatment have taken three key forms. First, there is what Crouch (following Levy) terms 'symbolic recognition' of certain ethnic nationalities and certain rights, a framework based in both representation and control. Secondly, Myanmar has developed a system of 'special representation' at state and regional levels, in which Ministers of National Race Affairs represent major ethnic groups in those areas. Crouch notes that this 'allows both for fragmentation and for Burman [majority ethnic group] representation in the ethnic-based states, although all such Ministers have their responsibilities controlled by the central Government'.[12] And, thirdly, some ethnic areas are now designated as Self-Administrative Zones or Divisions, in a process that Crouch calls 'limited self-governance'.[13]

In the Myanmar context, these steps appear to recognise and assuage both national and local power, and are directly related to historical conflicts. Such recognition, Crouch argues, in which the central government permits and recognises some ethnic and regional rights, is 'a concession that primarily, though not exclusively, relates to previous ceasefire deals in the late 1980s and early 1990s. The implication for all three forms of decentralisation, however, is that the central Government retains ultimate control under the terms of the 2008 Constitution.'[14] In these complex relationships the central Government and the dominant ethnic group continue to retain the upper hand, while ethnic and regional groups continue to demand more recognition and status.

Yet these institutional and geographic arrangements—both in terms of definitions and in terms of powers—may be in flux as a result of constitutional politics, ordinary politics and policy, a national census and other

[11] Ch 6, 'Conclusion'.
[12] ibid.
[13] Ch 6, 'Limited Self-governance: Self-administered Zones and Divisions'.
[14] Ch 6, 'Conclusion'.

factors. Power remains centrally held, but the future is not certain, and the granting of ethnic and regional rights, even though circumscribed, holds open some uncertainties for the future:

> [A]uthoritarian regimes may include provisions for special recognition of cultural rights for some ethnic groups as a means of facilitating negotiations and peace deals with such groups. The creation of these rights can therefore be used as part of the legitimising function of the constitution. Yet the meaning of these rights is dynamic, not static, and they must continue to be assessed, over the coming years, in order to gauge the impact of these provisions on the shifting nature of central-local relations more broadly.[15]

Given six decades of extreme ethnic conflict in Myanmar, which continues in spite of a cautious democratic opening, the issue of ethnic localism is deeply implicated in the future of the country.

LOCAL SELF-GOVERNMENT, LOCAL ELECTIONS AND LOCAL REGULATION: HOW MUCH AND HOW FAR?

Elected local self-government and the institutions of self-government are another important topic in the constitutional ordering of territorial governance and central-local relations. In Malaysia, a nation with a federal structure and what Andrew Harding terms 'a Westminster-type democratic Constitution embracing constitutional monarchy, with an ethnically divided society under an authoritarian state evolving, seemingly, into a two-party system',[16] the issues of local self-government are even more fraught than in other states.

The complex nature of developments in decentralisation is exacerbated by polarised views on local self-government. Malaysia's governments since 1957 have followed an authoritarian and centralised model in which local self-government is distrusted and kept weakened, with power resting in central authorities and states rather than moving, even slowly, to localities. Others, especially in the opposition coalition, seek more authority and power for local self-government and local elections, an

> opportunity for the exercise of autonomy that can help to lower the tensions of contestation over big prizes at the national level, empowering communities irrespective of ethnic composition, and empowering … fragile communities such as small indigenous groups … which have never had elected local government authorities.[17]

Thus the constitutional and normal politics of local elections and local self-government can be highly controversial, but so too are the practicalities of

[15] ibid.
[16] Ch 8, 'Introduction'.
[17] ibid.

three potentially active levels of government, particularly in smaller nations like Malaysia, even when, as in Penang, active state government seems to have had a beneficial effect. Yet the issues keep arising, in Malaysia and a number of other countries, for historical developments press forward the claims for local self-government. As Harding notes,

> while authoritarian government has been the norm in post-war Asia ... the progress towards constitutional government that we can see across most of the region raises new issues in central-local relations ... Can local communities take responsibility for their own local issues without arousing the Leviathan of authoritarian government? Would a reinvigoration of local government via [local elections] represent a significant shift in implementing democracy?[18]

Regardless of how the politics and practicalities of these issues are resolved, the controversies and struggles over local self-government and local elections can only increase in the decades ahead as citizens demand more government accountability, better provision of public services, better opportunities for their children and themselves, and even, in some states, explicitly more democracy. In the Malaysian case, then,

> the redefinition of central-local relations ... seems inevitably to be leading towards a more open and more democratic form of constitutional ordering in which local self-government will play a new and potentially creative role, as state government is already doing at a higher level. Ultimately, the issue of [local elections and local self-government] is a test of the reality of federalism within a structure that has been seen until recently as either quasi-federal, or as representing a highly centralised form of federalism.[19]

In Indonesia, the political momentum toward more decentralisation of central-local relations, or 'regional autonomy' as it is termed there, including regional power to issue regional regulations, results from an array of factors, as Simon Butt discusses in chapter five. The legacy of strong centralised power, a sense that the 'central government was predatory, or at least exploitative', particularly with respect to natural resources, ethnic, religious and cultural autonomy demands—all of these contributed toward policymaking in the direction of more decentralisation and regional autonomy.

The results of this process have, however, been nuanced and mixed: '[W]hile local governments have been given significant power to regulate and otherwise manage their affairs, the national Government has retained ultimate legal control over them.'[20] And yet the central Government and the judiciary have only rarely acted to block regional bylaws, a function of executive decision-making, 'unclear and overlapping ... division of power as between the various tiers of government',[21] and unclear and weak judicial

[18] ibid.
[19] Ch 8, 'Conclusion'.
[20] Ch 5, 'Introduction'.
[21] ibid.

jurisdiction. 'The net result of the failure of these mechanisms', Butt writes, 'is that, for the most part, local governments have had *carte blanche* to enact laws of virtually any subject matter without paying regard to national laws—even the Constitution—provided that they do not seek to encroach on central-government revenue streams.'[22] And in turn, what has resulted is significant legal inconsistency, 'a virtually impenetrable tangled mass of contradictory law, leaving citizens and legal entities unable to distinguish between laws they must follow and laws they can ignore'.[23]

Over a decade now after decentralisation took hold in Indonesia as part of *reformasi*, inconsistency, lack of executive exercise of power in reviewing regional regulations and weak judicial jurisdiction hamper the consistent development of a clear delineation of central and local power, in turn contributing to local governments exercising excessive rule-making, particularly to raise revenue, and the exercise of power with too much discretion, corruption and other problems. As Butt points out, while decentralisation can often be regarded as being of positive value, it can be used for the wrong purposes and in an unchecked manner, leading to abuses, lack of equity and severe legal inconsistency.

At times the exercise of national power is needed:

> Many important guarantees, such as human-rights protections, are provided to all citizens, regardless of the region in which they live, by national laws, including the Constitution, and local governments must be compelled to follow them and held to account if they do not.[24]

Where local power goes unchecked, and legal inconsistency reigns, broader constitutional values—such as basic rights—may be implicated and endangered as well. The recent election as President of Indonesia of a former Governor of Jakarta, Joko Widodo, with a strong record of local action on poverty and other issues, may indicate the possibility of these issues being addressed creatively in the next stage of *reformasi*.[25]

THE DILEMMAS OF CENTRAL AND LOCAL POWER

In chapter seven of this book, Shigenori Matsui looks at the state of central-local relations in Japan through a different lens. Positing the key role of central power in Japan's unitary and centralised state, and yet the significant (although still highly controlled) delegation of power from central to local

[22] ibid.
[23] ibid.
[24] Ch 5, 'Observations and Conclusions'.
[25] 'Local experience to benefit President elect Joko Widodo', *Wall Street Journal South East Asia*, 24 July 2014, available at <http://blogs.wsj.com/searealtime/2014/07/24/local-experience-to-benefit-president-elect-joko-widodo/>.

authorities to provide services and extend governmental authority, Matsui asks how the major Tohoku earthquake of March 2011 and the nuclear plant meltdown at Fukushima have affected central-local relations in Japan.

In the earthquake, despite local (municipal) obligations to respond to disasters, 'many municipalities suffered tremendous damage … far beyond their capacity to respond. Rescue, recovery and reconstruction thus necessitated a much stronger role for the central Government',[26] potentially stifling the exercise of local authority and decision-making. The case of the Fukushima tragedy, however, illustrated the lack of power—legal and political—that could be exercised by the central government, to the point that 'the central Government [had] to seek consent from local governments in order to build interim storage sites for nuclear waste and to restart the nuclear power plant … casting significant doubt on the ability of the central Government to carry out these national tasks'.[27]

It remains too early to say whether these tragedies will result in a significant reordering of power in central-local relations in Japan. The earthquake experience has spurred the Japanese Government to try to better align central and local obligations, and to mandate that prefectural and municipal governments revise disaster plans. The Fukushima accident has prompted the central Government to strengthen central capacity to deal with such events, through the establishment of a Nuclear Regulatory Authority, as well as higher safety standards for plant operators and revised mandates to local authorities on drafting evacuation plans.

At the same time, Matsui notes,

> no significant changes … alter the relationship between the central government and the local government. There still is no statute authorising the Prime Minister or the central Government to take over the tasks of the local government in times of emergency. Reconstruction is not left to the autonomous decision of the local government …
>
> [N]o consensus has yet been found on the proper relationship between the central Government and the local government, and there is no serious attempt to reconsider the proper relationship between the central Government and the local government on these disaster issues.[28]

In the end, Matsui tells us, the impact of tragedy on central-local relations may be a greater understanding of the need for both enhanced central power and strengthened local autonomy in times of disaster, along with considerably stronger central-local coordination.

'Historical legacies and geopolitical complications' affect territorial governance and central-local relations in many Asian territories, but perhaps no more so than in Taiwan. As Jiunn-rong Yeh writes in chapter three, there

[26] Ch 7, 'Introduction'.
[27] ibid.
[28] Ch 7, 'Lessons Learned'.

such legacies and complications 'are deeply embedded in Taiwan's constitutional journey'. The long political debate over Taiwan as a province of the People's Republic of China, and as a potential state in its own right, has further complicated the internal balancing of power between the central and the local. The traditional view was fairly clear—'limited autonomy within the highly centralised control of the national Government in the framework of a unitary state',[29] as Yeh describes it.

Yet constitutional and political provisions for central-local relations 'have been constructed and reconstructed over time against the dynamic relationship across the Taiwan Strait, as well as against the backdrop of democratic transition in Taiwan since the late 1980s'[30] and the rise of Taipei. And how the rapid economic and political transitions within Taiwan should affect the traditional constitutional ordering of central-local relations remains unclear; there is something of a gap between text and reality when the Constitution says one thing and reality seems to be showing us another. At the same time, also importantly, we witness 'the emerging significance of megacities, such as Taipei, that enjoy disproportionate powers and resources as against other autonomous localities'.[31]

Taiwan's democratisation has thus

> transformed the central-local relations in the Constitution from a limited autonomy in a unitary state into a hybrid and dynamic transitional federalism.... Against this backdrop, above all, Taipei's duel role of national capital on the one hand and local government on the other thus becomes the centre of political conflicts in the post-authoritarian era.[32]

Democratisation has altered the central-local balance, from the central in the Kuomintang area (which recognises the need for some local devolution) to more power at local levels today.

Under such pressures, 'limited autonomy within the highly centralised control of the national Government in the framework of a unitary state' has been transformed into a 'more hybrid and dynamic transitional federalism',[33] a series of developments in which local autonomy has been strengthened and, '[i]nstead of being positioned at the periphery of a big China, Taiwan is now placed at the centre of its own territorial imagination for constitutional design'.[34]

That new constitutional design has reduced the impact of 'rigid and complicated' regulation of local government; simplification of local government,

[29] Ch 3, 'Conclusion'.
[30] Ch 3, 'Introduction'.
[31] ibid.
[32] ibid.
[33] Ch 3, 'Conclusion'.
[34] ibid.

and simplification and reduction of some aspects of the role of the central (Taiwan) Government; new power to the municipalities; new authority for local governments over finances and other means toward more autonomy; and a better balance in regional development on Taiwan through the comparative empowering of more regions and regional officials. Judicial power has assisted these transitions, though not without significant complications for the courts.

And the Taiwanese story is not finished:

> Despite profound change over the last several decades, this evolution will likely continue as central-local relations evolve over time in new institutional settings and in the context of transitional politics. Dynamic central-local relations will continue to play a significant role in Taiwan's transitional constitutionalism.[35]

Similar dilemmas of central and local power play out in China, where, as Qianfan Zhang discusses in chapter two, territorial governance and central-local relations in this unitary state are characterised by 'political and administrative controls [that] flow from top to bottom, a mode of governance that has had a serious impact on democracy and the rule of law'.[36]

Reforms since the late 1970s have not changed that basic structure of top-down governance. That 'lack of local democracy', and growing local abuses of power, corruption and other problems, have even led to more centralisation of power on such issues. China's history shows both the dangers and the possibilities of decentralisation, including in the disastrous Great Leap Forward of the late 1950s. And even limited attempts at administrative and legislative decentralisation need to be accompanied by central efforts to reassert order in the legal and economic systems.

In recent years, along with some careful reforms in central-local relations and some cautious decentralisation, power has also become recentralised, especially after new Party leaders took office in 2013. Recentralisation now goes hand-in-hand with certain devolutionary reforms that loosened some land-holding restrictions and eased the formation of some local associations to a degree. 'This logic of centralisation', writes Qianfan Zhang, 'is easy enough to understand. One can readily see that many reform measures directly conflict with the interest of local officials, who have every reason to impede these salutary measures issued by the Central Government.'[37]

Such decentralising measures can be supported by more democracy and the rule of law, but that is not Party policy in China at this point. Instead,

> the Communist Party and the Central Government busy themselves with crushing civil movements, persecuting social activists, silencing dissenting voices in the press

[35] ibid.
[36] Ch 2, 'Introduction'.
[37] Ch 2, 'New Reforms Driven by Centralisation'.

> as well as on the Internet, and sponsoring anti-constitutionalist propaganda … Since society is not allowed to play a vital role in promoting reform, the moving force for reform against the status quo can come only from the very top.[38]

Reforms that are guaranteed by central control imply, however, a contradiction in terms that is difficult to overcome. The central state cannot effectively oversee all local governance in China, plus itself. In Qianfan Zhang's view, popular participation is the element that is so far unheeded and unwanted by a powerful central state, but which is necessary for devolutionary and any sort of democratic reforms to take place:

> Knowledge and information about local grievances that affect common people … depend on society, as do the courage and resolve to eradicate these grievances by institutional reform that is resisted almost uniformly by officials at all levels. Since 'reform' as commonly understood is for the benefit of the people, a reform without popular support is necessarily empty, and a reform program depending purely on centralisation can be nothing but a chimera.[39]

Despite this difficult predicament, the author finds hope:

> Even if China is to keep a unitary framework for such a vast territory, one-party despotism is far from being its only option. There is no reason why it cannot have local democracy, by which elected local officials are effectively prevented from abusing public power. Nor is there any reason to believe that it is obliged to confer plenary and supreme powers on the central Government and make it the wellspring of despotic abuses … Finally, in order to implement the division of powers between the central and local governments, and to ensure that national laws are effectively enforced throughout the country, China must establish some form of judicial review …[40]

Vietnam, like China, remains controlled by a single Communist Party, and here some of the dilemmas and challenges of central-local relations are similar, while other patterns show some differences. Fiscal and administrative decentralisation has proceeded to a significant decree since Vietnam's *doi moi* (opening) reforms began in 1986, but, until recently, broader forms of political decentralisation were a different matter altogether. As Bui Ngoc Son notes, and with the exception of a 'grassroots democratisation' program introduced after anti-corruption protests in 1997, Vietnam was 'willing to fiscally and administratively decentralise for effective public governance, but would only take cautious steps in regard to democratic or political decentralisation because of its anticipation of political difficulties'.[41]

The cautious moves toward some form of political decentralisation were first agreed upon and announced by the Vietnamese Communist Party in

[38] ibid.
[39] ibid.
[40] ibid.
[41] Ch 4, 'Political Decentralisation'.

January 2011, and then incorporated into a lengthy and controversy-laden process of constitutional revision that ended in late 2013. They were driven by a coalition of reformists, as Bui Ngoc Son describes, who called for 'popular election of local governors, removal of the People's Council at district level and judicial review of local legal documents'.[42]

After much debate, the revised Constitution that was adopted in November 2013 (effective January 2014), established

> principles reflect[ing] the discourse of political decentralisation. [On] specific proposals for political decentralisation, the Constitution explicitly rejects the call for a specialist institution of judicial review, but does not provide clear answers to other substantial questions, such as popular elections of local leaders or removal of the People's Council at district level, yet still opens the door for such practices.[43]

New legislation will need to concretise these new principles, and the debates over that legislation will determine much about how far Vietnam's political decentralisation proceeds.

CONCLUSION

From these important and revealing studies we can draw some conclusions.

It appears that local self-government is being increasingly recognised as a means of deepening and embedding democracy, or at least as taking the heat off central government from the viewpoint of accountability. It is also a means of alleviating intense struggles within societies divided politically, ethnically or religiously, providing a method of power-sharing. Further, it is a spur to effective delivery of services and programmes, matching central policies with local conditions and preferences.

There is clearly a growing desire amongst local communities across Asia to achieve or retain control over the decisions that affect them most locally. Shigenori Matsui's chapter cuts across many of the issues raised in the other chapters in this book by looking at a particular, and pressing, administrative issue that is increasingly being dealt with in an Asian context, namely, disaster response. Matsui finds, as we have seen, that there are problems in this example, and the piece may be of some direct importance in designing central-local relations more generally. It is a salient reminder that, in the end, it is national interests that need to be served by local government, and that attention needs to be paid to central-local relations in a multiplicity of contexts, not simply in ordinary cases. Thus far Asian constitutional

[42] Ch 4, 'Constitutional Discourse on Political Decentralisation in 21st-Century Vietnam'.
[43] Ch 4, 'Conclusion'.

systems have largely experimented with local self-government, and central-local relations remain uncertain in many ways. We can see this with the new initiatives in China, Vietnam, Malaysia, Indonesia and Myanmar. To this extent central-local relations have not, largely, been crystallised in constitutional terms, though recent developments in Vietnam are an exception, in part. Nor is there any obvious consistent Asian model for central-local relations.

This remains an issue for future discussion of constitutional design. How far can local self-government go? A balance needs to be struck between two forces: first, the demand for local democracy and political autonomy; and, secondly, the needs of national development. The spectre of corruption emphasises the need for some caution: in some ways more local government means more opportunities for corruption and a greater need for vigilance. In this sense more local government can be both an opportunity for better governance and a threat to better governance. It is not in our view wise to attempt to find generally applicable answers to these questions, because the context will invariably dictate the best solutions. The requirements of modern urban life in Malaysia will not be the same as those of nation-building in Myanmar.

One aspect that remains unclear at this stage is the definition of reserve powers of central government: in what circumstances and on what basis will central government be able to override local powers? This issue relates to the degree of entrenchment of local government systems within the constitutional structure. Do stakeholders even see local government as a constitutional issue? Clearly in Taiwan, Malaysia, Indonesia and Vietnam they do, but in China perhaps not—though in China, where the entire issue of constitutional revision is not yet back on the agenda for political reasons, we would not be surprised to see devolution as a major topic of constitutional debate when open debate and some guided revision are permitted to occur.

Yeh Jiunn-rong's chapter on Taiwan and Bui Ngoc Son's chapter on Vietnam (in its discussion of issues of constitutional review) remind us of an issue that is not explored very much in the other chapters, namely, that if local self-government is going to be pursued seriously, there is need for a good dispute resolution system. This might operate at two levels: first, the constitutional level, implicating the judiciary, as has happened in Taiwan; and, secondly, the executive/ informal level, where cooperation is required between levels of government in the overall national interest.

Ultimately it is clear that constitutionalism itself in its various aspects is deeply implicated in the problems of central-local relations. We can expect important and interesting further developments in Asia in the areas discussed in this book.

FURTHER READING

R Crook and J Manor, *Democracy and Decentralisation in South Asia and West Africa* (Cambridge, Cambridge University Press, 1998).

J Hatchard, M Ndulo, and P Slinn, *Comparative Constitutionalism and Good Governance in the Commonwealth: An Eastern and Southern African Perspective* (Cambridge, Cambridge University Press, 2004) ch 9.

P McCarney (ed), *The Changing Nature of Local Governments in Developing Countries* (Toronto, Centre for Urban and Community Studies, 1996).

S Mitra, 'Making local government work: Local elites, *panchayat raj* and governance in India' in A Kohli (ed), *The Success of India's Democracy* (Cambridge, Cambridge University Press, 2001).

T Sisk, *Democracy at the Local Level—The International IDEA Handbook on Participation, Representation, Conflict Management and Governance* (Stockholm, International IDEA, 2001).

M Turner (ed) *Central-Local Relations in Asia-Pacific: Convergence or Divergence?* (London, Macmillan Press Ltd, 1999).

2

Legalising Central-local Relations in China

ZHANG QIANFAN*

INTRODUCTION

LET ME BEGIN with Montesquieu's *Spirit of the Laws*, in which he declares that 'it is in the nature of a republic to have only a small territory', while 'a large empire presupposes a despotic authority in the one who governs'.[1] The Chinese empire was the paragon of his 'despotic government',[2] a form of government that China has maintained for over two millennia. The republican revolution in 1911 put an end to the last dynasty, but Montesquieu's Law remained applicable nevertheless. In essence the 'People's Republic' today is still a 'despotic' massive empire, where the political and administrative controls flow from top to bottom, a mode of governance that has had a serious impact on democracy and the rule of law in that country.

Montesquieu's Law is broken, of course, by federalism, first experimented with in the United States, where democracy is rather successfully practised over a vast territory. China has remained unitary, however, since the Qin dynasty (220 BC), except for very brief experiments with provincial federalism during the early 1920s. Since 1949, when the Communist Party defeated the Nationalists and took over power, China returned to being a united state with a regime more centralised than ever before, and the reforms that have taken place since 1978 have not changed the basic feature of top-down governance. And the lack of local democracy has made it all the more necessary to centralise control over abuses of public power at the local level.

Indeed, a limited devolution of the central power to local governments in an overall centralised structure could lead to unfortunate, even fatal,

* Professor of Law, Peking University. I thank Professors Andrew Harding and Mark Sidel for their valuable editorial advice. I am responsible for all remaining errors.

[1] Montesquieu, *The Spirit of the Laws*, AM Cohler, BC Miller and HS Stone (trans and eds) (Cambridge, Cambridge University Press, 1988) 124, 126.

[2] ibid, 127–28.

consequences. Contrary to the conventional wisdom, the Great Leap Forward Movement (1958–59) was carried out against the background of administrative decentralisation, by which local governments were given some discretion over local decision-making. In the area of food production, the central Government set the quotas for local conscrption, but the figures were based on local reports of the crop yield in that year. Since the performance and the opportunity for promotion of a local official were decided by superior officials and, ultimately, by the central Government, every local official had an incentive to exaggerate crop yields, leading to a gross overestimate of the national crop yield in 1959 and the amount of conscripted crops to be taken from the peasants. The local governments, far from challenging the unreasonable conscription orders, executed them relentlessly, depriving the peasants of the foodstuffs necessary for the basic maintenance of their lives and producing the greatest famine in human history. It has been estimated that roughly at least 30 million people died of starvation in the year 1960–61.[3]

This chapter reviews central-local relations in mainland China. It first describes the existing hierarchy of legal norms in China and the scope of power exercised by various levels of local government. It then explains the institutional causes of these pervasive legislative conflicts (or 'fighting', 打架, *dajia*), and the efforts made by the central Government to combat legislative conflict and bring order to the national legal system. The chapter ends with an update on the new centralisation efforts following the Third Plenum of the Eighteenth Congress of the Chinese Communist Party in 2013; a discussion of the inherent limits in the existing efforts; and a proposal for the solution of the undemocratic symptoms predicted by Montesquieu's Law.

THE HIERARCHY OF LEGAL NORMS

In January 2011 the Chairman of the National People's Congress Standing Committee (NPCSC) announced that a 'socialist legal system with Chinese characteristics' had been established, leaving China with 236 effective national laws (法律, *falü*); over 690 sets of administrative regulations (行政法规, *xingzheng fagui*); 8,600 sets of local regulations (地方性法规, *difangxing fagui*); and many more rules (规章, *guizhang*) and norms (规范, *guifan*) of lower rank.[4] It is the hallmark of a centralised state that these terms carry special significance, in the sense that they indicate the law-making power of various levels of government. While 'laws' can be enacted only by

[3] The death toll rose to 45 million, if deaths caused by torture and other mistreatments during this period were included. See F Dikötter, *Mao's Great Famine: The History of China's Most Devastating Catastrophe, 1958–1962* (New York, Walker, 2010).

[4] Chen Baocheng, 'Wu Bangguo Declares that the Chinese Legal System Has Been Established', *Southern Metropolitan Daily* (10 January 2011).

the NPC or the NPCSC, administrative regulations are made by the State Council, local regulations are made by the local People's Congress at the provincial level or the level of a city authorised to exercise such power, and rules are made by ministries and commissions of the State Council, or by provincial governments or authorised lower governments.

In the current hierarchy of legal norms, the 1982 Constitution theoretically occupies the highest place. The last paragraph of its Preamble states that the Constitution is 'the fundamental law of the state and has supreme legal authority'. In practice, however, the Constitution is not a 'law' in its complete sense, due to the lack of an effective enforcement mechanism. The Constitution is ineffective partly because courts and other judicial tribunals are not authorised to apply constitutional provisions in their decisions; rather, constitutional review of legal norms is entrusted to the NPCSC, which is given the function 'to interpret the Constitution and supervise its enforcement' (Article 67.1). However, this power has not been exercised by the NPCSC, at least in formal terms, since the Constitution came into force in 1982, even in in the face of cases that involve egregious violations of the Constitution.

Second in the hierarchy of legal norms are the 'laws' in their narrow sense—statutes enacted by the NPC or the NPCSC itself.[5] Unlike a federal framework, in which central legislation is required to lie within the scope of powers authorised by the federal constitution, China's unitary structure imposes no limits on the scope of national legislation. Though the word 'unitary' (单一制, *danyi zhi*) is not explicitly spelled out in the 1982 Constitution, it does provide a list of general areas in which the NPC or NPCSC may legislate, but they are not limited to legislation in these areas. Instead, any law will be deemed constitutionally valid as long as it does not contradict specific constitutional provisions. Indeed, Article 8 of the Law on Legislation specifically reserves several areas of competence to national laws. Those include matters with respect to state sovereignty; the structure and powers of governments at all levels; the autonomic governance of national (ethnic minority) Autonomous Regions and Special Administrative Regions (SARs); civil and criminal systems; 'deprivation of the political rights of citizens or compulsory measures and penalties that restrict personal freedom'; 'expropriation of non-state assets'; fundamentals of taxation and the economic system; and litigation and arbitration systems.

Below the Constitution and the laws are administrative regulations enacted by the State Council. Just as the function of China's Constitution is

[5] China is one of the few countries in which the Standing Committee of the national legislature is constitutionally authorised to make laws that become effective without the need for further approval of the full legislature. The Legislation Law provides that the NPC shall 'enact and amend criminal, civil, state-institutional and other basic laws', while the Standing Committee can make 'other laws'.

not fully to 'grant' (though it does 'limit') legislative powers, the function of these administrative regulations is not to 'grant' (though, again, they do 'limit') administrative powers. An administrative regulation is not required to be pre-authorised by laws but is deemed lawful as long as it does not contravene specific legal provisions. Even for areas reserved to the national legislatures, the NPC or NPCSC may pre-authorise the State Council to enact administrative regulations 'as needed', except in matters relating to criminal law, the judicial system, and deprivation of citizens' political rights or compulsory measures and penalties restricting citizens' personal freedom (Article 9). In these exceptional areas, a law must be enacted before the State Council may impose regulations. The national laws and administrative regulations are binding nationwide, and are superior both to local legislation and departmental rules of the central Government.

The structure of legal norms in China becomes less clear when one looks at the next level—local regulations enacted by the provincial People's Congresses (including those of municipalities and autonomous regions) and 'departmental rules' made by ministries and commissions under the State Council. Although an administrative regulation promulgated by the State Council always supersedes local regulations, this does not apply to a nationally applicable rule made by its department. In other words, the normative hierarchy as between central and local legislation becomes unclear for any rules or norms below the national laws and administrative regulation. In fact, not only is the hierarchy as between a provincial regulation and a departmental rule unable to be decided *a priori*, but even local regulations enacted by the local People's Congress of a 'relatively large city' (较大市, *jiaoda shi*) and local rules enacted by its government are not necessarily pre-empted by a national rule in the event of conflict,[6] though a local rule is supposed to conform to the local regulations of the same jurisdiction in addition to national laws and regulations (Article 73). The Law on Legislation explicitly provides that local rules have the 'same legal force' as departmental rules (Article 82).

Last, but by no means least, below regulations and rules is a massive body of 'normative documents' (规范性文件, *guifanxing wenjian*), such as orders, decisions, notices and instructions of general applicability made by a variety of government units at all levels. However, without even an assigned term, these Chinese 'red-headlined documents' (红头文件, *hongtou wenjian*) are marked not only by their sheer number, but also by the efficacy and strength of their implementation in practical life, especially in comparison

[6] According to the Law on Legislation, the category of 'relatively large cities' includes provincial capitals, special economic zones (SEZs) and 'any other city so approved by the State Council' (Article 63). The State Council has so far approved 36 such cities, including Qingdao, Dalian, Xuzhou, Ningbo, Suzhou, Wuxi, Changzhou and other relatively developed cities. Beijing, Shanghai and other even larger cities are in a separate category of 'specially administered (central) municipalities'.

with the Constitution and laws. For example, a local zoning plan aiming to take a piece of village land or demolish residential buildings in a city, or a local standard that minimises the compensation for such taking of property, would be implemented forcibly and swiftly because such a decision literally means revenue to the local government. Many of these 'red-headlined' orders are not published, even though the Regulation on Disclosure of Government Information (政府信息公开条例, *zhengfu xinxi gongkai tiaoli*), promulgated by the State Council in 2007, explicitly requires such publication by governments at all levels (Article 6).

LOCAL AUTONOMY IN A CENTRALISED FRAMEWORK

Although the national legislature enjoys supreme and plenary legislative powers in China's centralised legal framework, local legislation is not constrained in a straitjacket but is afforded plenty of room to adapt to local needs and circumstances. Article 63 of the Law on Legislation provides that a provincial People's Congress and its Standing Committee may 'enact local regulations according to the specific circumstances and actual needs of the jurisdiction, provided that such enactment does not contravene any provision of the Constitution, laws or administrative regulations'. The local People's Congress and its Standing Committee in a relatively large city may do the same, provided that the implementation is approved by the provincial local People's Congress Standing Committee, which is required to review the legality of the lower regulation and grant approval within four months if such regulation does not contravene provisions of the Constitution, laws, administrative regulations or provincial regulations (Article 63).

The Law on Legislation further provides that local regulations may be enacted for two types of matters. First, they can be made for the purpose of implementing a national law or regulation if more specific provisions are required in light of local circumstances (Article 64.1). Secondly, a local regulation can also be enacted with respect to 'local concerns', presumably referring to matters not covered by central legislation (Article 64.2). In addition, local People's Congresses and their Standing Committees in provinces and relatively large cities may, 'according to the specific situation and actual demands of the locality, make local regulations for those matters for which no laws or regulations have been enacted' (Article 64.3). Provisions of such regulations inconsistent with national laws or regulations enacted later shall be repealed or amended by the enacting body. A local rule is authorised to do by and large the same: to implement laws, administrative regulations or local regulations, and to enact independent rules 'within the regulatory scope of the local jurisdiction' (Article 73).

China's local autonomy is arguably severely, or even fatally, limited because of lack of trust in local governments, which leads to the abrogation of local competency and reservation to the national legislatures of certain key areas specified in Article 8 of the Law on Legislation. Although some of these areas—such as matters relating to 'state sovereignty', the organisation of the central Government, the division of competences between the central and local governments, and basic economic and legal institutions—may properly be said to fall within the remit of national legislation, some of these reservations plainly contradict a democratic principle of local autonomy. A typical example is the reservation of 'compulsory measures and penalties that restrict personal freedom' in Article 8.5 of the Law on Legislation (about which further details are given in the discussion of the case of Sun Zhigang below).

In other words, a local legislature may pass regulations on these compulsory measures or penalties only as an implementation of a pre-existing national law that involves these measures, and lacks independent authority to legislate for local needs without the authorisation of a national law. Personal freedom is undeniably an important individual right, but in mature democracies, local governments at the provincial level are generally entrusted with maintaining local order and promoting the legitimate public interest, perhaps in broader ways than are currently permitted in China. In some countries, for example, the central Government may at times intervene only when local legislation positively contravenes a provision in the national constitution or legislation. This may be achieved through judicial review rather than via direct legislative or executive intervention, though multiple models are used.

Trust in local governments is well deserved, however, only when they are held sufficiently accountable to the local people by effective electoral or judicial mechanisms. In China, where such mechanisms are simply unknown, and local officials are held responsible, if at all, to their superiors rather than to an electorate or the judiciary, distrust of local government is well founded, since such legislative powers, once delegated to local governments, certainly may be abused.[7] However, the remedy for such distrust is to establish more effective democratic and judicial controls over local government, rather than preventing them from exercising the powers necessary for local order and the public interest.

[7] In November 2009, for example, the Court, the Procuratorate, the Public Security Bureau and the Bureau of Justice of Shenzhen City in Guangdong Province, jointly issued a Notice Regarding Handling of Abnormal Petition Acts According to Law, which authorised the local police to place those who repeatedly engage in 'abnormal petitions' in 'education through labour' (*laodong jiaoyang*). This Notice was viewed by many as flagrantly infringing upon basic freedoms of the petitioners and as being inconsistent with Article 8 of the Law on Legislation. See 'Shenzhen Provides that Repeated "Abnormal Petitions" Will be Treated with Education Through Labour', *Guangzhou Daily* (12 November 2009).

CURBING 'LEGISLATIVE CONFLICTS' IN A UNITARY STATE

The unlimited competence of the central Government notwithstanding, a significant degree of conflict often remains between local legislation and the rules enacted by departments of the central Government. The result is a complex structure of legal norms.

Once local authorities gain freedom to provide for local interests, conflict between local and central legislation becomes inevitable. The problem is especially acute for a very large country like China, where central and local legislative competences are not constitutionally delimited. Article 3 of the 1982 Constitution merely states the vague principle of 'giving full scope to the initiative and enthusiasm of the local authorities under the unified leadership of the central authorities', which provides little guidance for dividing central and local functions. As a result, China's central-local relations have been trapped in a rather 'lawless' state, in which conflict between legislation at different levels, commonly known as 'legislative fighting' or legislative conflict—over both substance and the power to make rules—has been both pervasive and long-standing. In 2000, the Law on Legislation was enacted precisely to curb such legislative conflict by specifying the ordering of legal norms and law-making procedures, as well as ways of resolving conflicts. In this sense it is a 'law of laws', with a prominent status subsidiary only to that of the Constitution.[8]

The Law on Legislation does not provide an absolute principle of national legislative supremacy but employs a complex *ex post facto* review procedure to resolve conflicts between local regulations and national legislation that is below the level of administrative regulations. If a discrepancy occurs between a local rule and a central administrative rule, or between administrative rules concerning a similar matter, a ruling on that conflict shall be made by the State Council (Article 86.3). If a discrepancy occurs between a local regulation and a central administrative rule concerning the same matter, then the process becomes more cumbersome:

> The State Council shall give its opinion; where the State Council deems that the local regulation should apply, in the local jurisdiction the local regulation shall be applied; where the State Council deems that the administrative rule should apply, it shall request the Standing Committee of the National People's Congress to make a ruling.[9]

Since China lacks a centralised mechanism for reviewing the legality of legislation, the Law on Legislation is at pains to define a complex hierarchy of review authorities. Generally, a state institution has the authority to review

[8] For a concise explanation of the Chinese legal structure, see A Hongyi Chen, *An Introduction to the Legal System of the People's Republic of China*, 4th edn (Hong Kong, LexisNexis Butterworths, 2011) chs 1 and 2.

[9] Law on Legislation, art 86.2.

legislation enacted by another institution situated one level lower than it in the constitutional hierarchy, and an enabling agency has the authority to directly invalidate delegated legislation beyond the scope of authorisation or inconsistent with the objective of the enabling decision (Article 88.7). For example, while the NPC has the power to 'amend or withdraw any inappropriate law enacted by its Standing Committee' (Article 88.1) and to 'amend or withdraw any inappropriate administrative rule or local rule' (Article 88.3), the NPCSC has the power to invalidate, amongst other things, any administrative regulation that contravenes the Constitution or any law, and any local regulation that contravenes the Constitution or any law or administrative regulation (Article 88.2). Likewise, while the State Council has the authority to amend or invalidate an inappropriate departmental or provincial rule (Article 88.2), a provincial people's government has the power to amend or withdraw an inappropriate local rule enacted by the local people's government at the next lower level (Article 88.6). To facilitate legislative review, an inferior agency is obliged to report legislation made by it, within 30 days of its promulgation, to its superior (Articles 88 and 89). This complex mechanism of cascading review aims to ensure the legality (and, at least to some degree, consistency) of legislation at all levels.

Lastly, the Law on Legislation grants to state institutions, social organisations and individual citizens the right to request review of a legislative conflict. Unlike judicial review, which usually requires personal standing to initiate review procedures, China's legislative review process may be initiated by almost anyone. First, Article 90 of the Law on Legislation provides that certain state institutions can request and initiate the review process by right, even though no such request has been put forward since the promulgation of the Law on Legislation in 2000. The State Council, Central Military Commission, Supreme People's Court (最高人民法院, *zuigao renmin fayuan*), the Supreme People's Procuratorate (最高人民检察院, *zuigao renmin jianchayuan*), a special committee of the NPCSC, or a standing committee of a provincial People's Congress, may all make written requests to the NPCSC for review if they believe that an administrative regulation or a local regulation contravenes the Constitution or any law. The 'working office' of the NPCSC, its Legislative Affairs Commission (LAC) (法工委, *fagongwei*), distributes such requests to the relevant special committees of the NPC for review and comment, a process that may eventually lead to the NPCSC's deliberating on and deciding the matter.

Secondly, a private citizen or social group may also make written proposals to the NPCSC for review if any of the above types of legislation are deemed to contravene the Constitution or any law. Their proposals will be 'studied' by the LAC, and distributed to the relevant NPC committee for review and comments only 'where necessary' (Law on Legislation, Article 90(2)). So far, although hundreds and perhaps even thousands of such requests have been made, none of them has been deemed 'necessary' enough to initiate the review process. Even in the aftermath of the nationally prominent Sun Zhigang incident, discussed further below, the request made by legal scholars to invalidate the egregious Detention and Repatriation Measures—which were in fact repealed shortly afterwards by the State Council itself—failed to initiate the review process. In fact, although a special office was created for 'regulatory review and record' (法规审查备案室, *fagui shencha bei'an shi*) in 2005 under the LAC, it has never published a list of requests received, making it impossible to assess the number or nature of them. In any case, despite the minimal standing requirement, individuals and social organisations have never been able to trigger the seemingly well-designed, albeit convoluted, review process provided for in the Law of Legislation, while no public institution seems to have bothered to try.

COMBATTING LOCAL PROTECTIONISM WITHOUT THE COURTS?

As the 'law of laws', yet seldom used since its promulgation, the Law on Legislation suffers from several limitations. First, although its original purpose was to curb legislative fighting, the Law on Legislation has done little to strengthen the uniformity of national legislation or to clarify the order of different norms below administrative regulations. In contrast to a federal system such as that of the United States, where federal powers are limited to those granted in the Constitution but have supremacy vis-à-vis state and local legislation,[10] China's central legislation needs no constitutional grant; however, neither is it supreme over local legislation in the complete sense—a departmental rule is not necessarily superior to a local regulation or rule, even if it is entirely consistent with national laws and regulations that in turn comply with the Constitution. Far from curbing legislative fighting, then, the Law on Legislation runs the serious risk of encouraging conflict between legislative acts that sit below the level of administration regulations. While the Law on Legislation may accommodate local diversity and prevent 'cutting with a broad knife' (overly broad action) by departmental rules or decisions, it undermines legal uniformity as a basic requirement of the rule of law.

Secondly, it is not only impossible to decide *a priori* the rank of a departmental rule vis-à-vis a local regulation or rule, but also extremely difficult to apply the review mechanism in practice. If conflict between a departmental rule and provincial regulation or rule occurs, a request for review must be submitted to the State Council, an extremely busy bureaucratic centre that has a moderately staffed, arguably understaffed, multi-functional Legal Affairs Office (LAO) (法制办, *fazhiban*) to handle issues of legislative conflict. This results in long delays in conflict resolution. Added to those

[10] Constitution of the United States, art 6.

problems, if the State Council decides for its department against a provincial regulation, the matter will have to be appealed further to the NPCSC, which is preoccupied with its own legislative agenda. This process is meant both to temper the natural inclination of the State Council towards its own departments, which would disqualify it as a neutral arbitrator in dispute resolution, and to make up for any democratic deficiency inherent in a process in which the national administration imposes its decisions on locally elected People's Congresses. In reality, however, it simply prolongs an already lengthy process and creates further delays.

On the whole, both the State Council and the NPCSC are preoccupied with their own administrative and legislative work, and thus can hardly devote significant time to resolving pervasive legislative conflict in such a massive state as China, or to processing the great number of individual complaints that are made possible by the lack of a standing requirement. Timely resolution of legal conflicts requires a considerably more decentralised process, in which impartial judicial institutions across the country would be able to take up and speedily deal with complaints concerning local legislation.

This leads to the third and most important point: the conspicuous absence of the courts from the entire review process. Indeed, the Law on Legislation leaves out the courts entirely. This is consistent with the Administrative Litigation Law, which limits the scope of judicial review to 'concrete administrative acts' and does not extend to 'abstract administrative acts' such as laws, regulations, rules or any normative documents of a general nature. In fact, the courts are obliged to take laws and regulations as 'legal grounds' (法律依据, *falü yiju*) in adjudication (Article 51). That the courts play no role whatsoever in resolving legislation conflicts merely reinforces the impression that the review provided for in the Law on Legislation is purely legislative—or, more accurately, political rather than judicial in nature. Not only is the review of legislation directed to purely abstract norms, with no requirements regarding personal standing, and thus able to avoid the concrete cases and controversies normally associated with judicial review, but when review is conducted by a non-judicial institution without the guidance of any higher legal principles such as the supremacy of national legislation, legal criteria are absent. When the State Council or the NPCSC confronts a conflict between a departmental rule and a provincial regulation deemed to be of the same rank, what can possibly be the legal ground that predictably governs its ruling except *ad hoc* policy considerations?

As a result of these problems, the legislative review contemplated in Article 90 of the Law on Legislation is nothing but *ex post facto* law-making by the reviewing agency, which at best carries this out with a vague idea of the relevant situation at the time of review. Perhaps such clear violations of higher norms as found in the Detention and Repatriation Measures can be meaningfully reviewed even without a concrete case, but they are best conducted by an impartial institution of a judicial nature, since, as Chief

Justice Marshall pointed out in *Marbury v Madison*, '[i]t is emphatically the province and duty of the judicial department to say what the law is'.[11] Unfortunately, the courts in China are excluded from this task, leaving the basic objective of curbing legislative fights unfulfilled.

In fact, precisely two centuries after the *Marbury* decision, a similar case appeared in Luoyang, Henan province, but the very opposite result was reached. The case itself was simple enough: a seed company agreed with the plaintiff to provide an amount of corn seed, but defaulted by selling the seed to other parties at market price. The dispute came to the Luoyang City Court in 2003, focusing on the amount of damages due to the plaintiff. While the plaintiff insisted on payment of the market price according to the Seed Law enacted by the NPCSC, which would amount to damages of CNY700,000, the defendant, citing Article 36 of the Henan Provincial Regulation on Crop Seeds enacted by the provincial People's Congress Standing Committee, claimed that the 'government guidance price' should be the standard for calculating damages, which would amount to CNY20,000. The assistant judge presiding over the case, Li Huijuan, found for the plaintiff, interpreting the Seed Law as having established the principle requiring application of a market price standard. Since the Henan regulation was local legislation, which is below the level of national law in the legal hierarchy, the provision that conflicted with the national Seed Law was held null and void.[12]

The case did not even implicate any constitutional provisions, as *Marbury* had, although the nature of the question was similar: does the court have *any* power in reviewing abstract norms, if only to safeguard the supremacy of the Constitution and national laws? And the answer provided by the Luoyang court was commonsensical enough in any jurisdiction committed to rule of law: of course, the court, through the pivotal role of judicial review, is obliged to maintain a rational legal order, and reason dictates that a higher law be given effect, notwithstanding lower laws to the contrary. But the Henan provincial People's Congress Standing Committee reacted strongly against the decision and forced the Luoyang City Court to renounce the judgment. When the courts are unable to defend the law, local protectionism necessarily runs amok, seriously damaging the uniformity of the entire legal system.

A typical example of local protectionism was found in the *Preserved Fruits Case* (2005), in which the Beijing municipal government ordered local stores to remove from their shelves preserved fruits produced in Guangdong Province, on the ground that several brands of these products had been examined and found to have violated local criteria regulating harmful additives.[13]

[11] *Marbury v Madison* 5 US 137 (1803).

[12] See Guo Guosong, 'The Judge Struck Down a Local Regulation: Is She Violating the Law or Vindicating the Law', *Southern Weekend*, 20 November 2003.

[13] 'Beijing's Ban on Chao'an Dried Fruits Made National Impact', *Southern Daily*, 17 June 2005.

While these findings might have been well grounded, they failed to provide any rationale for a decision to prohibit the sale of all brands of Guangdong products. While the State Council explicitly prohibited local protectionism in an earlier notice, it took no action against such a discriminative measure. Nor did the affected enterprises in Guangdong take the issue to court. Had they done so, by bringing a case in Beijing, it is almost certain that they would have lost the case; or, even worse, the case might simply have been rejected by the court. The dispute was resolved only by Guangdong provincial government sending a high-level delegate to negotiate with Beijing municipality.

Another example of serious local protectionism concerns the criteria applying to the university entrance examination and admissions. In 2010 a joint letter was signed by over 10,000 parents of high-school seniors who had worked in Beijing for years without having obtained household registration in Beijing, demanding that the Beijing Education Commission allow their children to take the university entrance examination (高考, *gaokao*) in Beijing (rather than back in the province where their households were registered, and in which most had not lived for many years). The purpose of the letter was to allow the children of these parents, who lived in Beijing but did not have Beijing papers, to reap the benefits that China's university admissions system has long accorded to residents of Beijing and other municipalities or rich provinces. The event helped reveal what is hidden behind the bizarre undergraduate admissions system. Under the current scheme—an obstinate remnant of the planned economy era—each university allocates an admissions quota for each province. In 2010, for example, Peking University allocated a quota of 368 places for a total of 81,000 Beijing examinees, and a quota of a mere 60 places for 660,000 Shandong examinees, 78 places for 950,000 Henan examinees, and 30 places for 615,000 Guangdong examinees. The admissions ratio (the quota divided by the total number of examinees of that province) for an applicant whose parents are Beijing residents is 50, 55 and 93 times greater than the same ratio for a Shandong, Henan and Guangdong applicant, respectively.[14] Of course, Peking University and other 'national universities' in Beijing are far from the worst discriminators in terms of admissions. Virtually every university in China engages in such discriminative practices, and universities outside Beijing are much more protective as regards their local residents, who are discriminated against by universities in other provinces or municipalities.

In 2001, three students from Qingdao, Shandong province, brought litigation against the Ministry of Education for maintaining this discriminatory scheme of university admissions, but the Qingdao court declined to

[14] Zhang Qianfan and Yang Shijian, 'University Admission and Constitutional Equality' (2009) 11 *Legal Science Monthly* 15, and the accompanying articles in the same issue.

hear the case.[15] So far courts in China have played no role in remedying discrimination as regards university admissions or examinations. In 2012, the Ministry of Education, joined by other departments, issued a directive requiring that municipalities and provinces should in principle allow non-residents to take entrance examinations to attend local universities. While the vast majority of provinces implemented this directive reasonably well, Beijing and Shanghai by and large continued their discriminatory practices. Neither the courts nor the Ministry of Education itself intervened to order these recalcitrant authorities to comply with the national directive.

THE SUN ZHIGANG CASE: AN ILLUSTRATION OF CHINA'S CENTRAL-LOCAL RELATIONS

The irrelevance of the legal order as defined in the Law on Legislation was clearly illustrated by the Sun Zhigang (孙志刚) Case, which involved an administrative regulation that obviously violated the Law. In March 2003, when China and the rest of the world were grappling with the epidemic of severe acute respiratory syndrome (SARS), a personal tragedy struck Guangzhou and eventually triggered a public outcry against the age-old system for handling migrant populations in Chinese cities. Sun Zhigang, a 27-year-old graduate from the Wuhan Science and Technology College in Hubei province, came to work as a fashion designer in the economically booming city of Guangzhou, once known in the West as Canton. On the night of 17 March, he went to visit an Internet cafe, as he often did, without bringing his temporary Guangzhou residence permit as an identification document. He was mistakenly detained by police as an illegal immigrant to Guangzhou, and was brought to the Guangzhou internment and deportation transfer centre. Apparently having quarrelled with the management personnel about his treatment, he was battered by fellow inmates and died a few days later. The autopsy report displayed massive bruises on his back, indicating custodial brutality.

The institutional culprit in the Sun Zhigang tragedy was the Measures for Detention and Repatriation (收容遣送, *shourong qiansong*) of Urban Vagrants and Beggars (hereafter 'Detention and Repatriation Measures'), a regulation enacted by the State Council in 1982 that authorised widespread detentions and repatriation. Ironically, 1982 was the same year in which the current Constitution was brought into effect, which states that 'personal freedom … is inviolable. Unlawful detention or deprivation or restriction of citizen's freedom of the person by other means is prohibited'

[15] 'Admission According to National Uniform Exams Resulted in Disparate Admission Grades, Three Examinees in Qingdao Sued Ministry of Education', *Qilu Evening News*, 22 August 2001.

(Article 37). Detention and 'repatriation' as an institutional practice were, however, almost as old as the People's Republic itself, designed initially to clean up remaining Nationalist bandits, prostitutes and wandering beggars in the early 1950s, then to contain and settle the starved peasants pouring into the cities as a result of the radical Great Leap Forward movement in the early 1960s, and to curb the so-called 'blind migrations' (盲流, *mangliu*) of 'peasant workers' seeking employment in the cities during the 1980s. Over the years, detention and repatriation deteriorated into a practice that provided local polices with unchecked opportunities for profiteering and abuse of power, and it had caused several tragedies even before the Sun Zhigang incident.[16]

The Detention and Repatriation Measures ran directly into conflict with Article 8.5 of the Law on Legislation, which reserves 'compulsory measures and penalties that restrict personal freedom' to legislative action by the NPC and its Standing Committee. While detention and repatriation obviously involve 'compulsory measures … that restrict personal freedom', the Measures enacted by the State Council had never been legally authorised by the NPC or its Standing Committee in the form of law,[17] thus running counter to the Law on Legislation requirement. This time the Chinese public did not stop at morally condemning the official misconduct, but rather took a step further by questioning both the legality and the legitimacy of the Guangzhou police's authorisation to seize and detain Sun in the first place. Three young legal scholars initiated a constitutional review process as provided for in Article 90 of the Law on Legislation,[18] and sent to the LAC of the NPCSC a recommendation to review the constitutionality and legality of the Detention and Repatriation Measures. Their petition received overwhelming public support. The NPCSC failed to take any action, as usual, but the State Council, now under severe national pressure and under the leadership of a new Premier, Wen Jiabao, moved promptly to repeal the Detention and Repatriation Measures, which had authorised the compulsory relocation of 'vagrants and beggars'.

On 1 August 2003, less than five months after the Sun Zhigang tragedy occurred and within three months of its becoming publicly known, the State Council promulgated a new regulation of an entirely different nature: Measures for the Administration of Relief for Vagrants and Beggars without

[16] Zhang Qianfan, 'Chinese Legal Reforms in the Aftermath of the Sun Zhigang Incident' (2007) 4 *Asia Law Review* 1.

[17] Art 9 of the Law on Legislation does allow the State Council to develop certain regulations in the prohibited areas if it is authorised by the NPC/NPCSC, but such authorisation may not be given to enactments involving compulsory measures and penalties that restrict personal freedom, the deprivation of the political rights of citizens, or crimes and criminal penalties.

[18] Art 90 of the Law on Legislation confers a sort of 'citizen standing' that allows an ordinary person to request the NPCSC to review the constitutionality or legality of an administrative or local regulation even if that person is not directly concerned in a particular dispute.

Assured Living Sources in Cities. Based on the principles of 'receiving aid of one's own free will' and 'giving help gratis', relief for vagrants and beggars was now to be administered with compassion and according to individual circumstances, so that recipients could have access to food, lodging, medical care, means of communication and transportation to their home towns. In a surprisingly short period, a system that had been enforced for half a century and fraught with local interests was levelled, and an entirely new system of relief was built up.

The significance of the Sun Zhigang tragedy can be appreciated from a number of different perspectives. It illustrates how even positive laws such as the Law on Legislation can fail to produce any significant effect on such secondary norms as the State Council's Detention and Repatriation Measures. It is above all a vivid illustration of the working of China's intergovernmental relationships. The later action taken by the State Council now helps to save many potential victims from the fate suffered by Sun Zhigang, but the way by which it was accomplished reveals a serious dilemma that confronts rule of law in a centralised state, a dilemma that is all the more serious for a state as massive as China.

Keep in mind that the Detention and Repatriation Measures comprised central legislation uniformly implemented by local governments throughout a vast country, and that they were uniformly repealed by a single command from the same central Government. The local governments at various levels may to some extent adapt a regulation to local circumstances, but only within the regulatory framework and without contravening the basic spirit of the central regulation: with regard to the Detention and Repatriation Measures, they were as powerless to resist the uniform implementation of the national regulation prior to 2003 as they were to save it after the State Council pronounced its demise. Just as the central Government was positively promoting official misconduct when it uniformly enforced the Measures, it was efficiently promoting the national good when it uniformly repealed them. But even here, the national regulation may have inevitably compelled diversely situated local governments to operate on an equal footing, creating the pervasive 'one knife cuts all' (一刀切, *yidao qie*) problem of similar implementation without regard for local conditions. In other words, some local governments might well find themselves obliged to detain beggars and vagabonds, or adopt other compulsory measures restraining personal freedom under special circumstances, without the legislative authorisation of the NPC or its Standing Committee, since the necessity for these measures is found only in special local circumstances rather than felt nationwide; but it would have been both inadequate and inefficient for a national legislature to adopt regulations according to local interests, and indeed, it is practically impossible for the massive NPC (with nearly 3,000 representatives), in its short annual session (roughly 10 days), or for its overwhelmingly busy Standing Committee, to adopt any such measure.

As a result, local governments are left with two unappealing options: either to be handicapped and do nothing in the absence of central approval, or to step outside their legal competency in order to do good for the local community based on local circumstances. Yet Article 8 of the Law on Legislation, the very legal basis used to challenge the validity of the infamous Detention and Repatriation Measures, requires precisely such a result, and illustrates how a purpose is achieved in a unitary regime like China: powers are taken away from the local legislatures and invested in the central authority in order to prevent abuses and to protect certain fundamental rights. In this sense, the way in which the institutional cause of the Sun Zhigang tragedy was removed only revealed a deeper institutional pattern that left many more problems unresolved.

Only 10 years later was the rehabilitation through labour (*laodong jiaoyang*) program abolished on similar legal grounds. Under the now infamous program, a person could lose both his or her physical freedom and political rights for up to three years, extendable for one more year. Such onerous punishment was decided by an administrative board rather than a court, and the whole program, like the Detention and Repatriation Measures, was established by administrative regulation without authorisation of law. The Sun Zhigang case prompted the Chinese public to challenge the constitutionality of the equally long-standing rehabilitation through labour program, since both programs share the same legal infirmity of restricting personal freedom without authorisation of law, plainly contrary to the Law on Legislation. Unlike the voluntary relief program that took effect several months after the death of Sun Zhigang, however, legislation on rehabilitation through labour dragged on for years without producing a formal bill. It was formally abolished only in November 2013, when the Third Plenum of the Eighteenth Congress of the Chinese Communist Party published a major decision for comprehensive social reform.

NEW REFORMS DRIVEN BY CENTRALISATION

Precisely a decade after the death of Sun Zhigang, dilemmas in China's central-local relations were carried to a higher level. The Third Plenum (三中全会, *sanzhong quanhui*) of the Eighteenth Congress of the Chinese Communist Party, held in November 2013, introduced new elements to central-local relations in China, which are most likely to recentralise decision-making power in the hands of the Party's new General Secretary, Xi Jinping (习近平). The Third Plenum issued the Communist Party's Central Committee's Decision on Several Important Issues of Comprehensively Deepening Reforms, which encapsulated 60 reform measures covering socio-economic, legal and political issues. Some of these reform measures may be characterised as 'devolutionary', since they promised to build a stronger

Chinese civil society. For example, the Decision terminated the infamous rehabilitation through labour program, reduced controls on the transfer of lands held by peasants and simplified procedures for establishing associations in a few designated categories. Ironically, though, far from unconditional devolution, the keynote of the Third Plenum was centralisation.

In order to carry out the comprehensive reform program, the Decision also announced the establishment of two important institutions—the Leading Group for Deepening Reforms (深化改革领导小组, *shenhua gaige lingdao xiaozu*) and the National Security Commission (国家安全委员会, *guojia anquan weiyuanhui*)—both headed by the General Secretary Xi Jinping. While the Leading Group is to orchestrate reforms in various areas and overcome local and departmental impediments, the National Security Commission is to root out both domestic opposition and foreign threats, and guarantee a peaceful environment for the reforms. These two institutions seem to be the major driving force for the otherwise devolutionary reforms, aimed at leaving more freedom of action to the Chinese society and economy. And the Central Government has shown its resolve by introducing major anti-corruption measures directed at 'big tigers', ie cadres at the ministerial or provincial level, and now even higher.

This logic of centralisation is easy enough to understand. One can readily see that many reform measures may directly conflict with the interests of local officials, who have every reason to impede these often needed measures issued by the Central Government. Allowing peasants to transfer the right to use their lands, for example, strips the power of local government to take the same lands and make a huge profit by selling them to commercial developers at much higher prices. One way to resolve such problems is the traditional western-type approach based on democracy and the rule of law, by which the local government is made responsible to its electorate. The prospect of losing the next election might put an effective stop to land profiteering if the local official intends to continue his or her political career.

Despite the efforts to invigorate social organisations and reform the judiciary, however, the Decision merely paid lip service to democratic political reform and made no mention of freedom of the press. On the contrary, the Communist Party and the central Government continue to busy themselves with crushing civil movements, persecuting social activists, silencing dissenting voices in the press as well as on the Internet, and sponsoring anti-constitutionalist propaganda.[19] In fact, one of the three legal scholars who petitioned constitutional review in the Sun Zhigang case was even charged with the crime of disturbing public order for his lawful social activity.

[19] See Qianfan Zhang, 'The Past, Present, and Future of the "Public Opinion Struggle"' *Wall Street Jornal* (Chinese Edition), 9 October 2013, available at <http://cn.wsj.com/gb/20131009/ZQF072038.asp>.

Since society is not allowed to play a vital role in promoting reform, the moving force for reform against the status quo can come only from the very top.

And so thus far Montesquieu proves to be right once again. Yet this is only the beginning rather than the end of China's story on central-local relations, since the limitations of top-down reform pointed out previously hold true for the current reform. The very size of the state, which cripples direct democracy, cripples a highly centralised regime. Reform based on centralisation confronts many hard questions: How is the central Government to oversee the reform? And who are the members of the central Government? If local officials are prone to corruption and abuse of power, and thus need be checked by the central Government, do not the central officials need to be subject to the same checks with regard to their own ulterior motives? And who is in the right position to check them? Even if we could take for granted the complete benevolence of the General Secretary and six other members of the Standing Committee of the Party's Political Bureau—at the very top of China's power pyramid—it is impossible for them to oversee the giant bureaucracy necessary for supervising the many levels of local government throughout the country. If these questions cannot be answered seriously, the new reform is likely to dwindle into another episode of ambitious pronouncement without practical effect.

The Sun Zhigang incident shows that institutional progress cannot be achieved without popular participation. It is true that the Detention and Repatriation program was abolished by the central Government itself, but such a result could hardly have been imagined had the people failed to protest and exert pressure on the Government. Indeed, without press reports and civil protests on the Internet, the central Government might well have remained altogether ignorant of these events. Knowledge and information about local grievances that affect common people like Sun Zhigang depend on society, as do the courage and resolve to eradicate these grievances by institutional reform that is resisted almost uniformly by officials at all levels. Since 'reform' as commonly understood is for the benefit of the people, a reform without popular support is necessarily empty, and a reform program depending purely on centralisation can be nothing but a chimera.

Montesquieu was right when he predicted that a gigantic empire like China could be maintained only by despotism.[20] As the Sun Zhigang tragedy plainly illustrates, such a despotic empire is far from a felicitous paradise. A centralised regime organised from top to bottom necessarily relieves government at every level of the obligation to be accountable to the people. In China, the central Government itself has been the culprit in initiating such monstrous calamities as the Great Leap Forward and the Cultural Revolution, and for enacting such pernicious national policies as the household

[20] Montesquieu, above n 1, pt I, book 8, ch 16.

registration system, which discriminates against peasants, and the Detention and Repatriation Measures, which caused Sun Zhigang's death and pain to many more. Even if the central Government wishes to protect the people against exploitation by their local officials, it is inherently limited in its capacity to obtain the information necessary for enacting wise policies, or even discovering official misconduct, not to mention in its capacity to implement policies with consistency and efficiency. On its surface the empire may be at peace, even enjoying a degree of 'harmony', but how meaningful is such order to its potential victims like Sun Zhigang, who is representative of the vast majority of ordinary Chinese people? Without real democracy, which obliges government to 'represent the most fundamental interest of the overwhelming majority of the people',[21] the battle for the people has been lost even before it begins.

Montesquieu's Law about vast territories need not, however, be seen as casting a spell over China's political reform. Even if China is to keep a unitary framework for such a vast territory, one-party despotism is far from being its only option. There is no reason why it cannot have local democracy, by which elected local officials are effectively prevented from abusing public power. Nor is there any reason to believe that it is obliged to confer plenary and supreme powers on the central Government, making it the wellspring of despotic abuses. Even in a unitary framework, central and local governments may divide and share legislative powers, just as they are divided and shared in a federalist state.[22] Finally, in order to implement the division of powers between the central and local governments, and to ensure that national laws are enforced effectively throughout the country, China must establish some form of judicial review, empowering ordinary or special courts to resolve conflicts of legal norms, lest central-local relations are governed by the vissicitudes of political bargains and reduced to personal relations among central and local officials.

FURTHER READING

Jia Hao and Lin Zhimin (eds), *Chcanging Central–Local Relations in China: Reform and State Capacity* (Boulder, Col, Westview, 1993).

Li Yahong, 'The Law-Making Law: A Solution to the Problems in the Chinese Legislative System?' (2000) 30 *Hong Kong Law Journal* 120.

[21] This is one of the 'three represents', a theory proposed by Jiang Zemin that was inserted in the Preamble to the Constitution via the 2004 amendments.

[22] Japan, for example, is a unitary state, but the 1946 Constitution clearly partitions the powers of the national and local governments.

K Lieberthal, *Governing China: From Revolution through Reform*, 2nd edn (New York, WW Norton, 2003) ch 6.

PF Landry, *Decentralised Authoritarianism in China: The Communist Party's Control of Local Elites in the Post-Mao Era* (Cambridge, Cambridge University Press, 2008).

S Lubman, 'Looking for Law in China' (2006) 20 *Columbia Journal of Asian Law* 1.

Zhang Qianfan, *The Constitution of China: A Contextual Analysis* (Oxford, Hart Publishing, 2012) ch 3.

3

Evolving Central-local Relations in a Contested Constitutional Democracy: The Case of Taiwan

JIUNN-RONG YEH

INTRODUCTION

HISTORICAL LEGACIES AND geopolitical complications across the Taiwan Strait are deeply embedded in Taiwan's constitutional journey. The vertical separation of power in Taiwan reflects this complication squarely, witnessing the conflict between Taiwan as a state and Taiwan as a province of the Republic of China (ROC).[1] While the 1947 ROC Constitution stipulates a delicately balanced system of local autonomy and provides a sophisticated approach to power allocation, it has faced the challenges of applying in and accommodating the local context since regime relocation from the Chinese mainland to Taiwan in 1949. As a result, the central-local relations as stipulated in the Constitution have been constructed and reconstructed over time in light of the dynamic relationship across the Taiwan Strait, as well as against the backdrop of democratic transition in Taiwan since the late 1980s.[2] At the heart of the issue of central-local relations in Taiwan during its democratic transition has been the question of how to adapt the overly grand but constrained structure of local autonomy, as stipulated in the Constitution, to the use of the more transitional dynamics of Taiwan.[3]

[1] For a complete introduction to the problem of Taiwan in the historical tangles with China, see, eg, PL Hsieh, 'An Unrecognized State in Foreign and International Courts: The Case of the Republic of China on Taiwan' (2007) 28 *Michigan Journal of International Law* 765.

[2] Democratisation has been the major force driving constitutional and regulatory reforms. See Jiunn-rong Yeh, 'Changing Forces of Constitutional and Regulatory Reform in Taiwan' (1990) 4 *Columbia Journal of Chinese Law* 83; Jiunn-rong Yeh, 'Democracy-driven Transformation to Regulatory State: The Case of Taiwan' (2008) 3 *National Taiwan University Law Review* 31.

[3] For features of transitional constitutionalism, see Jiunn-rong Yeh and Wen-Chen Chang, 'The Changing Landscape of Modern Constitutionalism: Transitional Perspective' (2009) 4(1) *National Taiwan University Law Review* 145.

This chapter begins with a general survey of the ROC Constitution's provisions on local autonomy and power allocation among the different levels of government, followed by a contrasting picture of the reality of local autonomy in Taiwan. The disparity between constitutional text and reality is further exemplified by the downsizing of the Taiwan provincial government, as well as by the emerging significance of megacities, such as Taipei, which enjoy disproportionate powers and resources as against other autonomous localities.

I conclude that Taiwan presents a unique landscape of central-local relations against the backdrop of two constitutions: the textual one, designed for the whole of China, and the practical one, which evolved in tandem with Taiwan's path to democratisation. The transformation of local autonomy during the vibrant constitutional changes of the 1990s has also transformed the central-local relations as set out in the Constitution, from a limited autonomy in a unitary state into a hybrid and dynamic transitional federalism. Substantial reforms to the local autonomy system in the context of democratisation led to a new generation of central-local relations. Instead of being positioned at the periphery of a big China, Taiwan is now placed at the centre of its own territorial imagination for constitutional design. Against this backdrop, above all, Taipei's dual role, of national capital on the one hand and local government on the other, thus lies at the centre of political conflicts in the post-authoritarian era. Central-local relations will continue to play a significant role in the future of democratic transitional politics of Taiwan.

CONSTITUTIONAL REGULATION OF CENTRAL-LOCAL RELATIONS

The issue of central-local relations was an embedded controversy during constitution-making in the 1940s, against the backdrop of Japanese invasion, civil war and the disintegration of China.[4] In the conflict with the Communists, the Nationalists were concerned about localism, separatists and the remaining warlord forces, and regarded the multi-polar politics, which had lasted for decades since the establishment of the Republic, as the primary threat to it. These concerns were transformed into constitutional codification, in the form of a heightened level of centralised regulation of central-local relations.

Drafted by the Nationalists (*Kuomintang*, KMT), the ROC Constitution was adopted on 25 December 1946 by the National Assembly convened in

[4] For a more contextual introduction to the ROC Constitution's constitution-making background, see, eg, Suisheng Zhao, *Power by Design: Constitution-making in Nationalist China* (Honolulu, University of Hawaii Press, 1996).

Nanking. It was promulgated by the Government on 1 January 1947, and put into effect on 25 December of the same year. Prior to the drafting of the Constitution, in 1945, following the end of World War II, Taiwan had been handed back by the Japanese to China under the Nationalist regime as one of its provinces.[5] As a participating province, in 1946 Taiwan dispatched 17 delegates, along with those from other provinces, to engage in the drafting of the ROC Constitution. Not long after its promulgation, in 1949 the Nationalists retreated to Taiwan, making the Constitution a short-lived one on the mainland but, by chance, effectivein Taiwan right through to today.

Once conceived of as merely a peripheral province of China, Taiwan now became the only geographical base for the operation of the Constitution. In the early years of their rule in Taiwan, the Nationalists maintained the policy of 'striking back', and stuck to the framework of Greater China in the Constitution. However, as striking back apparently soon became impossible, and the Nationalists had to plan for permanent residence in Taiwan, the central-local relations as stipulated in the Constitution were bound to change. The only question was in what manner.

Central-local Relations in the ROC Constitution

Confronted with a nation covering a vast territory, regional diversity, multiple cultures and complicated factionalism, the framers of the Constitution found central-local relations a difficult issue. Though political concern had driven the Nationalist Government, in the constitution-making process, to pursue the goal for China of a full unitary state, it was nearly impossible for the central Government to govern without granting a degree of local autonomy. Therefore, the 1947 Constitution stipulated a unitary system with three levels of government for China, characterised by a centralised national Government and sub-levels of local autonomy with a limited degree of self-government. In addition, unusually, the Constitution clearly enumerated a wide range of matters over which powers of legislation and administration were granted. It took a total of two chapters (Chapters Ten and Eleven) and 22 articles of the Constitution to regulate central-local relations.

Chapter Eleven of the Constitution stipulated a two-tier local government system: provinces and counties.[6] The counties were further composed of lower townships and districts. In each province, there was to be a provincial council to exercise legislative power and a provincial government, with a Governor to exercise executive power. Members of the provincial council and the Governor were to be elected by the people of the province.

[5] See further Tay-sheng Wang, 'The Legal Development of Taiwan in the 20th Century: Toward a Liberal and Democratic Country' (2002) 11 *Pacific Rim Law & Policy Journal* 531.

[6] ROC Constitution, arts 112–136.

On the same level as the provinces in the Constitution were two special categories, reflecting the geopolitical complications of China in the 1940s. One was a special constitutional design called 'special municipalities'—megacities such as Beijing and Shanghai, along with the surrounding area—put under the direct jurisdiction of the central Executive Yuan. The other special category with provincial status concerned autonomy for the ethnic minorities. Here, the Constitution provided only that the local self-government system of the Mongolian Leagues (盟) and Banners (旗) should be prescribed by law (Article 119), and that the self-government system of Tibet should be safeguarded (Article 120).[7]

The county was the lowest level of constitutionally stipulated local autonomy, and was the basic unit of the government system under the Constitution. At the county level, the Constitution provided that there should be a county council to exercise legislative power, whose members should be elected by the people of the county. Also, there should be a county government with a Mayor, to be elected by the people of the county. The Mayor would have charge of county self-government and administer matters delegated to the county by the central or provincial government.

The Constitution provided special autonomous functions for counties. Each county would send a representative to the National Assembly. The National Assembly is by design a national organ similar to those found under democratic centralism, as it enjoys supremacy, represents the people and exercises higher legislative authority on their behalf. The National Assembly is also charged with the powers to elect and recall the President and the Vice-President, and to amend the Constitution.[8] Furthermore, the Constitution provides the rights of initiative and referendum, and powers of election and recall of the Mayor and other county self-government officials.

Chapter Ten of the Constitution regulated the division of power and responsibility between the central Government and local governments, and the settlement mechanism for any disputes between them.[9] Here the Constitution took four articles to specify four categories of powers, enumerating in detail the allocation of powers among the three levels of government. These four categories of powers covered:

(a) the powers of central Government (Article 107);
(b) the powers of the central Government, administration of which it might delegate to the provincial and county governments (Article 108);

[7] Ethnic minority has always been a critical issue within central-local relations in the unitary constitutional framework of Greater China, even under the rule of the People's Republic of China to date. See Zheng Ge, 'Economic Development and Cultural Autonomy in Tension: The Tibet Issue in China's Constitutional Framework' (2012) 42 *Hong Kong Law Journal* 195; B Sautman, 'Scaling Back Minority Rights?: The Debate about China's Ethnic Policies' (2010) 46 *Stanford Journal of International Law* 51.

[8] ROC Constitution, arts 25–34.

[9] ROC Constitution, arts 107–111.

(c) the powers of provinces, administration of which they might delegate to counties (Article 109); and
(d) the powers of counties (Article 110)

Article 107 listed 13 matters in category (a) above. As a result, the central Government was granted the most crucial powers, including, above all, financial measures. Article 108 set out 20 matters in category (b), which were powers of central Government but administration of which could be delegated to the provincial and county governments. Article 109 assigned 12 matters to category (c) above, over which the provincial governments would have the power of legislation and administration, but for which administrative powers might be delegated to counties. Any of the matters enumerated, in so far as they covered two or more provinces, might be undertaken jointly by the provinces concerned. If any province, in undertaking these matters, were to find its funds insufficient, it could, by resolution of the Legislative Yuan, obtain subsidies from the National Treasury. This regulation further granted the central Government the power of financial allocation. Article 110 listed 11 matters over which the county governments would have the power of legislation and administration (category (d) above). As with the third category, it was also provided that any of these matters, in so far as they covered two or more counties, might be undertaken jointly by the counties concerned.

While the Constitution allocated and delegated powers among the various levels of government, these divisions as set forth above were often overlapping and hard to disentangle. Article 111 provided that any matter not enumerated in these Articles would fall within the jurisdiction of the central Government if it was national in nature; within the jurisdiction of the province if it was provincial in nature; and within the jurisdiction of the county if it concerned the county. Disputes were to be settled by the Legislative Yuan. Notably, the Constitution, besides the enumeration of powers, allocated matters according to their 'nature', which, while meant to provide some degree of flexibility, nevertheless could cause further ambiguity.

As a result, central-local relations as set out under the ROC Constitution offered a form of limited local autonomy within a unitary state. The Republic of China in 1946, according to the Constitution, comprised 35 provinces with more than 3,000 counties, 12 special municipalities, two autonomous areas (Mongolia and Tibet) and one special administrative region (Hainan). However, such a design for territorial governance never had any chance of being implemented effectively throughout China. With the Nationalists' defeat in the Chinese civil war in 1949, and the relocation of the Nationalist Government to Taiwan, the Constitution encountered a completely different reality.

The Changing Landscape of Central-local Relations

The central-local government system as prescribed in the Constitution was never implemented. Instead it faced profound challenges when it was brought to Taiwan by the Nationalists. The framework set out in the Constitution was based on the vast territory of China. Although unfit for Taiwan, the Nationalist Government stuck to the ideology of claiming the sovereignty of China and applied the Constitution to Taiwan. During the martial-law era, democratic elections were limited to the local level; local autonomy began from lower levels under the Government's watch, but only to the extent that it did not threaten the stability of the Nationalists' rule. Later, supplementary elections to enlarge the seats in local legislatures were conducted to pacify dissidents and try to resolve the legitimacy crisis of the Government. Local politics thus became an important base, within which opponents managed to challenge the central Government's authoritarian rule.[10] In the early 1990s, as democratisation took off and constitutional reform was initiated, constitutionally stipulated central-local relations faced overall challenges in post-authoritarian Taiwan.

The system of local autonomy as set forth in the Constitution thus became unnecessarily complicated for Taiwan. Under this institution, for example, elections for administrators and legislators could occur at six or more levels, ranging from the central, provincial and county levels, to township levels. As a result, it became inevitable that the system of local autonomy, designed for a much larger state than Taiwan, must be changed. Constitutional revisions in Taiwan during the 1990s took an incremental approach. The second constitutional revision took place in 1992 and dealt with central-local relations.[11] Additional articles suspended Chapters Ten and Eleven so as to allow for more constitutional improvisation. Three levels of central-local government system were substantially modified, with the provincial level being downsized while special municipalities and counties were expanded, both geographically and as to their powers. Subsequently, in the early 1990s, a series of laws were introduced to pave the way for a new generation of central-local relations in Taiwan. Central-local relations were and remain one of the most significant issues on the road to Taiwan's democratic transition.

Local Self-Governance in the Era of Authoritarian Rule: 1945–89

Though the Constitution provided a foundation for the election of local governments, the self-governance afforded by it was close to a paper promise for two reasons. The first was the imposition of martial-law rule, which

[10] For the dissident movement in politics of the martial law era, see generally D Blundell (ed), *Taiwan since martial law: society. culture. politics. economy* (Taipei, National Taiwan University Press, 2012).

[11] For the incremental approach of Taiwan's constitutional revisions, see Jiunn-rong Yeh, 'Path Dependence or Collective Institutional Choice?: Modeling Constitutional Changes in the Context of Democratic Transition' (2006) 45(6) *Issues and Studies* 1 (in Chinese).

remained in place for 38 years until it was lifted in 1987. The second problem was the highly centralised financial power that created the continuing dependency of all local governments on the central Government. Article 107 of the Constitution stipulated matters over which powers of legislation and administration were assigned to the central Government, which also included 'central government finance and national revenues' and the 'demarcation of national, provincial and county revenues'.[12] Article 147 stipulated that 'the central government, in order to attain balanced economic development among the provinces, shall give appropriate aid to poor or unproductive provinces'.[13] As a result, the power over financial means was under the central Government's full control.

In the name of emergency powers during the Chinese civil war, the Nationalists compromised local autonomy as stipulated in the Constitution with a convenient means for undertaking social control.[14] During the martial-law period, the Government did not abide by the Constitution when passing a General Law of Provincial and County Self-Government, intended to provide a legal basis for local governments to embark on self-government. Instead, the Nationalist Government implemented a certain level of local autonomy through administrative rule, via the 1954 *Outline for the Implementation of Local Self-Government in every City and County of Taiwan* (Outline). Beginning in the 1960s, although the Outline was revised to enhance local self-government, local governments continued to lack autonomy, not only as regards powers in constitutionally guaranteed domains, but also in areas such as personnel and budgetary matters.[15]

Notably, in 1967 and 1979 respectively, Taipei City and Kaohsiung City were upgraded to become special municipalities, the special constitutional category intended for central control in China that was imposed in Taiwan. By designating the two major cities as special municipalities, the central Government had much stronger control over metropolitan areas of special economic and political significance. During the martial-law era, the governors of the Taiwan provincial governments and mayors of special municipalities were all appointed by the central Government. Elections were confined to trivial sub-level local governments, such as counties and lower-level townships. Even as late as 1990, the Constitutional Court denied the legislative power of the provinces and counties because of the lack of constitutionally stipulated general principles of provincial and county self-government.[16]

[12] ROC Constitution, art 107.

[13] ROC Constitution, art 147.

[14] For the KMT's policy in governing Taiwan, see P Chen-main Wang, 'Bastion created, a regime reformed, an economy reengineered 1949–1970' in MA Rubinstein (ed), *Taiwan: A New History* (New York, ME Sharpe, 1999) 320.

[15] D Fell, *Government and politics in Taiwan* (London and New York, Routledge, 2012) 144.

[16] *JY Interpretation No 260* [trans THY Taiwan International Law Offices], 19 April 1990.

Evading the constitutionally stipulated requirement for local autonomy with administrative rules, during the martial-law era the Nationalist Government manipulated 'local autonomy' through controlled local elections. This was political propaganda, designed to contrast Taiwan with mainland China under Communist rule.[17] Thanks to this make-believe local autonomy, however, political opponents, most of whom were local Taiwanese elites, emerged from local politics. Many dissidents who had started their political career through elections to local governments later became significant politicians in the opposition party.

Central-local Relations in Transitional Democracy: 1990–2010

Taiwan began a process of democratisation in 1987, when the major opposition party, the Democratic Progressive Party (DPP), was formed in the face of governmental intimidation, paving the way for a series of constitutional changes in the 1990s, which included central-local relations.[18] The framework of the ROC Constitution had apparently appeared too unrealistic for Taiwan. Above all, the transitional context created momentum in favour of modifying the local autonomy system.

First was the concern for political balance: with regard to the centralisation of power in the central Government, heads of local governments, regardless of party affiliation, now cried out for a larger share of powers. Second was the problem of allocating resources: with a growing population and urbanisation, inflexible financial means were unacceptable to local governments. Lastly, the drive for government efficiency in the face of global competitiveness was on the political agenda. The structure of three levels of government, plus lower-level local governing groups, was over-complicated in the new context of Taiwan.

The second constitutional revision of 1992 was a remarkable achievement, in which local self-government was granted a constitutional basis finally tailored to the Taiwanese context.[19] This constitutional revision suspended the requirement for a General Law on Provincial and County Self-Government to be made for undertaking local legislation, instead authorising local legislatures to enact self-governing law, and in so doing clearing a barrier imposed by the previous Constitutional Court interpretation, *JY Interpretation No 260*. Above all, centralised financial powers were replaced

[17] Regarding '*Fatung*', see Jiunn-rong Yeh, 'The Cult of *Fatung*, Representative Manipulation and Reconstruction in Taiwan' in G Hassall and C Saunders (eds), *The People Representatives: Electoral Systems in the Asia-Pacific Region* (Sydney, Allen & Unwin, 1997) 23.

[18] Jiunn-rong Yeh and Wen-Chen Chang, 'A Decade of Changing Constitutionalism in Taiwan: Transitional and Transnational Perspectives', presented at the Fourth Asian Forum for Constitutional Law, Hong Kong, 2011.12; Jiunn-rong Yeh, 'Constitutional Reform and Democratization in Taiwan: 1945–2000' in P Chow (ed), *Taiwan's Modernization in Global Perspective* (Westport, CN, Praeger, 2002) 47.

[19] Additional Articles of the ROC Constitution, art 9.

with more flexible arrangements. This round of constitutional revision also provided that provincial governors and municipal mayors should be elected by popular vote. And laws were introduced to put into practice a new generation of local autonomy. In 1994 the Self-Governance Act for Provinces and Counties and the Self-Governance Act for Special Municipalities were passed by the legislature, marking a new legal foundation for local self-government. In December 1994 the first popular elections were held for provincial governors and the mayors of Taipei and Kaohsiung cities, positions that had previously been government-appointed.

In the midst of this regime indigenisation and constitutional change, two constitutional institutions were further challenged, and the call for change intensified. The first was the National Assembly, designated in the Constitution as the supreme organ vested with the highest sovereignty and composed of delegates from counties all over the nation. It shouldered significant functions, such as electing and recalling the President and the Vice-President, and amending the Constitution.[20] Once it had been decided that sovereignty was to vest directly in the people and depart from undemocratic 'democratic centralism', and that universal suffrage for presidential elections should be provided for in the Constitution, the necessity for the National Assembly became less pressing. In the first round of constitutional revision, regular election of members of the National Assembly was stipulated, so as to replace those representatives elected during the mainland China era with new ones elected in Taiwan. Later constitutional revisions further shortened the terms of the members, and changed the National Assembly into a mission-orientated organ. Finally, in 2005, the last round of constitutional revision abolished the National Assembly altogether.[21]

The second institution was the Taiwan provincial government. Constructed on the model of a big China, the Taiwan government was but one provincial government out of more than 30. However, after 1949, Taiwan became the only province in which the ROC Constitution effectively reigned. Starting in the 1990s, a series of actions to streamline the government structure in the ROC Constitution, as well as the election of the President by universal suffrage, rendered the status of the Taiwan provincial government nothing but an embarrassment. Therefore, in 1997, the fourth constitutional revision substantially restrained its autonomous power. It stipulated that Taiwan provincial elections should be suspended; Taiwan Province would have a provincial government and a provincial advisory council; and the members of the provincial government, one of whom would be the provincial governor, would be nominated by the Premier and appointed by the President of the Republic. As a result, according to the current Constitution,

20 ROC Constitution, arts 25–34.

21 Additional Articles of the ROC Constitution, art 1.

the provincial government now serves only as a symbolic intermediate body between the central Government and local governments.

Finally, in 1999, the drafting of the Local Government System Act marked the completion of a body of legislation that enshrined local self-government in Taiwan. This marked the end of the past regime and a new era of central-local relations. The Local Government System Act, along with the Self-Governance Act for Provinces and Counties and the Self-Governance Act for Special Municipalities, served as the foundation for the new generation of local governance, with a system of local autonomy for Taiwan.

The Emergence of the Megacities: 2011–present

With the growing power of megacities like Taipei and Kaohsiung under the constitutionally safeguarded higher status of special municipalities, many counties argued insistently for an upgrade to the same status, reflecting a sense of regional disparity in post-democratisation Taiwan. In particular, national development-orientated strategy led to a divide between the north and the south: the north was generally more developed and urbanised than the south, empowering the national capital.[22] The Government's strategy was to pacify and suppress the growth of local governments, allocate financial resources unequally and support urbanisation in an unbalanced manner, against the background of rapid development—all of which contributed to over-investment in the north while ignoring the south. Furthermore, cooperation among levels of government is considerably more necessary in an era of globalisation. As early as the early 1990s, proposals had been made for adjusting administrative districts; after 2000, following the first regime change, when the DPP assumed power and the KMT became the opposition party, the redrawing of administrative districts became a hot issue that both major political parties sought to use to appeal to voters.

The status of the special municipalities became the envy of local governments. According to the ROC Constitution, the aim of designation of special municipalities is to subject strategically important and prime regions to the direct control of the central Government. The design of this institution recalls China's long history as a centralised empire, particularly in the context of the early Republic period, when warlords split territories to build up states within the state.

After 1949, when the KMT Government relocated to Taiwan, Taipei and Kaohsiung were designated as special municipalities by ordinance in 1967 and 1979 respectively. Subjecting the heads of special municipalities to the overall control of the central Government, the Government was able to utilise local resources to implement centralised control while pacifying

[22] See generally MA Rubinstein, 'Taiwan's Socioeconomic Modernization' in MA Rubinstein (ed), *Taiwan: A New History* (New York, ME Sharpe, 1999) 366.

local elites with official positions. However, compared with other local governments, their institutionally higher status and the capacity to direct the allocation of resources from the central Government allowed special municipalities to enjoy more benefits. Besides this, the heads of special municipalities, usually enjoying a high profile and esteem, have always been regarded as presidential hopefuls. As a result, other local governments strove to be upgraded to special municipalities.

In 2009, to pave the way for the redrawing of administrative districts, the Legislative Yuan revised the Local Government System Act. Article 4 of that Act stipulated that regions with a population of not less than 1,250,000, and that had special needs in their political, economic, cultural and metropolitan development, might establish special municipalities.[23] Article 7-1 stipulated that where a county or city was to be changed into a special municipality, the county/city government might formulate a plan for approval by the county/city council, which should be submitted by the Ministry of the Interior to the Executive Yuan for approval.[24] In 2010, besides Taipei City, which had already become a special municipality, Taipei County, Taichung County (merged with Taichung City), Tainan County (merged with Tainan City) and Kaohsiung City (merged with Kaohsiung county) were upgraded to special municipalities according to the Act. These five special municipalities are referred to as the 'Five Capitals'.

The formation of the Five Capitals marked a significant change from the previous 'Two Capitals' (Taipei and Kaohsiung) mode of power-sharing and resource allocation. This change not only reshuffled regional local politics, but also leaned towards more local autonomy. While the special municipality system was designed in China for better national control, as reflected in the Constitution, it evolved in Taiwan to serve the opposite function. It was anticipated that all the counties would, through merger between them, be upgraded to the special municipality level through an incremental process, and that the level of county government would hence forth be gradually replaced by the special municipalities.

CENTRAL-LOCAL RELATIONS IN A DEMOCRATIC TRANSITIONAL CONTEXT

Central-local relations are considered a significant issue during democratic transition. As early as the later stage of the martial-law period, the forces opposed to KMT rule had grown substantially, and they strove to win as many seats in local elections as possible, in order to show strength against the governing regime, despite the fact that national elections were not open

[23] Local Government System Act, art 4.
[24] Local Government System Act, art 7–1.

to full suffrage. With incremental introduction from local levels, opposition forces were thus growing much stronger, which finally culminated in the establishment of the first opposition party, the DPP.[25]

In the 1990s, with the lifting of martial law and the driving forces of democratisation, while the KMT Government maintained hold of power and control of the central Government, opposition parties still managed to break through and gain the edge in local elections.[26] Even within the KMT, the power struggle between the mainlanders and locals, and between the mainstream and the non-mainstream sections, took the form of a struggle between the central Government and local governments.

Stressful central-local relations continued, though the first regime change in 2000 brought Taiwan's politics into a new era. As from 2000, as fierce political divisions between pan-blue and pan-green camps took shape, coupled with a split Government, political struggle became even more confrontational.[27] As a result, controversial central-local disputes emerged amidst heightened political competition. Two disputes involving the central Government and Taipei City were later adjudicated by the Constitutional Court: they were cases where the head of a local government, a political star of the opposition party and regarded as a prospective presidential candidate, had challenged the central Government.[28]

As in the martial-law era, as well as in the transitional period, central-local relations can be expected to continue to play an important role in Taiwan's hyperactive politics of post-democratic transition.

Elections, Legitimacy and Sovereignty: The Downsizing of the Taiwan Provincial Government

The downsizing of the Taiwan provincial government was probably the most significant step in the renovation of central-local relations, as well as the most important event in the transitional politics of the 1990s. From the administrative point of view there was a need for organisational restructuring and reform. In this sense it was a way of enhancing administrative performance and national competitiveness, both of which required organisational

[25] MA Rubinstein, 'Political Taiwanization and pragmatic diplomacy: the eras of Chiang Ching-kuo and Lee Teng-hui, 1971–1994' in Rubinstein (ed) above n 22, 436; and D Roy, *Taiwan: A Political History* (Ithaca, NY, Cornell University Press, 2003) 152.

[26] For Taiwan's party politics in the 1990s and 2000s, see D Fell, *Party politics in Taiwan: party change and the democratic evolution of Taiwan, 1991–2004* (London and New York, Routledge, 2005).

[27] D Fell, *Government and politics in Taiwan* (London and New York, Routledge, 2012) 211.

[28] These two cases are discussed further in 'Partisan Politics, Taipei City and the Pro-Dialogue Court' below.

streamlining and the simplification of government administration.[29] In the original ROC Constitution, provincial government was the core unit under the central Government. An average province in China can contain more than 100 counties; as a result, the province becomes a very important intermediate form of local autonomy.

While Taiwan was but a peripheral and minor province in the ROC Constitution of 1947, it had been the only territory under effective constitutional control since 1949. During the martial-law era the central Government conducted its national rule through the Taiwan provincial government, so as to conform to the constitutional outlook of greater China. In the 1990s, however, the Taiwan provincial government overlapped with the national Government as regards population, constituency, power and legitimacy. This generally led to a subtle form of tension between the President and the Governor of Taiwan. Particularly following the second constitutional revision, when in 1994 the Taiwan Governor was directly elected by popular vote, there was constant friction between the democratically elected Governor and the unelected central Government. Indeed, the reputation of the Taiwan Governor, James CY Soong, and the popular support he attracted, surpassed that of the central Government. Soong became a political star within the KMT, and was touted as the political successor to President Lee Teng-hui. Their political relations soon deteriorated. As a result, in the eyes of some, the policy of downsizing provincial government amounted more to political suppression than constitutional reform. These political reasons not only provided legitimacy to a policy of downsizing provincial government, they also ensured that there was political impetus behind the restructuring of government.

The policy of downsizing provincial government can be traced to a consensus on the need for reform reached by the ruling and opposition political parties at a National Development Conference convened in December 1996, shortly after the first direct election of the ROC President. In July 1997, the National Assembly passed a constitutional amendment, adding key phrases such as:

> There will be no further elections for Taiwan Provincial Governor and provincial assemblymen and women as of December 21, 1998 ... The restructuring of the functions, business and organization of Taiwan Provincial Government will be conducted in accordance with special legal regulations ... The province will supervise matters to do with local government autonomy in accordance with instructions from the Executive Yuan.

The Executive Yuan even established a 'Committee for the Restructuring of the Functions, Business and Organization of Taiwan Provincial Government',

[29] See Jiunn-rong Yeh, 'Globalization, Government Reform and the Paradigm Shift of Administrative Law' (2010) 5(2) *National Taiwan University Law Review* 113.

to draft accompanying measures. In October 1998, the Legislative Yuan passed the Provisional Act for the Restructuring of the Functions, Business and Organization of Taiwan Government; and in January 1999, it passed the Local Government Systems Act and the Revised Act Governing the Allocation of Government Revenues and Expenditures, as various statutes accompanying the downsizing of the Taiwan provincial government were enacted.

Finally, as a result of the fourth constitutional revision of December 1998, the first democratically elected Taiwan Provincial Governor came to the end of his term in office and the Taiwan provincial government ceased to be a legal local government entity. The newly downsized provincial government became a field agency of the Executive Yuan. In addition, the democratically elected Taiwan Provincial Assembly was reorganised as the wholly-appointed Taiwan Provincial Consultative Council, stripped of its powers to make decisions on local government and supervise their implementation.

Besides serving the needs of government reform, the downsizing of the Taiwan provincial government was also significant politically, as it indicated that Taiwan was not just a province. The after-effects of downsizing the provincial government were also remarkable in the sense of electoral politics. James CY Soong later seceded from the KMT and competed in the 2000 presidential election; he split the KMT vote and helped hand the presidency to the DPP candidate Chen Shui-bian, resulting in the first regime change in Taiwan.[30] Besides, the downsizing of the provincial government now put the central Government in the front line of daily political relations with local governments. Power confrontations between political camps from now on tended to take shape more often in the form of disputes between central Government versus local governments.

Partisan Politics, Taipei City and the Pro-Dialogue Court

Power struggles concerning central-local relations did not disappear with the first regime change; instead, they intensified as a result of prior constitutional revisions that had helped forge a more dynamic local autonomy. Ever since the first direct presidential election in 1996, all elected presidents were former mayors of Taipei City, indicating that the mayor of the capital enjoyed a political advantage and usually played a crucial role in Taiwan's transitional power politics. In the first regime change (2000–08), incumbent President Chen Shui-bian did not enjoy a majority in the legislature, while facing a strong challenge from KMT political star and Taipei City Mayor Ma Ying-jeou. Many central-local disputes took the form of tension between the national Government and the Mayor of Taipei, requiring

[30] Roy, above n 25, 227.

Constitutional Court resolution. Two cases are of particular significance. The national health insurance case and the election postponement dispute were both appealed to the Constitutional Court, and in response the Court respectively rendered *Judicial Interpretations Nos 550 and 553*. Aware of the political sensitivity behind the legal issues presented, the Court deliberately took a cautious and pro-dialogue approach in resolving both cases.

The National Health Insurance Case

The establishment of the national health insurance program in 1996 was a great leap forward for social welfare policy in Taiwan. This ambitious compulsory health program was in general received positively, but the issue of allocating financial burdens remained controversial. One of the financial issues was the allocation of costs between the central Government and local governments. Though they enjoyed better financial resources as special municipalities, Taipei and Kaohsiung municipal governments constantly complained about their health insurance financial burdens. The Taipei municipal government refused to pay the contributions specified by the law, resulting in a series of administrative disputes and litigation. The tension between the central Government and local governments became worse because the Mayor of Taipei, Ma Ying-jeou, and the President, Chen Shui-bian, were major figures in opposing political parties. This made any judicial decision on the matter even more politically sensitive, and the dispute was finally appealed to the Constitutional Court for adjudication.

In *Interpretation No 550*, the Council of Grand Justices proclaimed that both the central Government and local governments bore constitutional duties of supporting a national health insurance program. The allocation of financial burdens to local governments such as Taipei City by the National Health Insurance Act was deemed constitutionally valid. The Court did not clearly indicate, however, how much of the financial cost borne by local governments was constitutionally permissible, the issue that had been appealed for resolution. Instead of indicating any concrete formula for allocation, the Court took an approach in favor of dialogue, as it has done in many similar cases. The Court further indicated that since local governments were required to share financial costs, they must be given sufficient opportunity to participate in policy formulation. The national Government must discuss and consult with local governments when drafting such policies to avoid possibly unreasonable outcomes, and must work out sound plans for the allocation of costs. In addition, the Court required that the legislature allow representatives of local governments to be present as observers during relevant legislative drafting sessions and to express their concerns.[31]

[31] *JY Interpretation No 550* [trans Raymond T Chu], 4 October 2002.

This ruling showed the consistent tendency of the Constitutional Court, in that it was unwilling to intervene in substantive policies but took a somewhat procedural approach. This case also revealed a disparity in resource allocation among local governments, particularly in favour of special megacities such as Taipei, and showed that in a contested democracy, the existence of multi-level governance provides incentives for levelling political rhetoric. Usually regarded as a potential prospective presidential candidate, the mayor of the national capital is usually able to challenge the central Government in favour of an already-favoured megacity such as Taipei, often at the expense of other local governments. With the new districting of the Five Capitals, the politics of Taiwan could change to a contest between the central Government and the five mayors.

The Postponement of the Local Election Case

The dispute on local elections was another case in which Taipei City was pitted against the central Government. In order to rearrange the lowest units of local governing bodies under district and township, the Taipei Municipal City Government postponed the election of lower-level local executives. According to the Local Government Act, such an election might be postponed in the light of special circumstances. However, the central Government considered that the rearrangement of the districts could be scheduled according to the settled election date, and thus there was no necessity for postponement, and no special circumstances. The City of Taipei is a protected local self-governance entity under Article 118 of the Constitution, and this petition concerned the delineation of jurisdictional boundaries and the dispute resolution mechanism between local governments and the central government. For these reasons this petition was not a mere dispute involving the interpretation of statutes among different government agencies; rather, it reached the constitutional level of correlation between the fundamental principles of democratic operation and the jurisdiction of local self-governance.[32]

In *Interpretation No 553*, the Court decided that since the Executive Yuan's decision to interfere with the exercise of local self-governance and override the Taipei municipal government's decision to postpone the election of district executives touched on specific fact-finding and statutory interpretation as to the applicability of a national statute over the exercise of local self-governance, the proper dispute resolution process for local government was to engage in administrative litigation regarding legality over the exercise of local self-governance authority. The proper agency and administrative court having jurisdiction over the petition should receive the case and render judgment accordingly. As a result, the Court referred to administrative litigation as the solution.

[32] *JY Interpretation No 553* [trans and ed Professor Andy Y Sun], 20 December 2002.

In this *Interpretation*, the Court was aware that even though the Local Governance Law provides mechanisms for communication and coordination, the failure of the local and supervisory governing agencies to implement such mechanisms in the local self-governance system has damaged the functionality of local governance. For the sake of constitutional protection over systematic local self-governance, the Court noted, the legislature ought to strengthen mechanisms in accordance with the meaning and purpose of the Constitution. As a result, once again, the Court took a reconciling and pro-dialogue approach; instead of pointing to the correct answer to the legal dispute, the Court referred both parties to a more dialectical mechanism to seek a solution. As can be seen in subsequent cases, with regard to the context of political confrontation after the first regime change, the Court would continue to take this approach to resolve a number of politically sensitive disputes during the first decade of this century.[33]

CONCLUSION

The textual stipulation of local autonomy in the ROC Constitution and its transformative development in Taiwan present two models of central-local relations, characterised by two distinctive pictures of political imagination. The vertical government system prescribed in the Constitution is rooted in the idea of a grand China, and stipulates limited autonomy within the highly centralised control of the national Government in the framework of a unitary state. The great changes rendered by the democratic transition in the 1990s, however, transformed this model of central-local relations into a more hybrid and dynamic transitional federalism. Amendments to the Constitution, as well as a series of landmark laws, resulted in substantial reforms to the local autonomy system and led to a new generation of central-local relations. Instead of being positioned at the periphery of a big China, Taiwan is now placed at the centre of its own territorial imagination for constitutional design.

A series of changes gave birth to this new model. First, the rigid and complicated regulation of local government stipulated in the Constitution was suspended; this allowed more room for legislative action in the later period, dealing with government re-adjustment. Secondly, the overly grand structuring of the levels of local government was reviewed; the National Assembly was simplified, transformed and finally abolished; the Taiwan

[33] Jiunn-rong Yeh, 'Presidential Politics and the Judicial Facilitation of Dialogue Between Political Actors in New Asian Democracies: Comparing the South Korean and Taiwanese Experiences' (2010) 8 *International Journal of Constitutional law* 911; and Wen-Chen Chang, 'Strategic Judicial Responses in Politically Charged Cases: East Asian Experiences' (2010) 8 *International Journal of Constitutional law* 885.

provincial government was downsized, and accordingly the effectiveness of local self-governing was enhanced; special municipalities are now no longer under the tight control of the central Government, and have even become major forces in local development. Thirdly, the highly centralised power of financial means was unlocked; local governments were thus given more space and more resources. Finally, the re-drawing of administrative districts signified another remarkable step in a new era for central-local relations; in contrast to the Two Capitals system, wherein the prime areas were subject to the control of the central Government while the leaders in local politics managed to challenge the central government and break the yoke of central control, the new system of Five Capitals now provides more balance in regional development, as well as in political competition.

This grand transformation can be appreciated further in the context of Taiwan's democratic transitional politics, for central-local relations have always been entangled with power politics in both authoritarian and transitional periods. Central-local relations in the martial-law era were a deliberate compromise between constitutional stipulation and reality. The KMT Government, while continuing to adhere to the ideology of a big China, permitted limited local autonomy through executive orders, out of political need, to evade constitutional stipulations. Besides, by designating special municipalities, the Government was able to control local politics and allocate resources to its own use. However, opponents and dissidents were able to break through in local elections and challenge the Government's authoritarian rule. These contested central-local relations continued into the transitional period. With the advent of democratisation, a series of constitutional revisions and legislation altered the local autonomy system to a significant degree. However, they also resulted in new rounds of political struggle between the central Government and local governments. The downsizing of the Taiwan provincial government and the two cases concerning legal disputes between central Government and Taipei City exemplified this same narrative: heavyweight politicians in opposition to the central Government. The strategic resolution over time of the transitional politics of these politically sensitive disputes tested the Court's capacity. In general, the Court has been able to advance the constitutionally mandated central-local relations into Taiwan's democratic geopolitical space through a call for a more engagement between the national Government and local governments.

The evolutionary path of Taiwan's central-local relations during all these periods can be attributed to the following four drivers: the political calculation of the power balance; the problem of allocating resources; concerns for administrative efficiency; and the rise of Taiwan's consciousness. Despite profound change over the last several decades, this forward momentum will likely continue, as central-local relations evolve over time in new institutional settings and in the context of transitional politics. Dynamic central-local relations will continue to play a significant role in Taiwan's transitional constitutionalism.

FURTHER READING

D Fell, *Party Politics in Taiwan: Party Change and the Democratic Evolution of Taiwan, 1991–2004* (London and New York, Routledge, 2005).

B He, B Galligan, and T Inoguchi (eds), *Federalism in Asia* (Cheltenham, Edward Elgar, 2007).

P Paolino and J Meernik (eds), *Democratization in Taiwan: Challenges in Transformation* (Aldershot, England and Burlington, VT, Ashgate, 2008)

SE Phillips, *Between Assimilation and Independence: The Taiwanese Encounter Nationalist China, 1945–1950* (Stanford, CA, Stanford University Press, 2003).

D Roy, *Taiwan: A Political History* (Ithaca, NY, Cornell University Press, 2003).

Jiunn-rong Yeh and Wen-Chen Chang, 'The changing landscape of modern constitutionalism: Transitional perspective (2009) 4:1 *National Taiwan University Law Review* 145.

Suisheng Zhao, *Power by Design: Constitution-Making in Nationalist China* (Honolulu, University of Hawaii Press, 1996).

4

Central-local Relations and the Constitutional Discourse on Political Decentralisation in 21st-Century Vietnam

BUI NGOC SON

Phep vua thua le lang ('The King's laws must yield to village rules')
[traditional Vietnamese saying]

INTRODUCTION

On 28 November 2013, the National Assembly of Vietnam enacted a new Constitution—the fifth to be enacted under the leadership of the Communist Party of Vietnam, although the original plan was a constitutional amendment rather than replacement.[1] One of contentious issues that caused a 'headache' to the constitution-makers, and which was controversially debated during the constitution-making process, was the issue of local government reform and central-local relations.[2] This chapter examines the discourse on local government and central-local relations in the latest Vietnamese constitution-making process from the perspective of political decentralisation.

[1] Under the leadership of the Communist Party, Vietnam has enacted five Constitutions: the 1946 Constitution after the August Revolution in 1945, the 1959 Constitution in North Vietnam after the Dien Bien Phu Victory, the 1980 Constitution after national unification, the 1992 Constitution after the *Doi moi* initiative and, most recently, the 2013 Constitution. For Vietnamese constitutional history in general, see M Sidel, *The Constitution of Vietnam* (New York and Oxford, Hart Publishing, 2009).

[2] Nguyen Le, 'Sửa Hiến pháp và sự "đau đầu" về chính quyền địa phương ['Constitutional Revision and the "Headache" for Local Government'], *VnEconomy* (19 August 2013), available at <http://vneconomy.vn/thoi-su/sua-hien-phap-va-su-dau-dau-ve-chinh-quyen-dia-phuong-20130819021510711.htm>.

Local government and central-local relations in post-1986 *Doi moi* (renovation) Vietnam have been considerably changed in the direction of decentralisation.[3] The Vietnamese Government had already practised fiscal and administrative decentralisation for several decades during the renovation period.[4] However, political decentralisation was not made part of any official agenda in a visible way until the latest constitutional revision process. The theme of local government and central-local relations has been among the most controversial themes in the debates over constitutional revision in Vietnam in the 2010s. Reformists clearly expressed support for further decentralisation by taking into account political demands. In contrast, conservatives harboured suspicions about political decentralisation. Consequently, the new Constitution includes several Delphic provisions, which both stipulate political decentralisation and insist on central control over local government. This discourse on political decentralisation and its constitutional consequence is an important move in a socialist regime, which is normally portrayed as having highly centralised power,[5] and deserves close scholarly attention.

Through the lens of democratic decentralisation, this chapter considers the discourse on central-local relations during the Vietnamese constitution-making process in the 2010s by examining its content, driving factors and influences. The structure of the chapter's argument is as follows: The rising discourse on political decentralisation is an important development in twenty-first-century Vietnam, and is derived from Vietnam's social complexity. Consequently, the new Constitution provides a base for the practice of political decentralisation, but does not abandon the attempt to centralise political power so as to balance competing reformist and conservative discourses. This requires rethinking of the conventional understanding of socialist power as being highly centralised, since political decentralisation for pragmatic reasons is possible within a socialist regime.

The remainder of this chapter unfolds in four further sections: the second section, 'Political Decentralisation', clarifies the conceptual framework of

[3] For pre-*Doi moi* central-local relations in Vietnam, see DG Marr, 'A Brief History of Local Government in Vietnam' in BJ Tria Kerkvliet and DG Marr (eds) *Beyond Hanoi: Local Government in Vietnam* (Singapore, NIAS Press, Institute of Southeast Asian Studies, 2004); Nguyen The Anh, 'Village Versus State: The Evolution of State-Local Relations in Vietnam Until 1945' (2003) 41(1) *Southeast Asian Studies* 101.

[4] Thaverporn Vasavakul, 'Rethinking the Philosophy of Central-Local Relations in Post-Central-Planning Vietnam' in M Turner (ed), *Central-Local Relations in Asia-Pacific: Convergence or Divergence?* (London, Macmillan Press Ltd, 1999) 166; CG Wescott, 'Hierarchies, Networks, and Local Government in Vietnam' (2003) 4(2) *International Public Management Review* 20; SA Fritzen, 'Probing System Limits: Decentralization and Local Political Accountability in Vietnam' (2006) 28(1) *The Asia Pacific Journal of Public Administration* 1.

[5] T Skocpol, *States and Social Revolutions: A Comparative Analysis of France, Russia, and China* (Cambridge and New York, Cambridge University Press, 1979); G Porter, *Vietnam: The Politics of Bureaucratic Socialism* (Ithaca, NY, Cornell University Press, 1993).

political decentralisation; the third section, 'Constitutional Discourse On Political Decentralisation in 21st-century Vietnam, describes the constitutional discourse on political decentralisation; the fourth section, 'Analysis', analyses its factors and influences; and the fifth section, 'Conclusion', concludes the chapter.

POLITICAL DECENTRALISATION

Political economists identify three forms of decentralisation: fiscal, administrative and political. Fiscal decentralisation refers to 'downward fiscal transfers, by which higher levels in a system cede influence over budgets and financial decisions to lower levels'.[6] Administrative decentralisation is defined as 'the dispersal of agents of higher levels of government into lower level arenas'.[7] Political decentralisation, also called 'devolution', refers to the transfer of resources and power to lower-level authorities. Political decentralisation supports 'democratization by giving citizens, or their representatives, more influence in the formulation and implementation of policies'.[8] It is hence sometimes called 'democratic decentralization'.[9] Political decentralisation implies that 'the selection of representatives from local electoral jurisdictions allows citizens to know better their political representatives and allows elected officials to know better the needs and desires of their constituents'.[10]

Mark Turner states that '[d]ecentralization is the conceptual framework that is most frequently employed to address central-local relations'.[11] This chapter adheres to this theory, but focuses on the political dimension of decentralisation for two reasons. First, the focus on political decentralisation is more congruent with the present general project of constitutional thematic studies. Secondly, the developmental potential and discourse on political decentralisation in Vietnam is underexplored, as scholars tend to focus on fiscal and administrative decentralisation, which have more empirical data.

Political or democratic decentralisation first involves direct or indirect elections of persons in authority at intermediate or local levels. It also needs

[6] J Manor, *The Political Economy of Democratic Decentralization* (Washington, DC, The International Bank for Reconstruction and Development/The World Bank, 1999) 9.

[7] ibid.

[8] The World Bank Group, 'Political Decentralization', *World Bank*, available at <www1.worldbank.org/publicsector/decentralization/political.htm>.

[9] Manor, above n 6.

[10] The World Bank Group, above n 8.

[11] M Turner, 'Central-Local Relations: Themes and Issues' in Turner (ed), above n 4.

community supervision or influence over projects or decisions by local authorities. Other varied democratic forms of decentralisation include

> efforts by local authorities to seek information on community needs and ways of addressing them, to establish local committees whose purpose is to foster active community participation, to organize and coordinate community involvement in projects (sometimes by hiring private firms to promote this), and to organize disenfranchised groups in order to assist them in voicing demands ...[12]

According to the World Bank,

> political decentralization often requires constitutional or statutory reforms ... The constitutions should be used to enshrine the broad principles on which decentralization is to operate, including the rights and responsibilities of all levels of government; the description and role of key institutions at central and local levels; and, the basis on which detailed rules may be established or changed. One or more laws should define the specific parameters of the intergovernmental fiscal system and the institutional details of the local government structure, including, key structures, procedures (including elections), accountabilities and remedies.[13]

Decentralisation is now a global trend. As James Manor observes, '[n]early all countries worldwide are now experimenting with decentralization'.[14] Developing countries experimented with it during the 1970s and early 1980s.[15] Vietnam has been riding the wave of decentralisation since 1991, as a component of the broader program of national 'renovation' (*Doi moi*).[16]

The *Doi moi* program, initiated in 1986 by the Sixth Congress of the Communist Party of Vietnam, was meant to transform the centrally planned economy into a socialist-orientated market economy. A new Constitution was enacted in 1992, amended once in 2001, and implemented during the *Doi moi* period, until its recent replacement by the 2013 Constitution. Under the *Doi moi* constitutional framework, three socialist constitutional principles deriving from the soviet pedigree, namely 'unity of powers', 'democratic centralism' and 'socialist legality', consistently shaped central-local relations. The principle of unity of power denies both horizontal and vertical separation of powers, which leads to the concentration of powers in the central Government. The principle of democratic centralism accentuates the idea that decisions must be eventually made by the central power, although it allows prior 'democratic' deliberations at lower levels. The principle of socialist legality requires strict implementation of central Government's law and policies nationwide, and in particular underlines the conformity of the actions of local government with the central Government's laws and policies.

[12] Manor, above n 6, 11.

[13] The World Bank Group, above n 8.

[14] Manor, above n 6, 4.

[15] DA Rondinelli and JR Nellis, 'Assessing Decentralization Policies in Developing Countries: The Case for Cautious Optimism' (1986) 4 *Development Policy Review* 3.

[16] Wescott, above n 4, at 22.

Within these directive principles, local governments were formulated in *Doi moi* Vietnam at communal, district and provincial levels. The two basic local bodies were People's Councils, representative local bodies, elected by the local people, and People's Committees, local administrative local bodies, created by the People's Councils at the same level. The ambitious centralised Government is obvious. To begin with, the National Assembly enjoyed the supreme power to supervise local government. Its Standing Committee could exercise supervision and control over the activities of, and give guidance to, the People's Councils at the provincial level, annul improper-resolutions passed by them and disband them whenever they caused serious harm to the interests of the people. In addition, the Government's control over local government was constitutionally guaranteed. The Government could direct, guide and control the People's Committees at all levels. The Prime Minister was vested with the power to approve the election, release from duty, secondment or dismissal of Chairmen and Deputy Chairmen of People's Committees at provincial level. In addition, the Prime Minister was authorised to suspend or annul decisions and directives of People's Councils and Chairmen of People's Committees at provincial level where they were inconsistent with the Constitution, the law or other formal written documents of superior state organs. However, local autonomy was also guaranteed to a certain degree. The People's Councils were allowed to issue resolutions to deal with local affairs.[17]

During the *Doi moi* period, central-local relations in Vietnam changed, characterised by a considerable degree of 'decentralisation' (*'phan cap, phan quyen'*). The Vietnamese phase *'phan cap, phan quyen'* includes two semantic elements: *'phan cap'* means allocating specific implementation duties to different levels, which captures the meaning of deconcentration or fiscal and administrative decentralisation; *'phan quyen'* means allocating powers, which is more associated with devolution or political decentralisation.[18] Scholars have demonstrated the remarkable fiscal and administrative decentralisation (*phan cap*) in Vietnam during the *Doi moi* period. Regarding fiscal decentralisation, as Fritzen observes,

> Vietnam is already fiscally decentralised to a significant degree to the provincial level, in the sense that the share of the economy controlled by the central government is not unusually high ... The share of the budget assigned to all local government levels has increased substantially ... This share of subnational expenditure would rank among the highest in the world.[19]

[17] This paragraph is drawn from the following articles of the 1992 Constitution, arts 83, 112, 114, 118, 119 and 120.

[18] Fritzen, above n 4, 9.

[19] ibid, 4.

Administrative decentralisation became evident in the emerging frameworks for managerial discretion and the Government's Public Administration Reform program.[20]

Compared to fiscal and administrative decentralisation, political decentralisation (*phan quyen*) was not on the official agenda during the *Doi moi* period until the last constitutional revision. The Vietnamese Government was willing to decentralise fiscally and administratively for effective public governance, but would only take cautious steps in regard to democratic or political decentralisation because of its anticipation of political difficulties. But the conceptually related program was called 'grassroots democratisation' (*dan chu hoa co so*).[21] Promoted in 1998 by Instruction No 30-CT/TW by the Politburo of the Communist Party and Decree No 71/1998/NĐ-CP by the Government, after unprecedented large-scale demonstrations against local officials' corruption in Thai Binh province in 1997, this program was meant to constrain local corruption and foster accountability and popular participation at grassroots level, under the slogan that 'the people know, the people discuss, the people do, and the people monitor'. On this view, the grassroots democratisation program stipulated that decisions of grassroots local governments (Commune People's Councils and Committees) must be communicated to the citizens, and must be subject to their supervision. Villagers were encouraged to engage in communal affairs through organisational fora, such as village conferences.[22]

In particular, the use of new *huong uoc* (communal contracts) was also encouraged. This practice has its roots in the tradition of *huong uoc* in Vietnam. Traditional *huong uoc* are a sort of 'social contract', the 'constitutions' of the village.[23] They set out general rules of communal governing machinery (consisting of a council of nobles and a village officer), and include customary, cultural and moral rules for the everyday behaviour of the villagers. Within the *huong uoc* framework, village communes dealt with their own affairs regarding culture, education, agriculture, finance and even local security. *Huong uoc* may include rules different from and even in contrast to official laws, as reflected in the traditional adage '*Phep vua thua le lang*' ('the King's laws must yield to village rules'). *Huong uoc* hence represent the village's autonomy in traditional Vietnam. New or modern *huong uoc* are drafted under the central power's regulatory guidance. They have been used, not to set up the communal governing machinery, but to

[20] ibid, 5.

[21] ibid, 7.

[22] RK Larsen, 'Reinventing Rural Development in Vietnam: Discursive Constructions of Grassroots Democracy During the Renovation Reform' (2011) 52(3), *Asia Pacific Viewpoint* 318.

[23] For traditional or 'old' *huong uoc*, see Bui Xuan Dinh, *Huong uoc va Quan ly Lang xa* [*Communal Contracts and the Management of Villages*] (Hanoi, Social Science Publishing House, 1998); Vu Duy Men, *Huong uoc co Dong bang Bac Bo* [*Ancient Communal Villages in North Vietnam*] (Hanoi, National Politics Publishing House, 2010).

continue to uphold the community's customs in compliance with state regulations, and to regulate local affairs, for example what the villagers must know and discuss according to the 'grassroots democratisation' program.[24] New *huong uoc* hence are an instrument for grassroots democratisation. In short, with the 'grassroots democratisation' program as the conceptually related attempt, *phan quyen* (political decentralisation) was not on the formal agenda in post-*Doi moi* Vietnam until the introduction of the last constitutional revision plan.

CONSTITUTIONAL DISCOURSE ON POLITICAL DECENTRALISATION IN 21ST-CENTURY VIETNAM

The situation changed following the latest constitutional revision. The Communist Party, at its XIth Congress in January 2011, included statements setting out the meaning of political decentralisation, directed towards the state's later constitutional revision program. The Party not only encouraged 'proper allocation (*phan cap*) to the local government', but also guaranteed 'the autonomy and self-accountability (of local government) in deciding and implementing policies within the allocated sphere'.[25]

Following the Party's direction, the proposal for constitutional amendment approved by the National Assembly in its 4 August 2011 session[26] referred to

> Amending, and supplementing provisions regarding local government in the direction that defines more clearly the legal position of local government, the organisational model, the authorities and duties of the local government, and the mechanism for *allocation and devolution* (*phan cap, phan quyen*) between central government and local government.[27]

For the first time, the idea of *phan quyen* (devolution) or political decentralisation was on the official agenda of the state, and more importantly on the constitutional reform agenda.

24 For the relation of new *huong uoc* to grassroots democratisation, see Dao Tri Uc (ed), *Huong uoc trong Qua trinh Thuc hien Dan chu o Nuoc ta Hien nay* [*Communal Contracts in the Process of Implementing Democracy in Our Nation today*] (Hanoi, National Politics Publishing House, 2003).

25 Party's Central Committee, 'Political Report at the XIth Congress of the Party, Section XI', available at <http://chinhphu.vn/portal/page/portal/chinhphu/NuocCHXHCNVietNam/ThongTinTongHop/noidungvankiendaihoidang?categoryId=10000716&articleId=10038382>.

26 'Nghị quyết về việc Sửa đổi, Bổ sung Hiến pháp năm 1992 và Thành lập Ủy ban Dự thảo Sửa đổi Hiến pháp năm 1992' ['Resolution on Amending and Complementing the 1992 Constitution and Establishing the Committee for Amending the 1992 Constitution'], *Duthaoonline*, available at <http://duthaoonline.quochoi.vn/DuThao/Lists/DT_DUTHAO_NGHIQUYET/View_Detail.aspx?ItemID=32&TabIndex=2&TaiLieuID=62>.

27 ibid (emphasis added).

Decentralisation in Vietnam is now expressed in constitutional terms. This implies possible decentralisation beyond fiscal and administrative aspects. The official commitment to development mechanisms for *phan quyen* opens the door for the rise of a liberalising discourse on political decentralisation. The various participants in this reformist discourse included constitution-makers, legislators, legal scholars, lawyers and actors within civil societies. They mobilised for *phan quyen* as the base for the organisation and operation of local government and for local-central relations. They then offered detailed proposals for political decentralisation, most notably popular election of local governors, removal of the People's Council at district level and judicial review of local legal documents.

Let us consider the reformist discourse in greater detail.

Three Constitutional Principles of Local Government

The issue of local government was one of three issues that resulted in serious divisions among the constitution-makers and Assembly deputies.[28] In debating local government, they were divided into conservative and reformist groups.[29] The conservatives relied on the conventional socialist rhetoric of unity of powers, democratic centralism and socialist legality, so as to defend the model of local government established by the 1992 Constitution. In contrast, the reformists proposed 'new' principles of local government to be mandated by the Constitution, which would direct the future concrete design of local government to be undertaken by legislation. Generally speaking, the proposed principles all reflect the spirit of organisational and functional autonomy of local government, which indicates a trend toward political decentralisation.

The first proposed principle may be called the *difference principle*. Basically, the 1992 Constitution and the related laws established a system of local government based on the model of central government. The creation, functions and relations of the People's Councils and People's Committees

[28] Two other issues are constitutional review and land ownership.

[29] This is reflected in the reports of the Constitutional Amendment Commission to the National Assembly, all available at the special online site of the National Assembly for constitution-making, *Duthaoonline*, at <http://duthaoonline.quochoi.vn/DuThao/Lists/DT_DUTHAO_NGHIQUYET/View_Detail.aspx?ItemID=32>. Comments of the Assembly deputies on the draft constitution were also posted on this website. Official media also disseminate different comments by the legislators on local government. See, eg, 'Chua nga ngu ve Chinh quyen dia phuong' ['The Issue of Local Government has not yet been Decided'], *NetLuat*, June 2013, available at <www.netluat.vn/vi-VN/print/zone/chua-nga-ngu-ve-chinh-quyen-dia-phuong/245/500>; 'Van Ban Khoan Thu hoi Dat, Chinh quyen dia Phuong' ['The Issues of Withdrawal of Lands and Local Government are Still in a Divided Mind'], *Sài gòn Giải phóng*, November 2013, available at <http://sggp.org.vn/chinhtri/2013/11/331826/>.

at all local levels basically mirror these of the National Assembly and the Government. For instance, according to the 1992 Constitution, the People's Committees are the administrative bodies, created by popularly elected People's Councils and responsible to the latter, which reflects the central arrangement in which the Government is the administrative body, created by a popularly elected National Assembly and responsible to the latter. Conservatives insisted on the consistency of local government with central government to ensure the unity and stability of the state apparatus, while reformers believe that local governments deal with different affairs that reflect local interests and hence need not replicate central arrangements.[30]

Consider, for example, the discussion by Le Thi Nga, Vice-Chairperson of the National Assembly's Judicial Committee, in the Assembly deputies' special meeting on constitutional revision on 14 March 2013.[31] She lamented that '[l]ocal governments are now too cumbersome, nearly a copy of the central Government in the way that what is available in the central model is available in the local model'.[32] She pointed out that in reality, by different ways, governments in different provinces and cities were often compelled to ask the central Government for special policies to 'release' them. In some cases, she continued, some local governments had even issued 'trespassing' policies to meet the imperative needs of local governance. She finally concluded that the Constitution should allow local governments to be organised and operated in a manner different from each other and from the central Government.[33]

The second proposed principle may be called the *diversity principle*. Under the 1992 Constitution and related laws, local government at all levels and at all regions throughout the country was organised in the same way. The Communist Party, at its XIth Congress, however, proposed the diversity principle. First, it encouraged the study of different possible arrangements of local government in different areas, namely rural, urban and the islands. Secondly, it stipulated that the People's Council need not be organised at the district level.[34] During the constitutional revision process conservatives consistently relied on the traditional rhetoric of unity and stability of the

[30] See, eg, different positions in a workshop on local government held by the Constitutional Amendment Commission on 28 August 2013: 'Tọa đàm về chế định chính quyền địa phương trong Dự thảo sửa đổi Hiến pháp năm 1992' ['Workshop on Local Government in the Draft Revised Constitution'], *Online Newspaper of the Communist Party* (August 2013), available at <http://dangcongsan.vn/cpv/Modules/News/NewsDetail.aspx?co_id=28340715&cn_id=605263#>.

[31] 'Trung ương có gì, dưới có cái đó' ['What is Available in the Centrality is Available at the Locality'], *Vietnamnet*, March 2013, available at <http://vietnamnet.vn/vn/chinh-tri/112843/trung-uong-co-gi--duoi-co-cai-do.html>.

[32] ibid.

[33] ibid.

[34] Party's Central Committee, above n 25.

state apparatus so as to defend the uniformity of local governments' organisation, whereas reformers strongly mobilised for the diversity alternative.[35]

To cite an example, Nguyen Sy Dung, a famous official and scholar, Vice-Chairman of the National Assembly's Office, acerbically commented:

> Our system of local government is basically designed following the Soviet model: all levels of government have similar functions and duties, like the [Russian] *matryoshka* dolls. All *matryoshka* dolls are beautiful, but the smaller are completely hidden by the bigger.[36]

He then proposed diversifying arrangements for local government.[37]

The third principle is *local self-government*. This principle reflects the essence of political decentralisation and deserves closer attention. In the plenary session of the National Assembly in late 2012, when the deputies discussed the draft Constitution, there were diverse positions on this principle. Such conservatives as Trieu La Phan insisted on retaining the system of local government as established in the 1992 Constitution. Yet many reformists, such as deputies Huynh Nghia, Hoang The Lien and Tran Du Lich, called strongly for local self-government.[38]

To illustrate this, consider the comments by Tran Du Lich from Ho Chi Minh City, an active legislator, economist and member of the Constitutional Amendment Drafting Board.[39] To begin with, Tran Du Lich proposed reconceptualising local government. According to him, 'local government (including the People's Councils) is a component of the administrative system, and has its own power to implement laws in the localities and protect the interests of the local people within the framework not contrary to national interests'.[40] This 'reconceptualisation' challenges the conventional conception in Vietnam, deriving from the soviet tradition, which regards the local People's Councils (the soviets) as a component of the soviet hierarchical system. The implication is that local People's Councils should have their

[35] See n 30 above; Thang Văn Phúc, 'Sửa đổi, bổ sung các quy định của Hiến pháp năm 1992 về Chính phủ và Chính quyền địa phương' ['Amending the Provisions in the 1992 Constitution on the Government and Local Government'], *Communist Review*, September 2013, available at <www.tapchicongsan.org.vn/Home/du-thao-sua-doi-nam-1992/2013/23405/Sua-doi-bo-sung-cac-quy-dinh-cua-Hien-phap-nam-1992.aspx>.

[36] Nguyen Sy Dung, 'Mô hình chính quyền địa phương đã lỗi mốt' ['Model of Local Government is Outdated'], *Vnexpress*, August 2013, available at <http://vnexpress.net/tin-tuc/thoi-su/mo-hinh-chinh-quyen-dia-phuong-da-loi-mot-2870853.html>.

[37] ibid.

[38] 'Mo hinh Chinh quyen Dia Phuong: Huong toi Bao dam Tinh Tu chu, Tu Chiu Trach nhiem' ['Model of Local Government: Toward Self-Government and Self-Accountability'], *Ministry of Justice*, March 2013, available at <http://moj.gov.vn/hienphap1992/News/Lists/giaidapthacmac/View_Detail.aspx?ItemID=5257>.

[39] Tran Du Lich, 'Phai lam ro ve Chinh quyen Dia phuong' ['Local Government Should be Clarified'], *Duthaoonline*, November 2012, available at <http://duthaoonline.quochoi.vn/DuThao/Lists/DT_DUTHAO_NGHIQUYET/View_Detail.aspx?ItemID=32&TabIndex=4&YKienID=875>.

[40] ibid.

own spaces independent from the central people's council—the National Assembly. The second point in Tran Du Lich's position suggests that local government as a whole should have its own power to implement laws for the benefit of the local people, given that this would not contravene general policies of the central Government. He proceeded to articulate the organisational principle of local government in light of the notion of local self-government, as follows:

> The general principle is to promote local self-government, and to promote the role of the local representatives in protecting local interests. It is unacceptable that a government of a city does not have even minor independent powers. For example, when Da Nang [a dynamic province in central Vietnam] wished to learn from the Capital [Hanoi], it had to ask the National Assembly for some powers regarding residential areas and administrative penalties. In fact, such powers are the self-governing powers of a city government at the local level, which should be provided in the Constitution. These powers are definitely within the local sphere, and not inconsistent with national interests. These powers are not state powers in general but the self-governing powers of the local people beyond any other framework. This principle should be provided in the Constitution to be realized.[41]

In early 2013, the draft Constitution was released to the public for debate, and the tendency towards support for local self-government was evident. Importantly, the Government's *Report on the Result of Collecting Opinions on the Draft Amendments to the 1992 Constitution* (dated 5 April 2013) demonstrated that numerous ministries and provinces supported local government autonomy and self-accountability.[42] On that basis, the Government (ambiguously) proposed to the National Assembly that the Constitution should present on one hand 'the principle that guarantees the autonomy and self-accountability of local government' and, on the other hand, 'the principle of the supervision and control of central government over local government'.[43]

Legal scholars in particular strongly advocated in public fora for devolution (*phan quyen*) and local self-government (*tu quan dia phuong*), the essence of political decentralisation. To illustrate this, we can consider the discussions in a special workshop on the draft Constitution's chapter on

[41] ibid.

[42] Vietnamese Government, 'Báo cáo Chính Phủ về kết quả lấy ý kiến vào Dự thảo sửa đổi Hiến pháp năm 1992' ['Government's Report on the Result of Collecting Opinions on the Draft Amendments to the 1992 Constitution'], *Duthaoonline*, April 2013, available at <http://duthaoonline.quochoi.vn/DuThao/Lists/DT_DUTHAO_NGHIQUYET/View_Detail.aspx?ItemID=32&TabIndex=2&TaiLieuID=1064>. The ministries supporting the trend included: Ministry of Internal Affairs, Ministry of Information and Communication, Ministry of Planning and Investment, Ministry of Medicine, Government's Office. The provinces and cities supporting the trend included: Bắc Ninh, Ninh Thuận, Quảng Trị, Sóc Trăng, Trà Vinh, Điện Biên, Hà Tĩnh, Nghệ An, An Giang, Tây Ninh, Điện Biên, Thái Bình and Hồ Chí Minh City.

[43] ibid.

local government, held in Ho Chi Minh in the midst of public constitutional consultation.[44] Speaking in this workshop, Truong Dac Linh, a law professor at Ho Chi Minh City University of Law, put forward the criticism that the chapter on local government was the weakest chapter in the draft Constitution, as it failed to articulate the principle of local self-government. That chapter, Linh continued, failed to appreciate the local people as the most important subject of local government, who practise their power directly or indirectly through their representatives. Linh then suggested that the Constitution should provide that '[l]ocal government be organized and operate according to the principle of autonomy and self-accountability within the legally allocated sphere. The local people practise their power in the localities directly and (indirectly) through local governments created by the law'.[45]

Commenting in the same meeting, Nguyen Cuu Viet, a distinguished law professor and former Dean of the Vietnam National University Law School at Hanoi, similarly called for local self-government. He critically noted that while the Party had agreed on the autonomy and self-accountability of local government, the draft Constitution failed to follow the Party's direction. He believed that autonomy and self-accountability constituted the essence of local self-government. He added that local self-government does not mean the absence of oversight or coordination. He then submitted that the chapter on local government in the Constitution should be 'rewritten' in a way that recognised local self-government as a fundamental principle.[46]

Tran Du Lich consistently defended his proposal for local self-government. He further underlined the position that the People's Councils are not the lower levels of the National Assembly. He even moved further to call for 'designing the model of local government in light of local self-government—not the lower level of anyone'.[47]

In the same workshop, Dao Tri Uc, a law distinguished professor who served for many years as Director of the Institute of State and Law, and a member of the Constitutional Amendment Drafting Board, argued that local self-government was the acme of devolution. He then proposed, 'We are in a transitional period. Therefore, [institutional] design should be taken in the way that facilitates rather than blocks the move forward. Meanwhile, the move to local self-government-devolution is the inevitable trend.'[48] In an article published by the *Communist Review* (*Tap chi Cong san*), Dao Tri Uc further argued that in the context of building up the 'rule of law state'

[44] Ta Lam, 'Dia Phuong Tu quan, Quan chuc het Ban dat' ['Local Self-Government, Authorities Cannot Sell Lands'], *Vietnamnet*, March 2013, available at <http://vietnamnet.vn/vn/chinh-tri/110864/dia-phuong-tu-quan--quan-chuc-het-ban-dat.html>.
[45] ibid.
[46] ibid.
[47] ibid.
[48] ibid.

and 'socialist-oriented market economy', Vietnam should promote not only *phan cap* (administrative and fiscal allocation) but also *phan quyen* (political devolution.) He stated:

> Vertical devolution includes the requirements of local autonomy and local self-government, which are the basis for the activeness and creativeness of local governments in their policy decisions regarding social, economic developments. It also includes the requirement of respecting the interests of local people.[49]

Legal scholars contrasted self-local government with the 'democratic centralist' model and highlighted the virtues of the former.[50] To illustrate this, Vũ Thư, a law professor at the Institute of State and Law, insists that local self-government is created by the local people and serves the interests of the local people, and that local self-government has independent powers and is not to be directed by central Government as is the practice in the democratic centralist model, because its authorities and duties have been defined by the law.[51] He points out several advantages of local self-government, such as enhancing local democracy, local administrative accountability, popular participation in local decision-making, and the creativeness and effectiveness of local governance.[52]

Specific Proposals for Political Decentralisation

There were essentially two trends in the debate over the specific organisation of local government. Conservatives insisted that local government should be organised over three local levels, as had been conventional in Vietnam, to ensure the stability and unity of state power.[53] In contrast, reformists, on the ground of the principles of difference and diversity, proposed that local

[49] Dao Tri Uc, 'Về mối quan hệ giữa Trung ương và địa phương trong sửa đổi Hiến pháp năm 1992' ['On the Central-Local Relations in Amending the 1992 Constitution'], *Communist Review*, February 2013, available at <www.tapchicongsan.org.vn/Home/du-thao-sua-doi-nam-1992/2013/20032/Ve-moi-quan-he-giua-Trung-uong-va-dia-phuong-trong-sua.aspx>.

[50] Nguyễn Minh Phương, 'Thực trạng phân cấp, phân quyền và vấn đề tự quản địa Phương tại Việt Nam' ['The Reality of Decentralization and Local Self-Government in Vietnam'], paper at *Hội thảo Tổ chức chính quyền địa phương ở Việt Nam: Những vấn đề lý luận và thực tiễn* [*Conference on Organization of Local Government in Vietnam: Theory and Practice*], Ninh Thuận, 6 April 2013, available at <http://duthaoonline.quochoi.vn/DuThao/Lists/DT_TAILIEU/Attachments/1188/02-Phanquyen-PhuongNM.pdf>; Vũ thư, 'Cải cách chính quyền địa phương ở Việt Nam hiện nay' ['Reforming Local Government in Today's Vietnam'], Institute for Science of Organization, available at <http://isos.gov.vn/Thongtinchitiet/tabid/84/ArticleId/294/language/vi-VN/C-i-cach-chinh-quy-n-d-a-ph-ng-Vi-t-Nam-hi-n-nay.aspx>.

[51] ibid.

[52] ibid.

[53] See Vietnamese Government, above n 42. They included the Ministry of Public Security and Ministry of Agriculture and Rural Development, and different provinces, such as Cao Bằng, Lào Cai, Bộ Nông nghiệp và Phát triển nông thôn, Vĩnh Long, Lạng Sơn, Bắc Ninh, Yên Bái, Nghệ An and Quảng Bình.

government in urban areas (especially in more developed cities like Hanoi City and Ho Chi Minh City) might have two levels (provincial and communal), while local government in rural and remote areas might include three levels (provincial, district and communal). It was explained that in urban areas, as public services can be provided smoothly and distances are small, the intermediate district level is unnecessary; meanwhile, in rural or remote areas, the intermediate district level is necessary because of the distance between the provinces and the communes.[54]

The overall proposal for the structure of local government follows the principle of local self-government. Consistently with the ideal that local self-government is created by the people, it was suggested that the local administrative governors be elected directly by the people themselves rather than being selected by the People's Councils. In terms of the People's Councils, reformists believe that these bodies can be removed at the intermediate level—the district level in the areas with three levels of local government. To supervise local government, legal rather than political or administrative means were invoked.

Let us consider in greater detail three specific proposals controversially debated during the cycle of constitutional revision.

Popular Election of Local Leaders

On 19 August 2013, when the constitution-makers were grappling with the difficult issue of local government, a group at the National Assembly's Office released an empirical report on the theme.[55] The group conducted interviews with 800 people at five localities, including representatives of the People's Councils, members of the People's Committees, officials of these bodies and ordinary people. The report demonstrated that most people agreed on the direct election of Chairmen of People's Committees. Reformists strongly supported this trend, and particularly focused on the possibility of popular elections of provincial and communal leaders, who have strong resonance with the local people.

In fact, in 2008 the Government had already submitted to the National Assembly a proposal for piloting the people's direct vote for the Chairmen of the Communal People's Committees, in the hope of enhancing the accountability of communal governance. Accordingly, it was proposed that 385 communes throughout the nation should directly elect their governors on 25 April 2009.[56] Many Assembly deputies supported the proposal, while

[54] Nguyen Sy Dung, above n 36.

[55] 'Kiến nghị dân bầu trực tiếp chủ tịch huyện, xã' ['The proposal for Popular Election of District and Communal Chairmen'], *Vietnamnet*, 19 August 2013, available at <http://vietnamnet.vn/vn/chinh-tri/136481/kien-nghi-dan-bau-truc-tiep-chu-tich-huyen--xa.html>.

[56] 'Vietnam Chua bau Chu tich xa' ['Vietnam Has not yet Practised Popular Election of Communal Chairmen'], *BBC* (16 November 2008), available at <www.bbc.co.uk/vietnamese/vietnam/story/2008/11/081116_direct_elex_scrapped.shtml>.

many others worried about this new practice. Uong Chu Luu, Vice-Chairman of the National Assembly, stated that '[t]he popular election of the Chairmen of communal People's Committees relates to the organization of government. The promotion of direct democracy at grassroots level should be cautious and needs appropriate steps'.[57] In the end, the proposal was not approved by the National Assembly.[58]

However, during the wave of constitutional revision in the 2010s, the issue returned to the table. Reformists called for revision of the Constitution in a way that would allow local people at communal level to elect their administrative governors directly.[59] In particular, the Fatherland Front, a socio-political organisation putatively presenting the popular voice, after collecting popular comments on the draft constitutional amendments undertaken in early 2013, proposed:

> To promote direct democracy, supplementing the provision that leaders of government in communes and wards shall be directly elected by the people rather than being indirectly selected by the People's Councils as is the present practice. This is useful both for promoting the power of the people and for enhancing effectiveness in the fight against corruption and bribery.[60]

Reformers also called for the popular election of leaders at the provincial level. The idea was first proposed in late 2008 by Nguyen Ba Thanh, the party leader and Chairman of the People's Council in Da Nang province at that time. Speaking in the session of the People's Council of Da Nang on 2 November 2008, he informed the members that this province would submit to the Government a proposal for a pilot scheme for the people's direct election of its leader.[61] This audacious proposal—a component of a larger project to develop Da Nang into a model of 'urban government'—was, however, ignored, since, among other things, it met with constitutional difficulties. In early 2012, when constitutional revision was firmly on the official agenda, Da Nang again put forward the proposal. In a lively public speech

[57] ibid.

[58] ibid.

[59] 'Đề xuất thí điểm dân bầu trực tiếp Chủ tịch UBND xã' ['Proposal for Pilot of Popular Election of Chairman of Communal People's Committees'], *An Ninh Thu Do*, 5 January 2012, available at <www.anninhthudo.vn/Thoi-su/De-xuat-thi-diem-dan-bau-truc-tiep-Chu-tich-UBND-xa/431660.antd>; 'Đề xuất nhân dân trực tiếp bầu chủ tịch UBND cấp xã' ['Proposal for Popular Election of Chairman of Communal People's Committees'], *Quang Nam Newspaper*, 9 April 2013, available at <http://baoquangnam.com.vn/chinh-tri/201304/de-xuat-nhan-dan-truc-tiep-bau-chu-tich-uBNd-cap-xa-277924/>.

[60] Vietnam Fatherland Front, 'Bao cao Tổng hợp ý kiến của nhân dân về Dự thảo sửa đổi Hiến pháp năm 1992' ['Synthetized Report on People's Opinions on the Draft Amendments to the 1992 Constitution'], *Duthaoonline*, 30 March 2013, available at <http://duthaoonline.quochoi.vn/DuThao/Lists/DT_DUTHAO_NGHIQUYET/View_Detail.aspx?ItemID=32&TabIndex=2&TaiLieuID=1014>.

[61] 'Đà Nẵng đề xuất để dân bầu chủ tịch TP' ['Da Nang Proposes People's Election of the Chairman of the Province'], *Vietbao*, 2 December 2008, available at <http://vietbao.vn/Chinh-Tri/Quy-12009-Da-Nang-de-xuat-de-dan-bau-chu-tich-TP/20816549/96/>.

televised on 24 February 2012, Nguyen Ba Thanh repeatedly called for direct election of the Chairman of the People's Committee of the province of Da Nang, following 'the model of mayor', through *open competition*.[62]

Da Nang's proposal was cited as the 'model' in debates about the possible popular election of provincial governors during the constitutional revision process.[63] Consider, for example, the interview carried out by *Tien Phong Newspaper* (one of the most popular newspapers in Vietnam) of Dinh Xuan Thao (an active Assembly deputy and Director of the Institute of Legislative Studies under the National Assembly's Standing Committee).[64] Strongly supporting the direct election of Chairmen of provincial People's Committees, he suggested that '[w]e should trust the people, since the people are completely intelligent to select the qualified persons if we provide the people with sufficient information and favourable conditions for them to communicate with the candidates'.[65] He even called for a 'change of thinking', in the sense that candidates need not to be party members, stating that 'I think we need further renovation. We need not require that all candidates [for the positions of provincial governors] must be party members, because we should trust the persons who are not party members but are devoted completely to the interests of the nation and of the people'.[66] Dinh Xuan Thao eventually proposed that there should be a mechanism for the people to remove from office those elected governors who were 'irresponsible, act illegally, harass the people for bribes, and commit corruption'.[67]

Removal of District People's Councils

The possible removal of the People's Councils at the district level—due to their purely symbolic position and ineffective operation—had been debated in the wave of constitutional revision in 2001, but there were no constitutional changes on this aspect then. While there was no constitutional basis for it, in 2008 the Government submitted to the National Assembly a proposal for a pilot scheme (*thi diem*) for abolishing the People's Councils in 67 districts, 32 urban districts and 438 precincts in 10 provinces and cities. The National Assembly approved the proposal in its Resolution No 26/2008/QH12 in force from 1 April 2009. The pilot scheme was

[62] Vo Tri Hao, 'Mô hình thị trưởng của Đà Nẵng—Hy vọng và Lực cản' ['The Model of Mayor in Da Nang: Hopes and Obstacles'] *TuanVietnam*, 1 March 2012, available at <http://tuanvietnam.net/2012-02-29-mo-hinh-thi-truong-cua-da-nang-hy-vong-va-luc-can>.

[63] ibid.

[64] 'Cần mạnh dạn bầu trực tiếp chủ tịch tỉnh' ['It is Necessary to Directly Elect Provincial Chairmen'], *Tien Phong Newspaper*, 26 December 2011, available at <www.tienphong.vn/xa-hoi/can-manh-dan-bau-truc-tiep-chu-tich-tinh-562331.tpo>.

[65] ibid.

[66] ibid.

[67] ibid.

implemented accordingly. In a national convention on the operation of local government in September 2010, the Government reported a positive result from the pilot scheme, and moved further to call for constitutionalising this practice. The possible elimination of the district People's Councils throughout the whole of the country was, then, one of the main reasons for the last constitutional revision, and was one of the contentious issues that caused serious divisions within the legislature.

During the constitutional revision process in the 2010s, diverse positions on whether to eliminate the district People's Councils employed the same rhetoric of 'democracy' in different ways. The opponents argued that to guarantee 'democracy', people need to create their representative bodies at all levels to supervise the administrative governors. If the district People's Councils are ineffective, the solution would be to make them more effective rather than to remove them, the opponents maintained. To remove the district People's Councils would be to remove an important instrument available to pursue 'democracy', they believed.[68] The proponents justified the possible elimination of the district People's Councils by viewing the same reasons associated with 'democracy' in a different light. They argued that the district People's Councils were intermediate bodies, and to remove them would allow the administrative systems to operate smoothly and effectively. Importantly, they argued that removing the district People's Councils could enhance local democracy, in the sense that this would enable local government to be closer to the local people, to serve them better and to be more responsible to them. This was because it would enable the local people to access the administrative governors directly, so as to bring before them their pressing issues, and supervise them.[69] This argument is not applicable to the People's Councils at the provincial and communal levels. It is argued that the provinces are the channels for the central Government to connect with the local governments, and hence they need a complete structure which includes both the representative body (the People's Council) and the administrative body (the People's Committee); and that the communes are the grassroots units closest to the local people, and that they equally need a complete structure.[70]

[68] Vũ Thy Huệ, 'Việc thí điểm không tổ chức Hội đồng nhân dân quận, huyện, phường' ['On the Pilot Not to Create the People's Councils at District Level'], *Ban noi chinh Trung uong*, 12 August 2013, available at <http://noichinh.vn/nghien-cuu-trao-doi/201308/viec-thi-diem-khong-to-chuc-hoi-dong-nhan-dan-quan-huyen-phuong-291989/>; 'Không nên bỏ HĐND quận, huyện, phường' ['The District People's Councils Should Not be Removed'], *Tien Phong Newspaper*, 20 September 2010, available at <www.tienphong.vn/Tuong-Tac-Dien-Dan/khong-nen-bo-hdnd-quan-huyen-phuong-512946.tpo>.

[69] Văn Tất Thu, 'Vì sao không tổ chức HĐND huyện, quận, phường?' ['Why Not Create the People's Councils at District Level'], *Vietnam+*, 1 January 2010, available at <www.vietnamplus.vn/vi-sao-khong-to-chuc-hdnd-huyen-quan-phuong/64342.vnp>.

[70] ibid.

The public tended to support the removal of the People's Councils at the district level. To illustrate this, on 28 March 2012, the Department of Local Government of the Ministry of Internal Affairs released an empirical survey of the opinion of the people in those places where the pilot scheme was implemented, according to which 79 per cent of interviewees supported the removal of the People's Councils at the district level.[71] The National Assembly's Office's empirical report, mentioned above, offered a similar popular position: only 7.9 per cent of interviewees agreed with the creation of People's Councils at the district level.[72]

Judicial Review

The 1992 Constitution and relevant laws allowed local governments to enact legal documents, variously called *nghi quyet* (resolutions) or *quyet dinh* (decrees), with general effect in the local areas, and established hierarchal political and administrative mechanisms to supervise these local legal documents. Accordingly, the National Assembly's Standing Committee and the Government supervise the constitutionality and legality of the documents enacted by provincial governments; the provincial governments supervise the legal documents enacted by district governments; and the district governments supervise the legal documents enacted by communal governments. The administrative courts at provincial level have relatively limited review powers. They are not allowed to review local legal documents with general effect; rather, they can only review local authorities' concrete decisions in individual cases.

Reformers pointed out that the hierarchal political and administrative mechanisms put in place to supervise these local legal documents were ineffective, as there were numerous local legal documents that were inconsistent with the Constitution and the central laws but ineffectively dealt with.[73] Alternatively, they called for legal or judicial mechanisms. Some suggested that the powers of administrative courts be extended to review local legal documents with general effect, but many others seemed less confident about

[71] 'Đa số dân ủng hộ không tổ chức HĐND quận, huyện, phường' ['The Majority of People Support Not Creating the People's Councils at District Level'], *Tien phong Newspaper*, 29 March 2012, available at <www.tienphong.vn/xa-hoi/da-so-dan-ung-ho-khong-to-chuc-hdnd-quan-huyen-phuong-571382.tpo>.

[72] 'Kiến nghị dân bầu trực tiếp chủ tịch huyện, xã' ['The Proposal for Popular Election of District and Communal Chairmen'], *Vietnamnet*, 19 August, 2013, available at <http://vietnamnet.vn/vn/chinh-tri/136481/kien-nghi-dan-bau-truc-tiep-chu-tich-huyen--xa.html>.

[73] A review report by the Ministry of Justice in 2013 indicates that among 485 legal documents (by different ministries and local governments) under review, 171 documents were enacted illegally. 'Hội nghị Triển khai công tác năm 2014 của Cục Kiểm tra văn bản QPPL' ['Conference on Implementation of the Works in 2014 of the Department for Reviewing Legal Documents'], Ministry of Justice, 7 February 2014, available at <www.moj.gov.vn/ktvb/Pages/hoat-dong-tw.aspx?ItemID=6213>.

vesting the ordinary judiciary with a review function, and moved to call for a special institution of constitutional review, like a constitutional court or council.[74]

Denouement: The Influence of the Discourse

The new Constitution was enacted by the National Assembly on 28 November 2013, with effect from 1 January 2014. The Constitution retains a three-level administrative system, namely provincial, district and communal levels, and supplements this with the creation of 'special administrative-economic units'.[75] The Constitution does not reify but provides the basic principles for organisation of local government, leaving the details to legislation. Generally speaking, these principles reflect the discourse on political decentralisation. As to specific proposals, the Constitution explicitly rejects the call for a specialist institution of judicial review, but does not provide clear answers to other important questions, such as the popular election of local leaders or the removal of the People's Council at district level, though it does open the door for such practices.

Regarding the problem of clarity, to begin with, the Constitution affirms the diversity principle in the following ambiguous provision:

> A level of local government consists of a People's Council and a People's Committee, organized consistently with the features of rural areas, cities, islands, and special administrative-economic units according to the law.[76]

The People's Council is elected by the local people, and 'the People's Committee at the level of local government is selected by the People's Council at the same level'.[77] The Constitution generally opens the door to diversifying the organisation of local government, in the sense that local government is created in all administrative units but in different ways in different areas. But ambiguity lies in the phrase 'level of local government' (*cap chinh quyen dia phuong*), an inconclusive response to the controversial debate on the possible removal of the People's Councils at district level.

Domestic scholars and officials explain that the Constitution does not mandate that all administrative units need necessarily include a complete 'level of local government'. For example, Hoang The Lien (Vice-Minister

[74] In fact, the draft Constitution released to the public for debate had included the institution of constitutional council (*Hoi dong Hien phap*), with the power to review the constitutionality of legal documents enacted by central (not local) authorities, but this institution was rejected in the Constitution adopted. For detailed discussion of constitutional review during the constitutional revision process, see Bui Ngoc Son, 'The Discourse of Constitutional Review in Vietnam' (2014) 9(2) *Journal of Comparative Law* 191–221.

[75] 2013 Constitution, art 110.

[76] 2013 Constitution, art 111.

[77] 2013 Constitution, arts 113, 114.

of Justice and the Government's spokesman on constitutional amendment issues) explained that there needs to be both People's Councils and People's Committees in a full 'level of local government', but in places where there is no full 'level of local government', there need only be administrative organs to provide public services, implying that People's Councils need not be created there.[78]

Apart from the diversity principle, the Constitution, for the first time in Vietnamese constitutional history, includes a separate article on the principle of decentralisation, as follows:

1. Local governments organize and ensure the implementation of the Constitution and the law in localities; decide on local issues according to the law; and are subject to the examination and supervision of the superior state organs.
2. The duties and competences of local governments shall be determined on the ground of differentiating authorities between central and local state organs and between different levels of local government.
3. In cases of need, local governments are allocated to exercise some duties of superior state organs, along with the necessary conditions to ensure the performance of those duties.[79]

Three important points about this article should be noted. First, the Constitution on one hand attempts to centralise powers, as it requires local governments to be supervised by central authorities (by conventional political-administrative mechanisms); but, on the other hand, it empowers local governments to decide their own affairs consistently with the law. The proposal for local self-government is reflected to a certain degree here. Secondly, the Constitution provides that authorities of central and local government and of the different levels of local government are different and shall be clearly defined by law. This actually opens the door to the practice of political devolution. These two points together indicate the constitutional basis for political decentralisation. The third point means that the administrative allocation, which has been practised in Vietnam for several decades now, becomes a constitutional principle.

To implement the Constitution, the revision or replacement of a number of organic laws has been on the official law-making agenda of the National Assembly pursuant to Resolution No 70/2014/QH13, including the enactment of a new Law on Organisation of Local Governmentto replace the Law on Organisation of People's Council and People's Committee of 2003. The Draft Law on Local Government was prepared by the Ministry of

[78] 'Hiến pháp năm 2013 Mở đường cho Việc Tiếp tục đổi mới thể chế về Chính quyền địa phương' ['The 2013 Constitution Opens the Door for Continuing Renovation of the Institutions of Local Government', *Phap Luat Vietnam*, 20 January 2014, available at <http://baophapluat.vn/trong-nuoc/hien-phap-nam-2013-mo-duong-cho-viec-tiep-tuc-doi-moi-the-che-ve-chinh-quyen-dia-phuong-175932.html.

[79] 2013 Constitution, art 112.

Internal Affairs. According to a commentator from the Government Office, 'the directive spirit of the Draft Law on Organization of Local Government fundamentally reforms the model of local government, strengthening allocation and devolution, enhancing autonomy and self-accountability, and upgrading the efficiency and effectiveness of local government'.[80] As the Constitution has provided inconclusive answers, a number of concrete organisational questions regarding local government in the light of political decentralisation, which had been debated during the period of constitution-making (such as the popular election of local leaders and possible removal of the People's Councils at district level), have been continuously debated in fora commenting on the Draft Law on Organisation of Local Government.[81] On 1 June 2015, the National Assembly debated on the draft, and these issues recurred.[82] According to the legislative schedule, the National Assembly voted on the Law on Organisation of Local Government on 19 June 2015.[83]

ANALYSIS

The Case for Reform

The discourse on political decentralisation is a new development in twenty-first-century Vietnam. Being firmly established on the formal agenda of constitutional reform, political decentralisation has been controversially debated and strongly supported by the Government, reformist legislators and constitution-makers, legal scholars and the public. Consequently, the 2013 Constitution includes general principles supportive of the future

[80] Nguyen Phuoc Tho, 'Xây dựng Luật Tổ chức chính quyền địa phương—Cơ hội và Thách thức' ['Drafting Law on Local Government: Chances and Challenges'], *Government's Online Newspaper*, 30 March 2014, available at <http://baodientu.chinhphu.vn/Trien-khai-Hien-phap-2013/Xay-dung-Luat-To-chuc-chinh-quyen-dia-phuong-co-hoi-va-thach-thuc/196235.vgp>.

[81] 'Dự thảo Luật Tổ chức Chính quyền địa phương' ['The Bill on Local Government'], *Government's Online Newspaper*, 11 August 2014, available at <http://baodientu.chinhphu.vn/Chinh-sach-moi/Du-thao-Luat-To-chuc-chinh-quyen-dia-phuong/205975.vgp>; 'Góp ý vào dự án Luật Tổ chức chính quyền địa phương' ['Comments on the Bill on Local Government'], *VOV Vietnam*, 30 June 2014, available at <http://vov.vn/chinh-tri/gop-y-vao-du-an-luat-to-chuc-chinh-quyen-dia-phuong-335688.vov>; 'Xây dựng Luật Tổ chức chính quyền địa phương' ['The Drafting of the Law on Local Government'], *Online Newspaper of the Communist Party*, 8 July 2014, available at <http://dangcongsan.vn/cpv/Modules/News/NewsDetail.aspx?co_id=30089&cn_id=662137>.

[82] The draft is available on the website of the National Assembly, available at <http://duthaoonline.quochoi.vn/DuThao/Lists/DT_DUTHAO_LUAT/View_Detail.aspx?ItemID=965&LanID=1063&TabIndex=1>.

[83] The the legislative schedule is available at <http://quochoi.vn/hoatdongcuaquochoi/cackyhopquochoi/quochoikhoaXIII/kyhopthuchin/Pages/chuong-trinh-lam-viec.aspx?ItemID=29572>.

development of political decentralisation in Vietnam. There are important factors behind the move, which can be explained from the perspective of complexity theory.[84]

One aspect of complexity theory focuses on the idea that the diffusion of global ideas and practices results in social complexity, which induces people to compel local actors to adopt new ideas and practices familiar to the global community.[85] Following this theorising model, the move to political decentralisation in Vietnam can be explained as having some connection with the global diffusion of political decentralisation. Entering the twenty-first century, when Vietnam has become deeply integrated into the global market, it has been compelled to adopt or learn from governance standards familiar to the international community, including political decentralisation. This motivates political leadership, domestic elites and the public to employ the global language of governance in their public discourse on reform.

Consequently, the Vietnamese discourse on political decentralisation—its condition, its nature, its content and its purposes—corresponds to the global discourse on this theme. To illustrate this, consistently with World Bank's observation that political decentralisation often requires constitutional reform, political decentralisation was among those crucial factors leading to the need for constitutional amendment, and featured strongly in the constitutional debates. The Vietnamese discourse reflects the nature of political decentralisation as giving more powers to the local people and their representatives, particularly evident in the calls for local self-government. This discourse also focuses on the substantial democratic content of political decentralisation that informs the global discourse, particularly the calls for popular election of local leaders and other reforms allowing the local people to know better and to supervise their local leaders (such as removing the district People's Council and instituting judicial review of local authorities' actions). The Vietnamese discourse also pursues the same purposes of political decentralisation as are informed by the global discourse, such as community participation, accountability and effective local governance.

Yet beyond the external global influence, there are substantial internal factors driving the move to political decentralisation in Vietnamese constitutional discourse. Another aspect of the complexity theory underlines the idea that social complexity is generated 'when there are strong interactions among its elements, so that current events heavily influence the probabilities

[84] To do this, I follow John Gillespie, who has employed the complexity theory to explain the evolution of human rights and religious freedom in Vietnam. See J Gillespie, 'Human Rights as a Larger Loyalty: The Evolution of Religious Freedom in Vietnam' (2014) 27 *Harvard Human Rights Journal* 107.

[85] A Giddens, *Modernity and Self-Identity: Self and Society in the Late Modern Age* (Stanford, CA, Stanford University Press, 1991) 32–36.

of many kinds of later events'.[86] From this perspective, the development of decentralisation in Vietnam and the recent emergence of the discourse on its political dimension are substantially associated with the nation's internal *Doi moi* (renovation).

At micro-level, several local factors driven by national renovation induce the need for political decentralisation. To begin with, the local dynamics (especially in major cities like Ho Chi Minh City, Hanoi and Da Nang) generated by the broader national dynamics of a (socialist-orientated) market economy result in the need for more local powers, autonomy and efficiency. On the other side, poor local performance, such as local corruption, generates the need for community participation and local accountability. Moreover, in 'the age of rights',[87] the local people's rising awareness of their rights, stemming from both the global diffusion of 'right talk' and internal privatisation as the result of the dynamics of a market economy, catalyses their demands for participation in deciding the fate of their local leaders and local affairs, and the accountability of those in power locally.

Yet the discourse on political decentralisation has a close connection with a broader macro-picture. The *Doi moi* program first introduced in 1986 by the Communist Party was originally meant to transform the centrally planned economy into a socialist-orientated market economy. However, beyond its original economic focus, nearly three decades of *Doi moi* have comprehensively transformed Vietnamese society and engendered social complexity. The implementation of the *Doi moi* program has generated not only economic but also social, cultural, legal, administrative and constitutional changes. These changes are complexly intertwined. More liberal governance concepts, which often go in tandem with a market economy, such as human rights, the rule of law and distribution of power, have been introduced and practised in Vietnam to a certain degree, and have consistently instigated further reforms. In this light, the discourse on the possibilities of political decentralisation is closely connected with the liberalisation of the national economy, individualist-orientated changes of the social structure, and the reform of the legal, administrative and constitutional systems in more liberal directions.

On closer inspection, the discourse on political decentralisation has not emerged on its own but is a part of a broader liberal discourse on constitutional issues. The calls for self-local government, popular election of local leaders, removal of district People's Councils, devolution and judicial review of local authorities' actions, all operate within the ambit of debates on more general constitutional issues, namely direct democracy (*dan chu truc tiep*),

[86] R Axelrod and MD Cohen, *Harnessing Complexity: Organizational Implications of a Scientific Frontier* (New York, Free Press, 1999) 7.

[87] L Henkin, *The Age of Rights* (New York, Columbia University Press, 1990).

constitutionalism (*chu nghia hop hien*), controlling state power (*kiem soat quyen luc nha nuoc*), distribution of state power (*phan cong quyen luc nha nuoc*) and constitutional review (*bao hien*). This broader discourse is able to take place thanks to the political leadership's commitment to 'comprehensive' constitutional reform and a more open and participatory constitution-making process, which stems from the need to restore political legitimacy in a context in which popular trust in the political leadership has declined, as described by the political leadership itself.[88] In short, the chances for 'comprehensive' constitutional reform, with a more open and participatory process, allows the rise of liberal discourse on constitutional issues, including political decentralisation.

The Case of the Conservatives

John Gillespie has disclosed the social complexity of Vietnam, stating that 'economic reforms, socialization, and globalization have brought about rapid changes in most facets of Vietnamese life. New ideas compete with old, creating contradictory and sometimes confusing public discourse'.[89] This observation holds true with respect to the public discourse on central-local relations. New liberal ideas of political decentralisation have to compete with a conventional socialist outlook emphasising centralised power. Conservatives' rejection of political decentralisation stems from both soviet-inspired ideology and practical calculations.

As to ideology, the new thinking about diversity, difference and the autonomy of local government that informs the discourse on political decentralisation substantially undermines the conventional outlooks on the 'unity of state power', 'democratic centralism', and 'socialist legality' and more general socialist ideology. This explains the conservatives' suspicion of the discourse on political decentralisation. Concrete proposals for political decentralisation also challenge the soviet-derived structure of local government. In particular, the rejection of the call to remove the district People's Councils connects more closely with official ideology and has less practical underpinning. The conservatives cannot deny that removing the district People's Councils may have practical advantages, but they worry that the practice would destroy the pyramid structure of soviets (councils)—an icon of socialism.

Other conservative arguments against political decentralisation are more closely associated with practical and political reasons. Central government

88 President of State Truong Tan Sang, 'Niềm tin với Đảng đang bị thách thức' ['Trust in the Party has been Challenged'], *Vnexpress*, 21 January 2013, available at <http://vnexpress.net/tin-tuc/thoi-su/niem-tin-voi-dang-dang-bi-thach-thuc-2416524.html>.

89 Gillespie, above n 84, 134.

may lose control over local government in the framework of political decentralisation. Local self-government may be an impediment to the nationwide implementation of socialist policies, as the history of Vietnamese socialism indicates that local government had to find its own way towards meeting the practical demands of local people while acknowledging that socialist policies are the ideal.[90] Concrete proposals for political decentralisation also meet with political difficulties. For example, the central Government may lose control over local governments if local leaders are popularly elected by the local people without approval or nomination by the central authority. The case is more serious when local people select a local leader who is not a party member.

The Delphic Outcomes

As the party leadership attempts to limit internal division in order to maintain party cohesion, they tend to decide constitutional issues only where there is broad agreement in the party and amongst the constitution-makers and legislators. Meanwhile, local government is the issue that has engendered the most serious divisions between the constitution-makers and legislators. As a result, both conclusive constitutional answers, which imply long-term consequences, and concrete issues, such as whether to remove the district People's Councils, or whether to allow popular election of local leaders, may aggravate political divisions. A more affordable alternative for the political leadership is to leave these issues to further deliberation at the legislative level, which allows the political leadership to reach more flexible and less consequential solutions. This explains why the Constitution merely includes general principles of local government, which on one hand tend to support political decentralisation to meet the aspiration for reform, but which on the other hand do not articulate in a concrete way any of the institutions of political decentralisation so as to appease the conservatives. Consequently, local-central relations in Vietnam now can potentially move in both a reforming and a conservative direction (political decentralisation and political centralisation) without constitutional difficulty.

The new Law on Organisation of Local Government does not include substantial organisational changes but confirms the principle of decentralisation, which may stipulate functional changes. The Vietnamese political leadership may promote political decentralisation to a certain degree for several reasons. First, political decentralisation might challenge some conventional socialist beliefs and local arrangements, but it would not substantially alter the nature of the socialist polity, which is fundamentally associated with central political institutional arrangements. This makes

[90] Marr, 'A Brief History of Local Government in Vietnam', above n 3.

political decentralisation a realistic option for the political leadership. In addition, while committing itself to devolution, the political leadership has no plans to abandon central supervision of local government. With political and administrative mechanisms of supervision, the central Government can ensure that political decentralisation cannot go so far as to undermine the unitary state and national goals. Last but not least, while the political leadership is grappling with a decline in popular trust, to promote political decentralisation so as to enhance local democracy, accountability and effective local governance, and to reduce local corruption, may become the way for it to gain more social legitimacy.

CONCLUSION

Twenty-first-century Vietnam is confronting a dilemma. On one hand it wishes to pursue socialist goals by using conventional socialist notions and institutions; but on the other hand it appeals to modernisation and global integration by employing some notions, institutions and practices shared by the international community, which are sometimes different from, or even conflict with, socialist goals. Reformists appeal to the latter, while conservatives appeal to the former. The political leadership has to balance competing visions, and may reach ambiguous solutions. The tale of political decentralisation illustrates that well. On one hand, the political leadership consistently maintains centralised power to pursue socialist goals nationwide; but on the other hand it permits a certain degree of political decentralisation to meet the practical demands of modernisation and global integration. The implication for understanding the socialist regime in the global age, at least in Vietnam, is that the conventional attribution of socialist power as highly centralised may need some revision, since for pragmatic purposes political decentralisation is, it appears from this study, possible within a socialist regime.

FURTHER READING

SA Fritzen, 'Probing System Limits: Decentralization and Local Political Accountability in Vietnam' (2006) 28(1) *The Asia Pacific Journal of Public Administration* 1.

M Sidel, *The Constitution of Vietnam* (Oxford, Hart Publishing, 2009).

N The Anh, 'Village Versus State: The Evolution of State-Local Relations in Vietnam Until 1945' (2003) 41(1) *Southeast Asian Studies* 101.

BJ Tria Kerkvliet and DG Marr (eds), *Beyond Hanoi: Local Government in Vietnam* (Singapore, NIAS Press, Institute of Southeast Asian Studies, 2004).

T Vasavakul, 'Rethinking the Philosophy of Central-Local Relations in Post-Central- Planning Vietnam' in M Turner (ed) *Central-Local Relations in Asia-Pacific: Convergence or Divergence?* (London, Macmillan Press Ltd, 1999) 166.

CG Wescott, 'Hierarchies, Networks, and Local Government in Vietnam' (2003) 4(2) *International Public Management Review* 20.

5

Central-local Relations in Indonesia: Reforming the Integralist State

SIMON BUTT

INTRODUCTION

IN MAY 1998, Indonesia's President Soeharto stepped aside amidst economic calamity and violent unrest across the country. Soeharto's immediate successor, Bacharuddin Jusuf Habibie, ordered fresh elections for the following year. Not since 1955 had free and fair elections been held in Indonesia and had the national parliament been comprised largely of democratically elected members.

These parliamentarians found themselves under great pressure to meet demands for change that had emerged during Soeharto's rule and had precipitated his fall.[1] There were fears that if these reforms were not made, or if they were made but were not genuine, then Indonesia might descend into violent unrest or even 'Balkanise'.[2] In any event, most of these lawmakers strongly supported reform, with many of them formerly being in opposition, from where they criticised elements of the authoritarian system they were now in a position to replace. Even former members of Soeharto's New Order elite who were re-elected to the new parliament recognised that they needed to support key reforms in order to avoid further unrest and to 'save themselves'.[3] Many of the reformist demands were met quickly, at least on paper, with a large swathe of statutory and constitutional enactments made to dismantle key components of authoritarianism.

One of the most important of these reforms was 'regional autonomy' (*otonomi daerah*) or decentralisation, under which local governments were given extensive powers to govern their own affairs, including by issuing by-laws, commonly referred to as *Perda* (*Peraturan Daerah*, usually translated

[1] E Aspinall, *Opposing Suharto: Compromise, Resistance, and Regime Change in Indonesia* (Stanford, CA, Stanford University Press, 2005).

[2] DL Horowitz, *Constitutional Change and Democracy in Indonesia* (Cambridge, Cambridge University Press, 2013) 34.

[3] H Crouch, *Political Reform in Indonesia after Soeharto* (Singapore, ISEAS, 2010) 7.

as 'regional regulation' or 'regional regulations'). Regional autonomy was important not only because of the anticipated improvements in standards of governance that were expected from it, but also because it helped assuage increasing resentment towards the strongly-centralised system established during the Soeharto period. Different regions had expressed different grievances. Some complained that central government control was excessively interfering and paternalistic. During the Soeharto period, the primary function of local governments had been to follow national policies and directives, with very little latitude given to the regions to govern their own affairs. Other regions, such as Aceh, Kalimantan and Papua, complained that the central Government was predatory, or at least exploitative, directing to itself the lion's share of the spoils from the exploitation of natural resources located in their provinces.[4] Despite their rich reserves of natural resources such as forests, minerals or fossil fuel, many of these 'outer' regions of Indonesia remained amongst Indonesia's most un- or under-developed. Yet other regions objected to central government control on ethnic or cultural grounds, complaining that the central Government was Java-centric and comprised primarily of moderate Muslims, and failed to respect ideological, cultural or religious differences. Local figures in Aceh, for example, sought a greater role for Islamic law in the province; Papuans and East Timorese, many of whom are Christians and ethnically distinct from many other Indonesians, claimed on historical grounds that they should never have been made part of Indonesia, and only joined as a result of military threats. Even Balinese groups sought to secede on cultural, religious and economic grounds. Bali is largely Hindu-Buddhist, and some argued that it could be administratively and economically self-sufficient, primarily because of its large tourism industry.

During the Soeharto period, the central Government had been able to thwart these types of complaints effectively in various ways. Ideologically, the state emphasised the need for national unity (a pillar of Indonesia's national ideology, *Pancasila*), and reinforced the importance of Indonesia's maintaining its territorial integrity as a 'unitary state' (*negara kesatuan*) and being an 'integralistic state', in which the people and their rulers were a single entity.[5] Soeharto and his ministers also continually reinforced the need for political stability (*stabilitas politik*) to further the primary objective of the state: economic development (*pembangunan*). Of course, these ideological mantras were backed by military force where necessary. For decades what were effectively civil wars took place across Indonesia, particularly in Aceh, West Papua and East Timor. However, with the fall of Soeharto, these

[4] T Lindsey, 'Indonesia: Devaluing Asian values, rewriting rule of law' in RP Peerenboom (ed), *Asian Discourses of Rule of Law* (London, Routledge Curzon, 2004).

[5] AB Nasution, *The Aspiration for Constitutional Government in Indonesia: A Socio-Legal Study of the Indonesian Konstituante, 1956-1959* (Jakarta, Pustaka Sinar Harapan, 1992).

ideologies 'faded',[6] as did their enforcement by a military slowly receding from the forefront of public life. In this environment, violence became more prevalent and secessionist threats had more potency. Genuine decentralisation appeared to be the only way to keep Indonesia peaceful, let alone whole.

This chapter demonstrates that while local governments have been given significant power to regulate and otherwise manage their affairs, the national Government has retained ultimate legal control over them. The central Government can, legally speaking, veto by-laws, and can override them by issuing national laws that are inconsistent with them. However, the central Government has rarely chosen to exercise this control. The Ministry of Home Affairs—the ministry charged with administering regional autonomy—has generally failed to review local laws for compliance with national laws, including national human rights norms, despite being legally required to do so under the statutes governing regional autonomy. For the most part, the Ministry has thus far only reviewed and sought to invalidate by-laws imposing user charges and taxes that are not authorised by national statute.

The judiciary, too, does not appear to have reviewed, let alone invalidated, many by-laws issued by local governments, despite many judicial-review applications having been lodged with it based on what appear to be strong arguments. On one view, this is inevitable, given two significant deficiencies in the legal infrastructure for decentralisation. First, the division of power as between the various tiers of government is unclear and overlapping, with only the central Government enjoying exclusive jurisdiction over some matters. Second, the mechanisms for the judicial resolution of jurisdictional disputes between the central Government and local governments are unclear and incomplete, effectively forcing the Supreme Court to throw out many cases. These deficiencies aside, the Supreme Court appears to have been reluctant to convincingly resolve even those disputes over which it clearly does have jurisdiction.

The net result of the failure of these mechanisms is that, for the most part, local governments have had *carte blanche* to enact laws on virtually any subject matter without paying regard to national laws—even the Constitution—provided that they do not seek to encroach on central-government revenue streams.[7] Of course, this might be a positive development if national laws were somehow lacking (such as if they provided no human-rights protections, or unduly hampered trade across regional borders), or if local politicians were primarily concerned with passing laws

[6] S Waddell, 'Shifting visions of the social and legal order in Indonesia: Implications for legislative style and form' (2005) 7 *Australian Journal of Asian Law* 43.

[7] S Butt and N Parsons, 'Reining in Regional Governments? Local Taxes and Investment in Decentralised Indonesia' (2012) 34 *Sydney Law Review* 91.

to further their communities' interests, such as by making advances in areas such as health, education and environmental standards. Many of these local parliamentarians are indeed well-intentioned and professional. As we shall see, however, other local lawmakers are regarded as incompetent, self-interested or corrupt, and have produced by-laws criticised for being predatory, discriminatory or illegal.

One result of the largely unchecked exercise of local law-making power is a lack of consistency between the laws enacted by the various tiers of government, creating a virtually impenetrable, tangled mass of contradictory law, leaving citizens and agencies unable to distinguish between laws they must follow and laws they can ignore.[8] Certainly this could not have been intended by those who designed and enacted the decentralisation laws the year after Soeharto fell.

This chapter is divided into four further sections. The second section provides a brief description of the decentralisation reforms within the context of other important post-Soeharto reforms. The third section discusses the way in which the decentralisation laws formally divide power as between the tiers of government. The fourth analyses the mechanisms established under the decentralisation law for the Ministry for Home Affairs to review and invalidate local by-laws, and for local governments to challenge those invalidations in the Supreme Court. It also assesses judicial review, as performed by Indonesia's Supreme Court, under which 'lower' laws, including many types of by-laws, can be reviewed for compliance with 'higher' laws, most of which are national. The fifth section then concludes the chapter by offering an explanation for the failure of the Indonesian legal system to provide a clear division of power between the various tiers of government, and for the inadequacies of central government executive and judicial review as currently performed.

REFORMASI AND DECENTRALISATION

Indonesia's regional autonomy reforms are perhaps best viewed as part of the catalogue of changes made to dismantle the authoritarian system during the period immediately after Soeharto fell—the so-called *reformasi* or reformation period. Authoritarianism had prevailed since mid-1959, when Soekarno, Indonesia's first President and Soeharto's predecessor, declared martial law in the face of unrest and perceived government failure. Assuming the presidency in 1966, Soeharto established a strongly centralised state without any of the fundamental prerequisites for democracy or checks on

[8] S Butt, 'Regional Autonomy and the Proliferation of Perda in Indonesia: An Assessment of Bureaucratic and Judicial Review Mechanisms' (2010) 32(2) *Sydney Law Review* 177.

the exercise of presidential power. Soeharto's parliamentary vehicle, *Golkar* (*Golongan Karya*, or 'functional groups'), held a majority in the national parliament, largely through rigged elections featuring 'a lot of dirty tricks, with the military, the bureaucracy, and *Golkar* colluding in all kinds of illegal and improper methods to preserve Soeharto's power'.[9] The Government monitored and suppressed opposition parties and non-governmental organisations, including by forcing *Golkar*'s political opponents to merge into two political parties in 1973.[10] A large number of seats were reserved for government appointees, including 100 seats for representatives from the armed forces.[11] Largely beholden to the executive, the parliament had little, if any, autonomy to introduce statutes, and was unable to monitor the executive effectively, let alone exercise any control over it. Political freedoms, including freedom of speech and association, were heavily restricted.[12] All this the Government did with military-backed force, both threatened and actual.

Soeharto had also sought to undermine and demoralise Indonesia's courts—a process Soekarno had begun in the last few years of his rule.[13] Indonesian judges were, like their counterparts in other civil-law countries, formally civil servants, but in Indonesia the Government used this to ensure judicial loyalty,[14] and very few cases were decided contrary to the interests of the Government or even individual officials. Corruption amongst officials, including the judiciary, became widespread and institutionalised.[15] The net result was a very strongly-centralised and tightly-controlled state, supported by a legal system that served the Government well but consistently failed citizens.

As mentioned at the outset, since the fall of Soeharto, significant progress has been made away from authoritarianism and towards democracy and the rule of law. Legally speaking, this progress was primarily effected through a series of constitutional amendments made each year from 1999–2002. The amendments, along with numerous statutory reforms made from 1999,[16]

[9] AB Nasution, 'Towards Constitutional Democracy in Indonesia' (Melbourne Law School, 2011) 19.

[10] *Partai Persatuan Pembangunan*, United Development Party, was created as an amalgamation of Islamic parties. *Partai Demokrasi Indonesia*, Indonesian Democracy Party, was an amalgam of nationalist, Christian and other non-Muslim parties.

[11] A Schwarz, *A Nation in Waiting: Indonesia's Search for Stability*, 2nd edn (Boulder, CO, Westview Press 2000).

[12] T Lubis, *In Search of Human Rights: Legal-political Dilemmas of Indonesia's New Order, 1966–1990* (Jakarta, PT Gramedia Pustaka Utama in cooperation with SPES Foundation, 1993).

[13] DS Lev, 'Judicial Institutions and Legal Culture in Indonesia' in C Holt (ed), *Culture and Politics in Indonesia* (Ithaca, NY, Cornell University Press, 1972).

[14] DS Lev, 'Judicial Authority and the Struggle for an Indonesian Rechtsstaat' (1978) 13 *Law and Society Review* 37.

[15] S Pompe, *The Indonesian Supreme Court: A Study of Institutional Collapse* (Ithaca, NY, Cornell University, 2005).

[16] N Hosen, *Human Rights, Politics and Corruption in Indonesia: A Critical Reflection on the Post Soeharto Era* (The Netherlands, Republic of Letters, 2010).

significantly reconfigured the powers of key state institutions and established new institutions. The primary aims were to disperse much of the power that had previously been centralised within Soeharto's presidency, and to introduce stronger checks and balances on the exercise of state power. Presidential powers were reduced and the exercise of them subject to greater parliamentary oversight; greater powers were transferred to the national parliament; an extensive bill of rights was inserted into the Constitution; and the judiciary was made institutionally independent of government under the so-called one-roof (*satu atap*) reforms. Important new institutions were established, including the Judicial Commission, Anti-corruption Commission and Constitutional Court.[17] The Constitutional Court was established in 2003 with several functions, including constitutional review, resolving electoral disputes and deciding impeachment motions. The Court's function and decision-making do not fall within the scope of this chapter, given that the Court formally lacks jurisdiction to review by-laws. Rather, the Court's review jurisdiction is strictly limited to reviewing statutes as against the Constitution.

The electoral system was also overhauled. *Golkar*'s parliamentary monopoly was dismantled and a multi-party system established. Forty-eight parties contested the 1999 general elections, and an independent electoral commission was established to oversee them—the *Komisi Pemilihan Umum* (KPU).[18] Indonesians now vote in a multitude of free, fair and highly-competitive elections.[19] In 2004 and 2009, more than 150 million of Indonesia's 250 million citizens voted for their local parliament and the national parliament, and for a national-level regional representative body (the *Dewan Perwakilan Daerah*, DPD) often referred to as a 'senate'. The President and Vice-President are now also directly elected, as are the heads of provinces, counties and cities.[20]

[17] For discussion of the Court's judicial-review function, see S Butt, 'Judicial Review in Indonesia: Between Civil Law and Accountability? A Study of Constitutional Court Decisions 2003–2005' (PhD Dissertation, Law Faculty, Melbourne University 2007); S Butt and T Lindsey, *The Indonesian Constitution: A Contextual Analysis* (Oxford, Hart Publishing, 2012). For analysis of its electoral dispute jurisprudence, see S Butt, 'Indonesian Constitutional Court decisions in regional head electoral disputes' (Canberra, Centre for Democratic Institutions, Australian National University, 2013).

[18] See Law 3 of 1999 on General Elections.

[19] D Ramage, 'Indonesia: Democracy first, good governance later' [2007] *Southeast Asian Affairs* 135, 136.

[20] Presidential and vice-presidential candidates are nominated in pairs by political parties with at least 20% of seats in the national parliament, or with 25% of the vote across the country in the previous legislative elections. Presidential and vice-presidential elections have, since 2004, been held around three months after legislative elections. However, in a recent decision, the Constitutional Court held that presidential and vice-presidential elections must be held at the same time as national legislative elections from 2019: Constitutional Court Decision 4 of 2013 reviewing Law 42 of 2008 on Presidential and Vice-Presidential Elections.

The first batch of decentralisation laws was enacted in 1999.[21] Their primary objective was to grant power to three levels of regional government to make policy and law—the *Perda* referred to in 'Introduction' above. The first tier is provincial government. The second is county (*kabupaten*) or city (*kota*) government. (Counties and cities are the same 'level' of government, distinguished primarily by their population density and the size of their territory).[22] The third tier is village government.[23] Provinces and counties/cities have legislatures and executives, both of which were granted powers to make law. These executive governments are led by regional heads (*kepala daerah*): governors (*gubernur*) in provinces, regents (*bupati*) in districts, and mayors (*walikota*) in cities.

One result of regional autonomy was, therefore, an almost immediate proliferation of law-making bodies. Their numbers have continued to increase. In 1998—the year before the first batch of decentralisation laws were passed—Indonesia had approximately 292 local governments outside Jakarta.[24] In subsequent years, the number has grown as various provinces, municipalities and cities split into two or more.[25] In 2003, this number had grown to around 440 municipalities and districts. By 2009 there were 33 provinces and 484 municipalities and districts.[26] By 2014, there were 34 provinces, 412 counties and 93 cities.[27] Almost 1,100 regional bodies and individuals had law-making powers.

Of course, the need to elect members of regional legislatures and regional heads democratically, as well as the national parliament, 'senate' and President/Vice-President, means that elections in Indonesia are commonplace. In 2013 alone, 15 provinces, 104 counties and 33 cities held elections for regional heads.[28] The large number of regional-head elections has significantly affected the workload of the Constitutional Court. Around 85 per cent of elections are challenged before the Court. The Court has

[21] See Law 22 of 1999 on Regional Government and Law 25 of 1999 on Fiscal Balance between the Central and Regional Governments. Aceh and Papua achieved 'special' regional autonomy. See Butt and Lindsey, above n 17.

[22] See art 1(4)(5) of Law 32 of 2004 on Regional Government; Government Regulation 38 of 2007 on the Division of Government Affairs between Central Government, Provinces, Regencies and Districts.

[23] Only limited powers were granted to village administrations. This chapter does not focus on them.

[24] F Fitrani, B Hofman and K Kaiser, 'Unity in diversity? The creation of new local governments in a decentralising Indonesia' (2005) 41 *Bulletin of Indonesian Economic Studies* 57.

[25] A Booth, 'Splitting, splitting and splitting again: A brief history of the development of regional government in Indonesia since independence' (2011) 167(1) *Bijdragen tot de Taal-, Land- en Volkenkunde*.

[26] See <http://kemendagri.go.id>.

[27] See <http://otda.kemendagri.go.id/images/file/data_dob/total%20daerah%20otonom%20 2013.pdf>.

[28] See <http://otda.kemendagri.go.id/images/file/seputar_pilkada/daftar%20pilkada%20 2013%20new.pdf>.

heard several hundred such disputes since it began hearing them in 2008.[29] However, the Constitutional Court has largely failed to resolve regional-head election disputes satisfactorily. Although having built a strong reputation for integrity and well-reasoned decisions in national electoral disputes and constitutional review cases, the Court has not provided legally convincing decisions in these regional disputes. Up until late 2013, this was not raised as a significant problem in Indonesian legal or political circles because the Court's decisions in these cases had been largely respected by the parties. However, in early October 2013, the Court's reputation took a nose-dive, when its newly-appointed Chief Justice, Akil Mochtar, who had served as a judge in the Court since 2008, was arrested by Indonesia's Anticorruption Commission for allegedly receiving bribes to fix several of these regional electoral disputes.

DISTRIBUTION OF POWER

Regional governments have broad jurisdiction to make laws regulating a wide variety of issues. Article 18(5) of the Constitution gives regional governments the 'broadest autonomy', and Article 18(6) gives regional governments the 'right' to issue regional laws (*Perda*) and other regulations to exercise this autonomy. Article 2(3) of Law 32 of 2004 on Regional Government—now the primary statute concerning decentralisation—specifies that this law-making power is to 'increase the prosperity of the community, public services and regional competitiveness'.

The 2004 Regional Government Law also lists the matters for which provincial governments and city/district governments are responsible. These so-called 'obligatory matters' (*urusan wajib*) include development planning, public order and security, public infrastructure, health, education, labour, small and medium enterprises, the environment, land affairs, public administration and investment.[30] However, the Law does not clearly distinguish between the obligations of provincial and county/city governments relative to each other. Most of their *urusan wajib*, such as to 'plan, use and monitor spatial planning' and to 'control the natural environment', are *identical*; others are distinguished only by the scale of those responsibilities, with cities/districts having jurisdiction over their own geographical territories and provinces having jurisdiction over cross-city/district matters.[31] The potential for overlap in the laws issued by various regional governments is, therefore, very high.

[29] Butt, 'Indonesian Constitutional Court decisions in regional head electoral disputes', above n 17.

[30] Articles 13(1) and 14(1) of the 2004 Regional Government Law.

[31] See Articles 13 and 14 of the 2004 Regional Government Law.

According to the 2004 Regional Government Law, *Perda* can be initiated by the regional head or the local legislature and should be directed towards 'implementing regional autonomy' (Article 136(2)), that is, addressing matters over which the 2004 Regional Government Law grants local governments jurisdiction. *Perda* should accommodate the special characteristics of the region in which they are enacted (Article 136(3)), and must not contravene the public interest or higher-level laws (Article 136(4)). Once deliberated and approved, they are brought into law (*ditetapkan*), or assented to, by the regional head (Article 136(1)). Also granted law-making powers are heads of the executive arm of regional governments, who can implement *Perda* by issuing regulations or decisions (Article 146(1)). A civil police unit (*pamong praja*) can be established to help the regional head enforce these laws (Article 148(1)).

Although the jurisdiction of regional governments is wide, it is certainly not unlimited. Article 18(5) of the Constitution specifies that the autonomy of regional governments is subject to 'matters reserved by statute for the central Government'. The areas over which the central Government has exclusive jurisdiction are listed in Article 10(3) of the 2004 Regional Autonomy Law. These areas are foreign affairs, defence and security, national monetary and fiscal matters, and religion. The central Government also has exclusive power over justice-sector matters (*urusan yustisi*), including establishing judicial institutions, appointing judges and prosecutors, determining justice-sector and immigration policy, and enacting statutes and other national laws (Elucidation to Article 10(3)). The central Government can, however, delegate its jurisdiction to regulate these matters to local governments (Article 10(4)).

Critically, Article 10(5) of the 2004 Regional Government Law also gives the central Government power legislate in the areas that Article 10(3) of the 2004 Law does not mention. In other words, the jurisdiction granted to local governments is not exclusive. Under Article 10(5), the central Government can itself exercise the jurisdiction granted to local governments, or delegate this to regional apparatuses and officials.

Article 10(5) appears to 'defeat the very goal'[32] of decentralisation, because many types of laws issued by the national Government will trump local laws, rendering them invalid to the extent of any inconsistency. Article 7(1) of Law 12 of 2011 on Law-making contains Indonesia's so-called 'hierarchy of laws', a list setting out various types of laws used in the Indonesian legal system and their relative status:

a. The 1945 Constitution (*Undang-undang Dasar 1945*);
b. Decrees of the People's Consultative Assembly (*Ketetapan MPR*);

[32] GF Bell, 'The new Indonesian laws relating to regional autonomy: Good intentions, confusing laws' (2001) 2 *Asian-Pacific Law & Policy Journal* 29.

c. Statutes/Interim Emergency Laws (*Undang-Undang/Peraturan Pemerintah Pengganti Undang-Undang*);
d. Government Regulations (*Peraturan Pemerintah*);
e. Presidential Regulations (*Peraturan Presiden*);
f. Provincial Regulations (*Peraturan Daerah Propinsi*); and
g. County/City Regulations (*Peraturan Daerah Kabupaten/Kota*).

In theory at least, lower-level laws are said to derive their authority from the laws higher than their type in the hierarchy. For example, government regulations are usually issued in response to a statutory provision that directs the Government to issue a government regulation to provide further details about a matter covered generally in the statute. Likewise, many regional regulations often cite provisions of national statutes as legal bases for their enactment. Each type of law must not conflict with any law higher than its own type in the hierarchy. So, for example, a provincial regulation will be legally valid—at least formally—only if, when passed, it does not contradict a presidential regulation, government regulation, statute, People's Consultative Assembly Decree or the Constitution.

Many types of laws very frequently employed in Indonesia are not specifically mentioned in the list contained in Article 7(1). Article 8 of Law 12 of 2011 recognises some of these, stating:

(1) Types of laws other than those referred to in Article 7(1) include regulations stipulated by the People's Consultative Assembly, the People's Representative Council, the Regional Representative Council, the Supreme Court, the Constitutional Court, the National Audit Agency, the Judicial Commission, Bank Indonesia, Ministers, or equivalent agencies, institutions or commissions established by statute or by the government as required by statute, Provincial People's Representative Councils, Governors, County/City People's Representative Councils, Mayor/County Heads, Village Heads or equivalent.
(2) The types of laws referred to in Article 8(1) are recognised and have binding legal force provided that they are required by higher level laws or on the basis of authority.

The precise legal authority of the types of laws given legal authority by virtue of Article 8(1), particularly vis-à-vis laws that *are* listed in the hierarchy, is unclear. Classic examples are ministerial regulations or decisions. They are amongst the most commonly-used national regulatory instruments, allowing ministers—including the Ministry of Home Affairs—to regulate matters falling within their portfolios without needing to seek parliamentary or other government approval. However, because they are not specifically mentioned in the hierarchy, different actors have voiced different views on their status compared with, for example, regional regulations (*Perda*). Some local-government officials, apparently disregarding Article 8(1), have expressed an inclination to ignore them completely because they are not mentioned in the hierarchy. The Minister of Justice and Human Rights, on the other hand, has attempted to decree that ministerial regulations and decrees prevail over *Perda*.[33] However, this view is not supported by the hierarchy itself, which is set out in a statute and hence prevails over this decree of the Minister of Justice and Human Rights.

Further, some types of commonly-employed legal instruments do not even appear to be recognised in Article 8. For example, Article 8(1) does not specifically refer to laws issued by the President. Yet Indonesian Presidents have long issued a variety of legal instruments other than regulations. The relative authority of these types of instruments—if they have any legal force at all—is therefore uncertain.

Nevertheless, the hierarchy makes it clear that the central Government can legally override laws issued by local governments, at least provided that it does so by issuing a legal instrument specifically mentioned on the hierarchy that appears above provincial and city/county regulations. These include statutes, government regulations and presidential regulations. However, as we shall see in 'Review Mechanisms', even though many of the central Government's laws legally predominate, it appears that the central Government rarely, if ever, seeks to 'enforce' the hierarchy.

REVIEW MECHANISMS

Invalidation by the Executive

The 2004 Regional Government Law gives power to the central Government to review *Perda* and, if necessary, invalidate them. For most types of *Perda*, local governments need not consult with the central Government during drafting or before enactment; review takes place after the local law-maker has enacted the *Perda*. Regional law-makers must send their *Perda* to the central Government within seven days of enactment. The central Government reviews the *Perda* against two criteria: whether the *Perda* breach the 'public interest' (*kepentingan umum*) or contradict a 'higher law' (*peraturan perundang-undangan yang lebih tinggi*) (Article 145(2) of the 2004 Regional Government Law). This is a reference to the hierarchy of laws discussed in 'Distribution of Power' above.

If the central Government considers that the *Perda* breach either of these criteria, the 2004 Autonomy Law allows it to invalidate the *Perda* by Presidential Regulation (Article 145(3)). If, however, the Government finds no fault with the *Perda* then the *Perda* remain in force (Article 145(7)).

[33] NM Aziz, *Laporan Akhir Pengkajiaan Hukum Tentang Eksistensi Peraturan Perundang-Undangan Di Luar Hierarki Berdasarkan UU No 10 2004 Tentang Pembentukan Peraturan Perundang-Undangan* (Jakarta, Pusat Penelitian dan Pengembangan Sistem Hukum Nasional Badan Pembinaan Hukum Nasional Kementerian Hukum dan HAM RI, 2010).

Significantly, the central Government's right of review expires after 60 days (Article 145(3)), so if it does not invalidate the *Perda* within this time, they continue in force by default (Article 145(7)). If the central Government decides to invalidate, it must inform the relevant regional head—whether provincial, district or municipal—who is obliged to prevent the *Perda* from being further implemented or enforced, and must revoke the *Perda* within seven days (Article 145(4)). If dissatisfied with the central Government's decision, the local law-maker can lodge an application for review with the Supreme Court (Article 145(5)), as mentioned above. Different procedures apply for the review of *Perda* that set local government budgets, impose regional taxes or user charges, or relate to spatial planning.[34] These types of *Perda* need the prior approval of central Government, and are also subject to post-enactment review.

In 2013, the *Jakarta Post* reported the Minister of Home Affairs as announcing that the Ministry had partially or completely rejected 951 of 15,000 by-laws that it had reviewed between 2009 and 2012, and that it had annulled 1,878 by-laws between 2002 and 2009.[35] The Minister also predicted that his Ministry would review more than 2,500 by-laws, 'both old and new', in 2013.[36] While these statistics might appear to indicate that the review process is comprehensive and rigorous, there are indications that executive review does not function effectively.[37] One of the most significant problems is that the central Government's primary, if not exclusive, concern is to prevent local governments from raising revenue in breach of national law.[38] Though complete statistics are hard to obtain, it appears that almost all of the *Perda* invalidated thus far under the executive review process have had this purpose. For example, it appears that most, if not all, of the by-laws invalidated between 2002 and 2009 were primarily concerned with raising revenue. According to the Minister, 1,800 of them sought to impose regional taxes and levies, 29 dealt with third-party political donations and 22 pertained to alcoholic beverage regulation. Although the author was unable to obtain these laws to verify their content, it seems reasonable to speculate that the by-laws regulating both third-party donations and alcoholic beverages had revenue-raising as an objective. The same could be said of the 758 by-laws being evaluated by the Ministry in early 2013, 589 of

[34] Butt and Parsons, above n 7.

[35] I Parlina and M Aritonang, 'After straddling proposal, ministry to review bylaws', *Jakarta Post*, 18 January 2013.

[36] ibid.

[37] For an early analysis, see D Ray, 'Decentralization, regulatory reform, and the business climate', *Decentralization, regulatory reform, and the business climate* (Jakarta, Partnership for Economic Growth 2003).

[38] Butt, above n 8, 2.

which imposed regional taxes and levies, 19 of which concerned alcoholic beverages, and 71 of which concerned third-party political donations.[39]

Presumably this focus helps guard central Government revenue flows. Laws covering other subject matter appear to have escaped invalidation, perhaps even any form of review, even if, on their face, thy contradict central-government laws or the public interest. The National Women's Rights Commission (*Komnas Perempuan*) has conducted an annual review of the *Perda* in force in Indonesia's regions in past years. In early 2014, the Commission announced that it had identified 342 by-laws that were discriminatory against women in 2013, up from 282 in 2012.[40] Discrimination on the basis of gender is prohibited by 'higher laws', namely, the 1999 Human Rights Law and the Constitution,[41] yet the central Government did not detect these problems in the review process. Possible explanations are that some regional governments have not conveyed their new *Perda* to the central Government, often as a deliberate strategy to avoid revocation,[42] and that the central Government lacks the capacity to review all of the *Perda* it receives within 60 days.[43] As mentioned, if the central Government has not invalidated a *Perda* submitted to it by a local government within 60 days, that *Perda* automatically comes into force, and, in the case of most categories of *Perda*, the central Government loses its power of annulment.

For *Perda* that are problematic as a result of escaping executive review, the remaining alternatives for invalidation are enactment of a higher-level law to revoke the *Perda*, or the launching of judicial review proceedings in the Supreme Court. It is to this role of the Supreme Court in central-local jurisdictional disputes that I now turn.

Invalidation by the Supreme Court

Article 24A(1) of the Constitution grants the Supreme Court power to review legal instruments below the level of a statute to ensure that they comply with statutes. This jurisdiction is confirmed both in Law 4 of 2004 on the Judiciary (Article 11(2)(b)) and Law 14 of 1985 on the Supreme Court

[39] Seventy-nine other by-laws on 'other matters' were also under review. It is, of course, impossible to speculate on their subject matter, and on whether they were revenue-raising.

[40] M Muhyiddin, 'Komnas Perempuan: Perda diskriminatif meningkat' *Tempo.co* (20 January 2014).

[41] Law 39 of 1999 on Human Rights, arts 1(3), 3(3).

[42] *Panduan praktis memahami perancangan peraturan daerah* (Jakarta, Direktorat Jenderal Peraturan Perundang-undangan Departemen Hukum dan HAM bekerjasama dengan United National Development Programme; CAPPLER Project, 2008); 'Banyak Perda abaikan kaidah yang berlaku' *Hukumonline* (16 March 2012).

[43] See Ray, above n 37, 18.

(Article 31(1)).[44] These Laws authorise the Supreme Court to invalidate a legal instrument below the level of statute if:

a) it conflicts with a higher legislative instrument; or
b) the process by which it was enacted did not conform to legislative requirements.[45]

Legal instruments invalidated by the Supreme Court will no longer be legally binding.[46] No appeals against Supreme Court review decisions are permitted.[47]

Article 145(5) of the 2004 Regional Government Law also grants powers of review to the Supreme Court, albeit that they are narrower in scope than the 'general' review power described above. This provision allows local law-makers whose laws are revoked by the central Government (under the executive review process, discussed in 'Invalidation by the executive' above) to challenge the revocation, presumably on the basis that the grounds for the revocation did not exist at the time the revocation was made.[48]

The Court's formal jurisdiction does not extend to cover most of the possible conflicts or disputes that arise from the hierarchy of laws, let alone those conflicts between laws that have an unclear status, such as between ministerial regulations and presidential instructions. In particular, there is no judicial avenue provided by the Constitution or by statute to challenge lower-level laws against laws below the level of statute listed in the hierarchy—such as presidential regulations, government regulations and regional regulations—or even directly as against the Constitution. Likewise, there are no legal mechanisms formally available for the review of local laws (*Perda*) with ministerial decrees. Also missing is a mechanism for the review of country/city *Perda* as against provincial *Perda*. Lastly, there are no avenues to resolve conflicts between legislation from different provinces, such as might occur if two *Perda* from neighbouring provinces purported to regulate trade between those two provinces, or the management or use of natural resources that cross provincial borders.

The Court has, in many cases, rejected applications for the review of lower-level laws as against other lower-level laws on the ground that it only has jurisdiction to review lower-level laws as against statutes.[49] However,

[44] Law 14 of 1985 on the Supreme Court has been amended twice, first by Law 5 of 2004 Amending Law 14 of 1985 on the Supreme Court, and then by Law 3 of 2009 Amending for the Second Time Law 14 of 1985 on the Supreme Court.

[45] Art 31(2) of Law 14 of 1985.

[46] Art 31(4) of Law 14 of 1985.

[47] Art 9 of Supreme Court Regulation 1 of 2004 on Material Review.

[48] This type of review appears to be distinct from the Supreme Court's general review power because it does not involve a lower-level law being reviewed as against a 'statute'. Rather, the revoked *Perda* is reviewed against the instrument that revoked it: either a ministerial or a presidential decision.

[49] See, eg, Supreme Court Decision No 19.P/HUM/2002.

the Court has not always considered itself strictly bound by the limitations on the exercise of its judicial review jurisdiction, even though those limitations appear to be imposed unambiguously by both Constitution and statute. Successive regulations issued since 1993 by the Supreme Court Chief Justice governing judicial review procedures appear to have ignored these constitutional and statutory restraints. The regulations declare that Supreme Court judicial review applications can be brought 'against a legal instrument suspected of being inconsistent with a higher-level legal instrument'.[50] In other words, the regulations allow applicants to challenge a lower-level law against a higher-level law, even if that higher-level law is not a statute. The Court has, in fact, struck down *Perda* for conflicting with government regulations and presidential regulations in several cases.[51] The result is uncertainty about a fundamental issue: whether the Supreme Court will, in any given case, refuse to hear disputes about conflicting lower-level laws, or whether it will decide them, in apparent contravention of both the Constitution and statute.

Even those conflicts that do fall within the Supreme Court's judicial review jurisdiction have rarely been resolved convincingly. Generally speaking, the Supreme Court's reasoning in judicial review cases is simplistic and superficial. In many *Perda* review cases, the Court has not, in its judgments, discussed the substance of the relevant by-law, the arguments of the parties, or even whether the by-law contradicts any higher laws.[52] In other words, the Court has been reluctant to consider the 'merits' of the case openly. The Court has, in some cases, been content to simply declare that the *Perda* is regional in scope and within the jurisdiction of the relevant local government 'on the basis of Regional Autonomy'.[53] In the eyes of the Supreme Court, it seems that regional governments should and do have a broad discretion to pass laws to implement a very wide range of policies.

Lastly, fundamental questions remain unanswered in both the Court's decisions and in the Indonesian legal literature about the degree to which laws must overlap to be 'inconsistent'. Are laws 'inconsistent' simply because they cover the same subject matter, even if they are quite different in their details? The Supreme Court appears to have answered this question in the affirmative in some cases, invalidating *Perda* for regulating an issue that had been touched upon in a presidential decision, even though the *Perda* and the presidential decision did not appear to contradict each other

[50] Art 2(2) of Supreme Court Regulations No 1 of 2004 and 2011; art 3(1) of Supreme Court Regulation No 1 of 1993.

[51] See, eg, Supreme Court Decision Nos 01.P/HUM/2001, 20.P/HUM/2002 and 25. P/HUM/2008.

[52] See, eg, Supreme Court Decision Nos 03 G/HUM/2002, 06 P/HUM/2003 and 06 P/HUM/2006.

[53] See, eg, Supreme Court Decision No 03 G/HUM/2002.

directly.[54] Another important unresolved question is whether a lower-level law should be deemed inconsistent with a higher-level law if it simply adds certain requirements or preconditions to that higher-level law. One view is that additions are both expected and necessary when higher-level laws are cast in general terms, leaving detail to be fleshed out by local governments, as recognition that they are best placed to 'fit' rules to local conditions.

OBSERVATIONS AND CONCLUSIONS

Decentralisation has now been in operation for well over a decade in Indonesia. Yet, as this chapter has shown, critical elements of both law and practice are still 'missing', which prevents the system from functioning. As for the legal 'gaps', there remains no clear division of power between the various tiers of government on any matter, except those reserved for the central Government, leading to legal conflict in many areas, both actual and potential. And while the legal framework for review of most types of by-laws by the Ministry of Home Affairs appears to be reasonably complete, if not laden with overambitious time limits, reviews are rarely, if ever, conducted in practice, unless the relevant by-law might potentially affect central-government revenue. The result is that each tier of government can regulate the same matter in different ways, leading to confusion amongst citizens and businesses alike as to which law they are required to follow. Unfortunately, rather than helping to create order within the legal system, Indonesia's courts appear, for the most part, to be adding to the confusion and dysfunction. The Supreme Court's judicial review jurisdiction is 'incomplete' in that, legally, it lacks power to review anything other than central-government invalidation of a *Perda*, on the one hand, and a 'lower' law as against a statute, on the other. As mentioned, the Court will sometimes ignore the constitutional and statutory limits on its jurisdiction and review *Perda* as against government regulations rather than statutes, but it does not always do so, leading to significant uncertainty about whether the Court will accept such cases or simply throw them out.

One explanation for the lack of clarity about the division of power between tiers of government is that the first batch of decentralisation laws of 1999 were drafted and put into effect too quickly—in less than two years. Law-makers were simultaneously considering many other important reforms. With the overwhelming concern appearing to be to provide genuine and wide authority to local governments to govern for themselves, drafters might not have identified these potential jurisdictional conflicts, let alone conceived of ways to handle them. Jurisdictional divisions and disputes are

[54] Supreme Court Decision No 20.P/HUM/2002 and No 25.P/HUM/2008.

unlikely to have been priority issues for drafters in any event. After all, most of them had lived within an authoritarian system. It seems reasonable to speculate that they might not have foreseen the need for the state to fight *itself* in decentralised and democratic Indonesia.[55] In the integralistic state proposed at Indonesia's independence by Professor Soepomo, and then apparently adopted by Soeharto, there had been no need for a delineation of power between tiers of government or mechanisms for challenge, because the state was 'one'.

However, even if this explanation accounts for initial deficiencies in design, it does not appear to explain why, after years of legal problems and conflicts, those deficiencies have not since been remedied. The 1999 decentralisation laws were, as mentioned, replaced in 2004, and even though regional government jurisdiction was regulated more in the 2004 Law,[56] the jurisdictional overlaps remained. The 2004 laws also failed to clarify the Supreme Court's jurisdiction, and appeared to tighten the executive review process, imposing the strict time limits that the Ministry of Home Affairs appears to be unable to meet, thereby allowing many *Perda* to 'slip through' without review.

Yet by 2004 it was already clear that regional autonomy had produced an inordinately complex and dysfunctional legal system. Many local governments had reportedly exercised their new powers by passing masses of new laws, many of which were unworkably unclear, met no apparent regulatory need and were not preceded by any public consultation.[57] A large number of these laws were said to have exacted taxes and user charges, some of which duplicated those imposed by another tier of government, without providing commensurate services.[58] This, as the Indonesian Chamber of Industry (*Kamar Dagang dan Industri Indonesia*, KADIN) and many other commentators have long argued, created a 'high cost economy' that has damaged Indonesia's investment climate.[59] By that time also, various non-governmental organisations had identified hundreds of oppressive or

[55] S Butt and N Parsons, 'Judicial review and the Supreme Court in Indonesia: A new space for law?' (2014) 97 *Indonesia* 55.

[56] Under art 7 of the 1999 Law, jurisdiction to regions was given over 'all fields of government', except for those reserved for the central Government.

[57] Ray, above n 37.

[58] In the first six years of decentralisation, local governments established, between them, around 1,000 new taxes and user charges (*retribusi*) per year. See BD Lewis and Bambang Suharnoko Sjahir, 'Local Tax Effects on the Business Climate' in N McCulloch (ed), *Rural Investment Climate in Indonesia* (Singapore, SEAS, 2009) 224, 231.

[59] Pratikno, 'Exercising freedom: Local autonomy and democracy in Indonesia, 1999–2001' in P Sulistiyanto, M Erb and C Faucher (eds), *Regionalism in Post-Suharto Indonesia* (USA, Routledge Curzon, 2005) 21; I Saad, 'Implementasi otonomi daerah sudah mengarah pada penciptaan distorsi dan high cost economy', *Decentralization, Regulatory Reform, and the Business Climate* (Jakarta, Partnership for Economic Growth, 2003); B Brodjonegoro, 'Three years of fiscal decentralization in Indonesia: Its impacts on regional economic development and fiscal sustainability' in M Chatib Basri and P van der Eng (eds), *Business in Indonesia: New Challenges, Old Problems* (Institute of Southeast Asian Studies, 2004) 276; Agus Maryono,

discriminatory by-laws in operation across Indonesia. Worse, it had also become clear that many local officials had been using their office for private commercial gain, rather than to improve public services for their constituents.[60]

The precise reason for this continuing dysfunction is unclear. However, the central Government is under very little pressure to address these problems. Most local governments, and many central-government officials, including some within the Ministry of Home Affairs itself, contend that the primary purpose of decentralisation was to hand over genuine autonomy to local governments, and that local governments should therefore be allowed to govern with minimal interference, unless they intrude on central-government interests. Local legislators are democratically elected, so they should be able to enact any laws that they wish. Local law-makers can be voted out by their constituents if they fail to perform, such as if they enact laws that are exploitative or discriminatory.

However, this position is difficult to sustain from a legal perspective. Many important guarantees, such as human-rights protections, are provided to all citizens, regardless of the region in which they live, by national laws, including the Constitution, and local governments must be compelled to follow them and be held to account if they do not. Of course, the national Government is also afflicted by its own set of governance problems: it is certainly not renowned for professionalism in law-making, and dozens of parliamentarians and other officials have been embroiled in recent corruption scandals.[61] However, the current legal system is becoming increasingly unworkable, and central-government officials are probably in a better position than local governments themselves to ensure that local governments maintain Indonesia-wide standards of governance. If the central Government does not begin taking its function of review more seriously, then other reforms made when Soeharto fell in 1998—including the insertion of a Bill of Rights into the Constitution—might ultimately have little or no real effect.

'Thousands of bylaws halt investment: BKPM', *Jakarta Post*, 23 October 2009; OECD, *OECD Investment Policy Reviews* (Paris, Organisation for Economic Cooperation and Development, 2010) 21.

[60] Pratikno, above n 59; VR Hadiz, 'Decentralization and democracy in Indonesia: A critique of neo-institutionlist perspectives' (2004) 35 *Development and Change* 697; V Hadiz and R Robison, 'Neo-liberal reforms and illiberal consolidations: The Indonesian paradox' (2005) 41 *The Journal of Development Studies* 220. These claims seem to be borne out in Anti-corruption Commission (*Komisi Pemberantasan Korupsi*, KPK) investigation and prosecution statistics. In early March 2011, the KPK announced that it had investigated or was investigating 13 former and four serving governors, and 158 regents and mayors for corruption. In only five of Indonesia's 33 provinces were there no ongoing corruption investigations or prosecutions involving local government officials: Kompas, 'Aceh Sampai Papua Tersandera Korupsi', *Kompas*, 24 January 2011.

[61] S Butt, 'Anti-Corruption reform in Indonesia: An obituary?' (2011) 47 *Bulletin of Indonesian Economic Studies* 381.

FURTHER READING

A Booth, 'Splitting, splitting and splitting again: A brief history of the development of regional government in Indonesia since independence' (2011) 167(1) *Bijdragen tot de Taal-, Land- et Volkenkunde* 31.

GF Bell, 'The new Indonesian laws relating to regional autonomy: Good intentions, confusing laws' (2001) 2 *Asian-Pacific Law & Policy Journal* 29.

S Butt and T Lindsey, *The Indonesian Constitution: A Contextual Analysis* (Oxford, Hart Publishing, 2012).

S Butt and N Parsons, 'Judicial review and the Supreme Court in Indonesia: A new space for law?' (2014) 97 *Indonesia* 55.

6

Ethnic Rights and Constitutional Change: The Recognition of Ethnic Nationalities in Myanmar/Burma

MELISSA CROUCH*

INTRODUCTION

ONE WAY IN which a government may accommodate the unique claims of cultural groups is by legally conferring certain recognition or status on such groups through the constitution. The accommodation of the rights of ethnic minorities and the need to manage diversity are often crucial to democratisation and political stability.[1] In Myanmar,[2] the Government recognises that it needs to resolve conflict with ethnic armed groups as part of the process of transition to a quasi-civilian government under the 2008 Constitution. The political and legal reform process,[3] and the process of constitutional amendment, has renewed discussions about options such as federalism. Yet the 2008 Constitution already contains numerous provisions that build on the past recognition of some ethnic groups.

Under the 2008 Constitution, there are several levels of administration, beginning with the village and village-tract,[4] to wards, townships (some

* This chapter is based on field research conducted in Yangon, Shan State, and Naypyidaw, supported by the Centre for Asian Legal Studies, Law Faculty, National University of Singapore. I would like to thank Katherine Southwick and Ricky Yue for their comments on an earlier version of this chapter. All errors remain my own.

[1] See generally W Kymlicka and Baogang He (eds), *Multiculturalism in Asia* (Oxford, Oxford University Press, 2005).

[2] In this chapter I use Myanmar to refer to the country post-1988, and Burma to refer to the country as it was known from independence in 1947 up until 1988.

[3] On the development of the legal system generally, see M Crouch, 'The Layers of Legal Development in Myanmar' in M Crouch and T Lindsey (eds), *Law, Society and Transition in Myanmar* (Oxford, Hart Publishing, 2014) 33–58.

[4] For a preliminary analysis of village governance, see S Kempel, *Village Institutions and Leadership in Myanmar: A View from Below* (Yangon, Myanmar Development Research, 2012).

of which are organised into self-administered zones), districts, and States or Regions. At the national-level, representation in the *Pyithu Hluttaw* (People's Assembly, the lower house) is drawn from the townships, while members of the *Amyotha Hluttaw* (Nationalities Assembly, the upper house) represent the States and Regions. The ways in which ethnic nationalities are represented at the national level, and the extent to which they have powers of governance at the local level, are based on past constitutional configurations of central-local relations. Further, the very concept of 'ethnic nationality' is a construct, as this term is used by the Government to refer to a list of 135 races classified into eight groups. While I recognise that this list is highly problematic in many respects, I am interested in understanding the way that law has been used to reinforce and cement this arbitrary classification and the very idea of an 'ethnic nationality'.

In this chapter I explore the constitutional arrangement of central-local relations in Myanmar and its implications for the capacity of law in authoritarian regimes to accommodate diversity. In Myanmar a key determinant in central-local relations is ethnicity. While a majority of the population are ethnic Burmans, the country is also home to a diverse range of ethnic groups. I therefore focus on how and why the current Constitution recognises the rights of ethnic minorities. That is, I am concerned with why a military regime would grant forms of special recognition to ethnic nationalities in a Constitution drafted under its control, and the meaning that constitutions take on in authoritarian regimes.[5]

From one perspective, constitutional recognition of ethnic rights can be understood through the literature on cultural rights and multiculturalism. Kymlicka and Norman define 'minority rights' as 'public policies, legal rights and constitutional provisions sought by … groups for the accommodation of cultural differences'.[6] In order to clarify the kinds of constitutional rights that ethnic nationalities in Myanmar have been given, I rely on Levy's classification of legal rights sought by minorities. His list includes eight different, though at times overlapping, rights, including: support to do things the majority can do; self-government for particular groups; rules that aim to protect a group by imposing restrictions on those outside the group; internal rules of a group; incorporation of a legal code into law, such as customary law; special representation of a group, and symbolic recognition of a group.[7] I recognise that his definition presumes a Western liberal democratic context. But these forms of recognition may also be adopted by non-democratic regimes, which requires careful consideration of the implications of such

[5] See, eg, T Ginsburg (ed), *Constitutions in Authoritarian Regimes* (Cambridge, Cambridge University Press, 2014); T Ginsburg and T Moustafa (eds), *Rule by Law: The Politics of Courts in Authoritarian Regimes* (Cambridge, Cambridge University Press, 2008).

[6] W Kymlicka and W Norman, *Citizenship in Diverse Societies* (Oxford, Oxford University Press, 2000) 2.

[7] JT Levy, *The Multiculturalism of Fear* (Oxford, Oxford University Press, 1997) 25.

recognition in light of local context, history and politics. Drawing on this classification, I identify three aspects of the formal recognition of select ethnic nationalities under the 2008 Constitution, in order to expose the way in which cultural rights may be used by authoritarian regimes to legitimise their rule.[8]

SYMBOLIC RECOGNITION: TERRITORIAL DIVISIONS OF THE SEVEN STATES AND REGIONS

The form of constitutional recognition that has endured the longest is the designation of seven ethnic-based States and seven Burman-based Regions. This arrangement emerged from discussions leading up to independence, as well as from subsequent discussions between the Government and ethnic nationalities such as the Mon and Arakan in the 1950s and 1960s. The establishment of these seven States and Regions has been a key way in which law has reinforced ideas of ethnic difference and associated ethnic difference with territorial claims over land.

Since independence in 1947, the Government has struggled to incorporate ethnic nationalities, and this is partly because of the colonial legacy. Burma was annexed to Britain in three stages (from 1825 to 1885), and was organised at two administrative levels: 'ministerial Burma' in Burma proper, and the 'scheduled' or 'excluded' frontier areas.[9] Certain ethnic areas were therefore never under complete colonial control. As part of the political negotiations towards independence from British colonial rule that took place in the late 1940s, discussions were also held with some ethnic nationalities. The most historic was the Panglong Agreement, which recognised the need for separate governance arrangements with ethnic nationalities. On 12 February 1947, this was signed by General Aung San and leaders of the Shan, Kachin and Chin ethnic nationalities. Despite the fact that not all major ethnic nationalities were included in this meeting, the Panglong Agreement remains a symbolic political pact between the majority Burmans and the plethora of ethnic nationalities.

The drafting of the 1947 Constitution took place not long after this, and several features of the Constitution demonstrate an awareness of the need to accommodate some ethnic nationalities. The 1947 Constitution provided for the creation of special areas for five ethnic groups: the Federated Shan States, Kachin State, Karen State (also known as Kaw-thu-lay), Karenni State and the Special Division of the Chins. Two groups, the Shan and

[8] I only focus on special rights. I do not focus on human rights or cultural rights given to all groups under the Constitution.

[9] M Charney, *A History of Modern Burma* (Cambridge, Cambridge University Press, 2009); A Smith, 'Burma/Myanmar: Struggle for Democracy and Ethnic Rights' in W Kymlicka and Baogang He (eds), above n 1, 262.

Karenni, were given a constitutional guarantee that they could opt to leave the Union after 10 years if such a decision was approved by a plebiscite. After 1948, however, armed insurgencies against the government began across the country, including in Karenni State (1948), Karen State (1948), Shan State (1959) and Kachin State (1961).[10]

Some of the constitutional provisions concerning ethnic nationalities were later abolished through constitutional amendments based on negotiations and deals made with ethnic nationality leaders. The first, which took place in 1951, provided for the governance of Karen State and stated that the right to secession no longer applied.[11] The Second Schedule was also amended to reduce Karen representation in the Chamber of Nationalities from 24 to 16 seats, while Burman seats increased. Other ethnic groups that were not recognised in the Constitution were nevertheless given some recognition, such as through the appointment of the Mon Affairs Minister and Arakan Affairs Minister in March 1961, which was to be in preparation for the formal establishment of Mon State and Arakan State respectively.[12]

Another step that reduced the special constitutional rights of some ethnic nationalities was the change in the administration of Shan State. After part of Shan State was put under military administration in 1952, negotiations took place between the Government and Shan State leaders.[13] Subsequently, the rights of Shan chiefs and their representation in the Chamber of Nationalities were annulled.[14] This was followed by the 1962 coup, the abolition of the Shan State Council and the arrest of some of its leaders.

Several years later, under the 1974 socialist Constitution, the recognition of the seven States and Divisons was formalised, although it did not make any special provisions for ethnic groups. The ethnic nationalities previously given some forms of special recognition in the 1947 Constitution were formally promoted to the status of States (Kayah State, Karen State, Chin State, Kachin State, Shan State), along with the addition of two more: Mon State and Arakan State. These are all based on, or at least named after, the dominant ethnic group in the particular area. These seven States were on the same administrative level as the seven Divisions, and it covered what British authorities previously termed 'the excluded areas'.[15] The 1974 Constitution

[10] See generally M Smith, *Burma: Insurgency and the Politics of Ethnicity*, 2nd edn (Bangkok, White Lotus, 1991).

[11] The Constitution Amendment Act 1951, 7 November 1951, replacing art 180 with art 181.

[12] Kyaw Yin, *The Foundations of Public Administration in Burma: A Study in Social and Historical Perspectives* (New York, University Microfilms, 1968) 299. These Ministries were later abolished after General Ne Win's coup in 1962.

[13] Sai Aung Tu, *History of the Shan State: From its Origins to 1962* (Thailand, Silkworm Books, 2009) 317, 338.

[14] The Constitution Amendment Act 1959 (second) repealed s 154(2).

[15] M Callahan, *Political Authority in Burma's Ethnic Minority States: Devolution, Occupation and Co-existence* (Washington, DC, East-West Center, 2007) 12.

can therefore be seen as solidifying a historical division of administrative power, yet without the original promise of secession for some nationalities that was present in the 1947 Constitution. The States and Divisions also had few substantive powers, because, for example, it was the central unicameral parliament that retained all legislative power for the entire country under the socialist regime.

The organisation of seven States and Divisions/Regions has been retained in the 2008 Constitution. From 1993, while Myanmar was still under military rule without a constitution, the military orchestrated a constitution-drafting process that was not complete until 2007. As part of this process, representatives of some ethnic nationalities attended the proceedings. For example, in 2004 representatives of ethnic nationalities made up more than half of the 1,088 delegates at the National Convention.[16] The resulting 2008 Constitution retained the distinction between seven Divisions that were renamed as 'Regions', and the seven States, with the addition of the new capital, Naypyidaw, as a union territory. This raises the question of whether and how powers given to the States and Regions under the 2008 Constitution have been exercised.

Prior to 2014, the States and Regions had rarely exercised their legislative power, and remnants of the administrative structures of the previous regime remained intact.[17] Under the previous military regime there were no State and Region governments with the power to pass laws, so the State and Region governments must therefore be regarded as new developments. In late 2013, there were indications from the President's Office that greater expectations would be placed on the States and Regions to increase the scope of their involvement in administration and governance. The unicameral State and Region Hluttaw primarily consist of representatives from townships, with 25 per cent of seats still reserved for the military. At the level of administration, up until late 2013, while State and Region ministers had been appointed to various ministries, there were essentially no ministries, because pre-existing departments of the military administration had been put under the realm of State and Region control. The General Administration Department, established by the State Law and Order Restoration Council (SLORC) in 1988 as a bureaucratic means to control village-level administration, remains in operation.

Further, Union Government control over State and Region leadership appointments is ensured because, according to the Constitution, the Chief Ministers are selected by the President from amongst elected *Hluttaw* members. Among these, 10 out of the 14 are former military officers, and all

[16] M Smith, 'Ethnic Participation and National Reconciliation in Myanmar: Challenges in a Transitional Landscape' in T Wilson (ed), *Myanmar's Long Road to National Reconciliation* (Singapore, ISEAS, 2006) 38.

[17] See generally H Nixon *et al*, *State and Region Governments in Myanmar* (Yangon, The Asian Foundation, MDRI-CESD, 2013).

are affiliated with the Government political party, the Union Solidarity and Development Party (USDP), rather than ethnic-based political parties. The States and Regions are granted legislative power over a limited range of areas specified in the Constitution, although little attention has been given to the legislative activity of the State and Region parliaments.[18]

Lastly, in addition to central control of the parliament and executive, the Government also retains control over the State and Region courts. The Chief Justice of the High Court in each State and Region is chosen by the Chief Justice of the Union Supreme Court on the advice of the President (the latter being chosen by the President). The symbolic recognition of seven ethnic-based States and seven Burman-majority Regions largely endures as a convenient way for the Government to allow a basic form of unicameral government while maintaining its control over the State and Region branches of government. While governance at the State and Region level has not yet been a major focus of the post-2011 reform process, it is likely to become more significant after the 2015 national elections.

SPECIAL REPRESENTATION: MINISTERS OF NATIONAL RACES AFFAIRS

The second way in which the 2008 Constitution provides for ethnic nationalities is through the appointment of 'Ministers of National Races Affairs',[19] which can be characterised as a form of *special representation*. But why this form of special representation, and special representation for whom? This special representation partly functions to divide State and Region parliaments and allows Burmans to have a representative in those areas where ethnic nationalities are in a majority. The effect of this is to limit the power of State and Region governments.

Levy distinguishes between two main types of special representation in legislatures: representation based on the identity of the voters, and representation that is based on the identity of the members of parliament.[20] Under the 1947 Constitution, the latter type of representation was in place, and the Chamber of Nationalities reserved 125 seats on the basis of ethnicity in proportion to the population, which included 25 Shan, 8 Chin, 3 Kayah, 12 Kachin and 15 Karen representatives. The other 62 representatives were Burmans. This design was intended to give a voice and recognition to some ethnic nationalities. The subsequent 1974 Constitution did not follow this model of representation, but replaced the bicameral parliament with a unicameral parliament as part of the centralised socialist order.

18 But see a forthcoming report by Asia Foundation on State and Region law-making (2015).

19 2008 Constitution, s 15.

20 Levy, above n 7, 45.

The 2008 Constitution introduced a new category of Ministers for National Races Affairs, which fits with Levy's form of representation based on the identity of the voters, although one criticism of this approach is how the identity of voters is decided. At the National Convention to draft a new constitution in the 1990s, the creation of positions for Ministers for National Races Affairs appeared to be a concession proposed for inclusion in the Constitution for ethnic nationalities that could not satisfy the criteria for a 'Zone' (discussed in the following section).

As a result, the 2008 Constitution provides for a national race recognised by the Government to have representation at the State/Region or Zone level, if it forms at least 0.1 per cent or more of the population in that Region.[21] Like the States and Regions, the Ministers for National Races Affairs remain under close control of the central Government, as their role is determined by the President.[22] The Constitution also places several obligations on the Government and on national races with respect to national races matters, but here I concentrate on how this formal designation of a Minister for National Races Affairs has been allocated in practice.[23]

For the period 2011–2015, the election of 29 Ministers of National Races Affairs at the State and Region level provides an indication of the purpose and distribution of this form of representation (although again it is based on unreliable statistics prior to the 2014 census). The number of Ministers is one indication of the ethnic diversity within each State and Region. Shan State has the most with seven representatives, which is not surprising given that the Shan barely constitute a majority in that area; Kachin State has four Ministers; Karen and Mon State each have three. The Irrawaddy, Rangoon and Saigang Regions have two Ministers each. Lastly, there are two States—Arakan and Karenni State—and four Regions—Magwe, Mandalay, Pegu and Tenasserim Regions—that have just one representative. Chin State is the only one that does not have any representatives, which is an indication that its population is primarily of Chin ethnicity (or one of the Chin subgroups recognised by the government).

Of the 29 Ministers for National Races Affairs, two ethnic groups, the Burman and the Karen, each have five Ministers to represent them across the States and Regions. The crucial point is that this allows the Burmans to have representation in the parliaments of five out of seven ethnic-based States. The Chin and Shan both have three representatives; the Pa-O, Rakhine and

[21] 2008 Constitution, s 161(b) and (c). This presumably only applies to the 135 ethnic nationalities recognised by the Government.

[22] 2008 Constitution, s 262(g).

[23] For example, the Union Government must facilitate the development of local dialects and the preservation of culture, and promote socio-economic development of disadvantaged races (ss 22, 27).

Lisu have two each; and then a handful of ethnic nationalities have one representative.[24]

The political affiliation of the Ministers for National Races Affairs suggests that most of them are closely affiliated with the military. A majority of the representatives (17) are members of the USDP. Another two Ministers are from the National Unity Party, a political party also known to support the military. Of the remaining Ministers, nine are from ethnic-based political parties. This includes two from the Kayin People's Party; two from the Shan Nationals Democratic Party; and one from the All Mon Region Democracy Party; the Chin Progressive Party; the Inn National Development Party; the Kayan National Party; and the Rakhine Nationals Progressive Party. The remaining Minister is independent.

In addition to indicating which ethnic group has been granted representation through these positions, it is also important to consider how these Ministers have been perceived in relation to other members of parliament. There are preliminary indications that in some States and Regions, these Ministers were given subordinate portfolios, or were even considered to be in an inferior position to other Ministers.[25] This came to national public attention through a case heard by the Constitutional Tribunal regarding the Ministers of National Races Affairs,[26] which concerned the benefits given to these Ministers in comparison to those given to State and Region Ministers. A group of parliamentarians from the *Amyotha Hluttaw* lodged the case with the Constitutional Tribunal in order to challenge legislation that would have effectively prevented Ministers of National Races Affairs from receiving the same privileges as other State and Region Ministers. In December 2011, the Constitutional Tribunal agreed that Ministers for National Races Affairs were of the same status as other Ministers and struck out the related sections of the law under review.

There are several criticisms of such forms of special representation more generally, as identified in the literature on cultural rights, which need to be kept in mind if the position of Minister for National Races Affairs is retained. For example, one concern is that special representation may create a false veneer of unity within an ethnic group, when in reality its members may not share the same political interests. It may be 'self-fulfilling', in the sense that it may only further encourage political support to gather along ethnic lines, and therefore undermine the need to form multi-ethnic coalitions. In addition, it requires officials to identify voters on the basis of race, and this process could be open to discrimination.[27] For example, the future allocation of Ministers for National Races Affairs will be determined

[24] These are the Kayan (Padaung); Kachin; Mon; Rawang; Lahu; Akha; and Inn.
[25] Nixon *et al*, above n 17, 56.
[26] Constitutional Tribunal Submission No 2/2011, dated 14 December 2011.
[27] Levy, above n 7, 43.

based on the 2014 census. But the census has been mired in controversy due, among other matters, to the central Government's insistence on retaining the 135 recognised categories of ethnic nationalities. Many ethnic groups feel that they have not been classified appropriately, while other groups are not recognised on the list at all.

As the Ministers for National Races Affairs operate only at the State and Region or Zone level, they clearly remain under the control of the central Government. In the future it will be necessary not only to evaluate what 'responsibilities' are allocated to these Ministers by the President, but also how these Ministers use their position, and whether it is for the benefit of people they represent.

LIMITED SELF-GOVERNANCE: SELF-ADMINISTERED ZONES AND DIVISIONS

The third aspect of constitutional recognition for ethnic nationalities is the designation of Self-administered Zones and Divisions (hereafter 'Zones'), a form of *limited self-governance*, which did not feature in the 1947 or 1974 Constitutions. As Levy notes, the introduction of forms of self-governance are often in response to the need to address demands for greater local control over land.[28] This is true in Myanmar, where land rights remains a central issue of ongoing concern. In order to understand these Zones as a limited form of self-governance, in this section I analyse the selection process for the Zones and the constitutional powers each Zone has in theory. I then focus on the history and background of the six areas in order to explain why these areas were successfully designated as Zones.

Selection Process for the Zones

The process of determining which ethnic groups received Zone status was partly mathematical and relied on population data (although this data is considered to be unreliable).[29] At the National Convention in the 1990s, there were 16 groups that applied for self-administered status. The conditions that a group was required to meet in order to obtain this status were largely numerical: first, an ethnic group must make up the majority of the population in at least two townships; and, second, the townships must be located adjacent to each other. If the application included more than two townships, the ethnic group had to form a majority of the population in *all*

[28] Levy, above n 7, 32–33.

[29] This section is drawn from documentation on the National Convention on the Online Burma/Myanmar library, <www.burmalibrary.org>.

of these townships. The final two conditions that needed to be satisfied were that the application could only be made by one ethnic group, that is, it could not be a coalition of groups. A further limitation is that ethnic groups that already had a State were not allowed to apply for this status (even if they satisfied the above criteria in areas outside their States).

In the 1994 sessions of the National Convention, 10 of the 16 applications for self-administered status failed. Some were rejected because they only applied for status over one township, instead of two or more, such as Lahu and Inntha in Shan State. Others failed because they proposed two townships in two different States, like the application for Kayah Zone in relation to several townships in Shan and Kayah States. Some failed because they did not meet the criteria of a majority population in two townships, such as the attempt to form a Paletwa Hills Division for the Khumi in Chin State.

Some ethnic nationalities attempted to achieve this status by combining with other ethnic nationalities to meet the requirements. For example, an Akha Zone was rejected because it proposed to group the Akha, Shan and Lwela races together, which are considered by the government to be distinct ethnic groups. Further, groups that already had recognition as a State were effectively ruled out of claiming status recognised in another State. Therefore, the Kachin population in Shan State North Special Region 5 and the Kayin population that lived outside of Kayin State were unsuccessful.

As a result of this application process, the Self-administered Zones were announced as early as 1995.[30] Fifteen years later, on 20 August 2010, the Zones were officially proclaimed.[31] Not long after the 2008 Constitution came into force, on 30 March 2011, the President issued a notification to clarify the areas covered by these Zones, and to announce that they had begun operation.[32] Six Zones were established: the Naga, Kokang, Danu, Palaung, Pa-O and Wa Zones.[33] Each of these Zones includes between two and six townships. The Zones, in theory, have legislative, executive and judicial power;[34] in the following section I explore the potential scope of these powers.

[30] The Detailed Basic Principles for Prescribing Self-administered Divisions or Self-administered Zones as laid down by the National Convention Plenary Session held on 7 April 1995.

[31] The Union of Myanmar, The State Peace and Development Council Notification No 33/2010, 20 August 2010, Delineation of Self-administered Division and Self-administered Zones and their Seats of Government.

[32] Republic of the Union of Myanmar State Peace and Development Council, Presidential Notification No 7/2011, 30 March 2011.

[33] 2008 Constitution, s 56.

[34] 2008 Constitution, ss 12, 17, 18.

Constitutional Powers of the Zones

The Zones as a form of limited self-governance are allocated certain powers and functions under the Constitution. Legislative and executive power is administered by the Leading Body of the Zone.[35] The Leading Body has at least 10 members, including military personnel and Ministers for National Races Affairs (discussed in 'Special Representation: Ministers of National Races Affairs' above). These members are elected for a period of five years by a Scrutiny Body, originally established by the former State Peace and Development Council (SPDC). The Leading Body is coordinated by a chairperson who is chosen on the consensus of the Body itself, or by a secret vote if there is a dispute. One of the privileges of this position is that the chairperson has the power to submit a question to the Constitutional Tribunal, the newly established tribunal that can decide on constitutional law matters.

The role of the chairperson is to oversee the function and activities of the Leading Body, and the President can also assign responsibilities to the chairperson, in the same way that the President determines the duties of the Ministers for National Races Affairs. The position of the chairperson is not secure, as the President has the authority to dismiss him or her before the end of the five-year term on ambiguous grounds, such as if the chairperson is not carrying out his or her duties 'efficiently'.[36] This is similar to the grounds for dismissal of judges of the Supreme Court and High Courts.

Within the Leading Body, a smaller unit known as the Executive Committee must be formed, which consists of between three and five members. All of the existing Zones have three members, except for Naga Zone and Pa-O Zone, which have five each. The Executive Committee has responsibility for 'administrative functions', oversees the civil service and is also supposed to be responsible for drafting the annual budget.[37]

In terms of legislative power, the power to pass laws is granted to the Leading Body of the Zone.[38] According to Schedule III to the 2008 Constitution, the legislative power covers a narrow list that includes matters such as the provision of electricity and the prevention of fires. The list is composed of three types of matters: local development and public services; the environment; and the local economy. Even if a Zone does legislate in these areas—and to date there is no evidence of any such legislation—a Zone law is subordinate to both State and Region law, as well as Union Government laws, to the extent that there are any inconsistencies.[39]

[35] The powers of the Leading Body of the Zone are set out in the Constitution (arts 274–283) and mirrored in the Self-administered Division or Self-administered Zone Leading Body Law No 17/2010.

[36] 2008 Constitution, s 61(a); Law 17/2010, s 53.

[37] Law 17/2010, ss 38, 45, 41.

[38] 2008 Constitution, s 275.

[39] 2008 Constitution, s 198(c) and (d).

In terms of the judiciary, the courts are supposed to include a Zone-level court, the District Court (in Wa Division) and the township courts.[40] However, none of the Zone-level courts have been established to date. This suggests that any disputes that arise are resolved through non-State or informal means. Lastly, the Constitution is clear that the Zones, like the ethnic-based States, have no right to secede from the Union.[41]

The Concentration of Zones in Shan State

Five of the six Zones are located in just one state in Myanmar, Shan State. Shan State is important because it is the largest state in terms of land mass and covers almost a quarter of the area of Myanmar. Most of Shan State is rural, rich in mineral resources and famous for its precious stones, metals and horticulture. Shan State produces a large portion of the world's opium and heroin,[42] which contributes to Myanmar's position as the second largest opium producing country in the world. Due to the borders it shares with China, Shan State is a key state for strategic, security and economic reasons.

Today, the Shan are the largest minority group in Myanmar, most of whom are Buddhist. Only about half of the population of Shan State are ethnic Shan, while other major ethnic groups that live in Shan State include the Pa-O, Palaung, Kachin, Danu, Lahu, Inthar, Wa, Kokang and Akha.[43] Yet the differences within the population of Shan State are more geographical than linguistic or religious. As a result of this diversity, Shan State has never been united but, if it was, it could rival Burman interests and power. Since independence, the central Government has therefore encouraged divisions among ethnic groups in order to hamper any attempts to establish a national movement in Shan State.[44]

The history of the relationship between the Shan and the Burmans is part of the reason that five of the six Zones are located in present-day Shan State. The period from late 1200s to early 1500s is generally acknowledged as a time when the Shan rulers, known as *saopha*, were the dominant power in the area now known as Myanmar.[45] This came to an end only after the reassertion of power by Burman Kings, beginning with the Toungoo Dynasty in 1531. In 1885, after the last king, Thibaw, was deposed and exiled by British colonial authorities, Upper Burma was annexed as part of British India. The extent of engagement between British authorities and the Shan varied

[40] Union Judiciary Law 20/2010, s 42(b) and (c).

[41] 2008 Constitution, s 9.

[42] On the history of Shan state, and the use of drugs and US foreign policy in particular, see B Linter, 'The Shans and the Shan State' (1984) 5(4) *Contemporary Southeast Asia* 403–45.

[43] Maung Thawnghmung, above n 27, 15.

[44] ibid, 16.

[45] See, eg, GE Harvey, *History of Burma: From the Earliest Times to 10 March 1824* (London, Frank Cass & Co Ltd, 1967) 71–126.

under colonialism,[46] and from 1922 the Shan were under a federated form of administration. By 1937, when the Government of Burma Act 1935 came into effect to separate the administration of Burma from British India, the *Saopha* were given representation in the Government.[47]

As part of negotiations for the drafting of the 1947 Constitution, it was clearly recognised that the Shan should be afforded special rights. As a result, the 1947 Constitution provided that the Shan had the right to secession from 10 years after independence. But in 1952 the Government declared a large part of southern Shan State under military administration. This was on the pretext of suppressing Kuomintang forces, but also worked to undermine the power of the Shan leaders, the *saophas*, and a large number of Burmese troops moved into Shan State.[48] Fighting between the Government and various ethnic armed groups in Shan State broke out in the 1960s, and continued in the following decades, until a number of ceasefire agreements in the late 1980s and early 1990s.[49] The social, economic and political history of Shan State needs to be considered in order to understand how the Zones were created and which areas were given Zone status.

I now turn to examine why each of these Zones was established, emphasising the history of relations between these ethnic nationalities and the central Government, particularly since the late 1980s.

Round 1 Ceasefires: Wa and Kokang Zones

The Wa and Kokang Zones share a similar history in terms of their relations with the central Government and both are located in Shan State. Up until the late 1980s, both were part of the Communist Party of Burma (CPB), until they entered into ceasefire deals with SLORC and received certain concessions in return. The constitutional status as a Zone was granted to these two groups as part of the broader process of the ceasefire deals with these ethnic armed groups.

From the 1960s until late 1980s, the Wa were one of the biggest forces in the CPB, which posed the most significant military threat to the Government of Burma at the time.[50] By January 1968 the CPB had also entered the Kokang area. Support for the CPB waned in the late 1980s, however, after it took steps to oppose the drug trade, which many ethnic nationalities relied on as a source of income. In March 1989, the Kokang opposed the

[46] Sai Aung Tun, *History of the Shan State: From its Origins to 1962* (Washington, DC, University of Washington Press, 2009) 171.

[47] ibid, 224.

[48] Linter, above n 42, 403, 411.

[49] See generally, Smith, above n 10.

[50] The most comprehensive account of the CPB in Burma is B Linter, *The Rise and Fall of the Communist Party of Burma* (Ithaca, NY, Cornell University Press, 1990) 35.

leadership of the CPB. In April 1989, Wa troops took the strategic base of Panghsang and drove the CPB leadership across the border into China.

As a result of the break with the CPB, new lines of communication were opened up with the military junta. In 1989 the Kokang entered into a ceasefire agreement with the junta, and their area became known as the Shan State Special Region 1 (North).[51] The Kokang were allowed to keep their arms and control of all their territory. The military junta also provided the Kokang army with money, cars and food, and allowed opium growing.[52]

In 1989 the Wa also entered into a ceasefire deal with the junta, as represented by General Khin Nyunt with the assistance of Lo Hsing-han, a former drug lord from Shan State. The Wa area became known as Shan State Special Region 2 (North). The United Wa State Army (UWSA) was similarly given food, fuel and funding by SLORC, and was allowed to continue its drugs trade and the extraction of natural resources.[53] As the Wa were part of the first round of ceasefires, they benefited from higher rewards and a lack of restrictions in comparison to those entering into later ceasefire deals. In particular, the Wa and Kokang were given the profitable jade mines in Kachin State, because areas like the Wa Hills have no minerals of its own.

Aside from these concessions, by the late 1990s, the ceasefire deals also allowed room for international non-governmental organisations to establish development projects in these areas.[54] By the mid-2000s, a new partnership was established, known as the Kokang and Wa Initiative, which aimed to help poppy farmers and families meet basic needs without income from opium. Yet from a governance perspective, institutions of the Union Government in these regions are minimal or non-existent. Up until 2007, one development practitioner observed that in the Wa Region '[t]here was no court structure and no system of appealing decision … There was and is no legal profession and there never have been any practising Wa lawyers in the Wa Region'.[55]

One characteristic of both the Wa and Kokang political parties and armies, and a reason that the central Government needs a strategic alliance, is their strong connections to China. Some leaders of the Wa and Kokang do not speak Burmese.[56] There are an estimated 700,000–800,000 Wa living in Myanmar, but another 350,000 in China.[57] Both the Wa and Kokang

[51] ibid, 83–85.

[52] Zaw Oo and Win Min, *Assessing Burma's Ceasefire Accords* (Washington, DC, East-West Center, 2007) 15; Linter, above n 50, 53.

[53] On the Wa and Kokang ceasefire deals, see Zaw Oo and Win Min, ibid.

[54] On the Wa political party, see T Kramer, *The United Wa State Party* (Washington, DC, East-West Center, 2007).

[55] RD Renard, 'The Wa Authority and Good Governance 1989–2007' (2013) 17(1) *Journal of Burma Studies* 141, 152.

[56] Linter, above n 50, 85.

[57] Myo Myo and Soe Than Lynn, 'Wa party to contest few home seats' *Myanmar Times*, 21–27 June 2010, available at <www.mmtimes.com/index.php/national-news/5234-wa-party-to-contest-few-home-seats.html>.

maintain close ties with China, including officials and intelligence agents from Yunnan. It is also common knowledge that some Chinese were granted Wa or Kokang identity cards in order to live in Myanmar (at least during the period of General Khin Nyunt).[58]

The UWSA is estimated to have 30,000 troops, which makes it the largest ethnic force in Myanmar. There continue to be disputes between the central Government and the Wa. For example, in 2008, the Wa Region was the only part of the country that returned a majority 'no' vote in the constitutional referendum, even refusing access to election authorities prior to the poll, resulting in the ballot being cancelled in areas not under central Government control.[59]

In 2010, the UWSA submitted a proposal to the Burmese Army for the inclusion of three more townships as part of the Wa Zone, on the ground that in 1948 these Regions were marked as inhabited by Wa people.[60] While a new ceasefire was signed with the Government in September 2011,[61] there have since been calls for greater independence.[62] Despite the ceasefire deals and Zone status, there remain ongoing demands for greater recognition.

Round 2 Ceasefires: Pa-O Zone and Palaung Zone

Similar to the Wa and Kokang, the Pa-O and Palaung also share a history of opposition to the central Government that since the 1990s has been mediated by a ceasefire, and which again resulted in the constitutional recognition of Zone status.

The Pa-O are related ethnically to the Karen; most adhere to Buddhism and primarily live in south-west Shan State. The Pa-O National Liberation Organisation (PNLO) was formed in 1949 and has at times fought against both the Shan and the Government.[63] In the late 1950s, the PNLO was one of the ethnic armies that took up U Nu's offer of 'arms for democracy' and formed a political party known as the Pa-O National Party (PNO).[64] But

[58] Callahan, above n 15, 21.

[59] Transnational Institute, 'A Changing Ethnic Landscape: Analysis of Burma's 2010 Polls' (Burma Policy Briefing No 4, 2010), available at <www.tni.org/files/download/bpb4final.pdf>.

[60] 'UWSAs proposal on transformation of itself into Border Guard Force', *Mizzima*, 7 January 2010, available at <http://archive-2.mizzima.com/research/3326-uwsas-proposal-on-transformation-of-itself-into-border-guard-force.html>.

[61] Burma News International, *Deciphering Myanmar's Peace Process 2013*, available at www.themimu.info/sites/themimu.info/files/documents/Ref%20Doc_DecipheringMyanmar%27sPeaceProcess_BNI_2013.pdf>, 180.

[62] See, eg, 'Wa Army Pledges to Continue Push for Independence', *The Irrawaddy*, 28 March 2013, available at <www.irrawaddy.org/ethnic/wa-army-pledges-to-continue-push-for-independence.html>.

[63] Callahan, above n 15, 45.

[64] Zaw Oo and Win Min, above n 52, 8. Smith claims that the Pa-O were offered a State in return: M Smith, *State of Strife: The Dynamics of Ethnic Conflict in Burma* (Washington, DC, East-West Center, 2007) 168–69.

in the mid-1960s, some PNO leaders were arrested after the breakdown of the ceasefires. The CPB formed links with the Pa-O and entered into an understanding that the CPB would supply arms in return for being allowed to operate in the Pa-O area.[65] Following the retreat of the CPB to China, in February 1991, the PNO agreed to a ceasefire with the military government.[66] As part of the ceasefire deal, the PNO was granted logging permits and concessions in the gem-mining industry.[67] It was also allowed to retain control of what was then known as Shan State Special Region 6 (South).

The Palaung did not form a resistance army immediately after independence, as the Pa-O did, but they eventually took up arms against the Government after the coup in 1962. The Palaung people are related to the Mon-Khmer, and most identify themselves as Buddhist, with a small percentage being Animist or Christian. The population is estimated to number over one million, spread across Shan State with a concentration in the north-west, although there are also Palaung refugees in northern Thailand and a Palaung population in south-west China. In the late 1980s the Palaung State Liberation Party (PSLP), like many other ethnic armed groups, was affected by the junta's 'four cuts' program, a strategy that aimed to target ethnic armies' supplies of food, finances, information and recruits. The Palaung State Liberation Army (PSLA) entered into a ceasefire in 1991,[68] and the area it controlled came to be known as Shan State Special Region 7. The agreement allowed the PSLP to maintain the area it already held, and was also based on promises of greater financial and development assistance.

The area of concern for the central Government is the ongoing conflict with the Ta'ang National Liberation Army (TNLA). In 2012 this led to the displacement of over 2,000 people, and fighting continued in 2013.[69] The Palaung has also accused government forces of crimes against its people, such as the murder of three off-duty Palaung soldiers in northern Shan State.[70] In addition to conflict, in 2013 the TNLA also called for the expansion of the Palaung Zone from two to 12 townships, and it contested the Government's estimate of population figures.[71] Similar to the Wa, the Palaung continue to call on the central Government for greater recognition than has currently been granted, such as by adding more townships as part of existing Zones.

[65] Linter, above n 50, 29.

[66] Callahan, above n 15, 46.

[67] Zaw Oo and Win Min, above n 52, 44.

[68] On the Palaung ceasefire, see ibid, 12, 18.

[69] Burma News International, above n 62, 8; and Burma News International, *Deciphering Myanmar's Peace Process 2014*, available at <http://mmpeacemonitor.org/images/pdf/deciphering_myanmar_peace_process_2014.pdf>, 7–10.

[70] '3 killed 2 raped by Myanmar army says Palaung group', *Mizzima News*, 3 May 2013, available at <http://mizzima.com/news/ethnic-issues/9327-3-killed-2-raped-by-myanmar-army-says-palaung-group.html>.

[71] Nan Tin Htwe, 'No ceasefire but govt and Palaung agree to further talks', *The Myanmar Times*, 4 August 2013.

The Exceptions: Danu Zone and Naga Zone

The last two Zones are grouped together as exceptions that seek to legitimise this form of special representation beyond mere ceasefire agreements. While the Danu Zone is located in Shan State, it is the only ethnic nationality of the six that was not in armed conflict with the Government. The Naga Zone is located outside of Shan State, and its status therefore reduces the perception that the aim of the creation of the Zones was simply to undermine unity in Shan State.

The Danu Zone appears to be largely the result of the numerical formulae for Zone status and the population count in the 1990s. The Danu Self-administered Zone includes two townships, Pindaya township and Ywangan township. The current Chief Minister of Shan State, Sao Aung Myatt, is Danu,[72] and one of the members of the executive committee is from the Danu political party. When conducting field research, my informants questioned why Danu was recognised as a Zone because it does not fit the ceasefire concession narrative. As one Danu informant put it, the Danu had never had an armed group, the Danu can speak Burmese and, in his opinion, they have a good relationship with the Government. The responses I received as to whether status as a Zone made any difference were largely ambivalent. One informant, however, showed me a book on Danu cultural identity that had been published locally. When I sought to clarify whether he meant that the central Government was now funding initiatives to publish materials on cultural affairs and local languages, the response I received was, 'Oh no, it was not funded by the Government. The central Government simply gave us permission to publish.' In contrast, the government-run media claimed that Union Ministers had made donations to a Danu Education Foundation.[73] While on one level obtaining permission to print material on the culture and tradition of ethnic nationalities is a break from the past, it may be attributed to the general lifting of restrictions on media publications and censorship, rather than to the creation of the Danu Zone in particular.

Outside of Shan State, the Naga Self-administered Zone is located in Sagaing Region and includes three townships, with Lahe as the capital. The Naga were one of the ethnic nationalities who served in World War II alongside the British.[74] The area populated by the Naga has had a history of conflict, and includes the Naga on both sides of the border with India. While there have been past attempts to unite the Naga across the borders,[75] in 1988

[72] Maung Thawnghmung, above n 27, 34.
[73] 'Union Minister meets members of Danu Self-Administered Zone Leading Body', *New Light of Myanmar*, 22 September 2012, 2.
[74] Maung Thawnghmung, above n 27, 3.
[75] Burma News International, above n 62, 151–52.

the Burmese Naga drove the Indian Naga out of their base.[76] Although the National Socialist Council of Nagaland had entered into conflict with the Government, it was never to the same extent as the Wa, Kokang, Pa-O or Palaung. A ceasefire agreement was signed on 9 April 2012, which included an agreement to stop all fighting and provided for further discussions on steps towards settlement.

The Naga Zone has received some development assistance for education, health and infrastructure projects from the Indian Government and India-based companies. Similarly, China's support for the Wa Zones and Kokang Zones is also evident, although it is not proclaimed in terms of development aid. The designation of the Naga Zone has also seen a renewal of overt central Government sponsorship of annual ethnic celebrations. For example, on 15 January 2013, as part of the Naga New Year celebration hosted at Lahe Township attended by Zone members,[77] the Deputy Minister for Border Affairs reportedly gave financial assistance for the development of Naga Zone. But this practice of publicly reported displays of gifts to ethnic nationalities is not new, and from one perspective it only fosters a sense of dependency on the central Government and requires the Zone to ensure it maintains its focus on pleasing Naypyidaw.[78]

There remain issues of contention between the central Government and the Naga concerns the categorisation of the Naga ethnic group. For example, the Naga contest their classification as one of the 53 Chin tribes. In March 2013, a public statement issued by several Naga organisations based in Rangoon called on the Government to list the Naga as a separate ethnic tribe on the official government list.[79] The status as a Zone has therefore not necessarily reduced the demands of ethnic nationalities for greater recognition.

CONCLUSION

The relationship between the national Union Government and 'recognised' ethnic nationalities is of crucial significance to the agenda of the Myanmar Government. Levy's framework on cultural rights provides one lens through which to understand how central-local relations in Myanmar are

[76] Linter, above n 50, 107.

[77] *Myanmar Update*, 'Naga Self-Administered Zone Organises New Year Celebration on 15 January', 23 January 2013, <www.myanmarupdate.com/naga-self-administered-zone-organizes-new-year-celebration-on-15-january>.

[78] 'Naga Self-administered Zone sees health care services, development works', *The New Light of Myanmar*, 16 January 2014, 16.

[79] Thawng Zel Thang, 'We are an indigenous people in Burma, Naga', *Chinland Guardian*, 16 March 2013, available at <www.chinlandguardian.com/index.php/cartoons/item/1832-we-are-an-indigenous-people-in-burma-naga>.

determined in part on the basis of a constructed idea of ethnicity through the Constitution. The organisation between States and Regions is a form of *symbolic recognition*, which allows the Government to maintain a sense of continuity in recognition provided for select ethnic nationalities.

Secondly, there is a system of *special representation* at the State and Region level for Ministers of National Race Affairs to represent other major ethnic groups in the area. This allows both for fragmentation of power between ethnic groups and for Burman representation in the ethnic-based States, although all such Ministers have their responsibilities controlled by the central Government. Given that some ethnic groups have actively sought to be represented at the State and Region level through the appointment of a Minister for National Race Affairs, this suggests that it is seen as a potentially valuable form of representation at least by some groups.

Thirdly, certain ethnic nationality areas are now recognised as Self-administered Zones or Divisions, which I have identified as a new form of *limited self-governance*.

Overall, these forms of recognition, as set out in the 2008 Constitution, can be understood as a means of 'constitutional business', whereby the central Government (previously the military junta) conferred certain constitutional privileges or created opportunities for leaders of ethnic nationalities as a concession that primarily, though not exclusively, related to previous ceasefire deals in the late 1980s and early 1990s. The implications for all three forms, however, is that the central Government retains ultimate control under the terms of the 2008 Constitution. This has led to the emergence of a 'Look to Naypyidaw' approach, in which ethnic nationalities remain conscious of the need to appease the central quasi-civilian Government, while at the same time focusing on Naypyidaw to demand increased forms of recognition.

One indication that these forms of recognition provide for continuity, in terms of the way in which the central Government has sought to subordinate ethnic nationalities, is the periodic public gestures of dialogue and donations, as reported in the government-controlled newspaper, *The New Light of Myanmar*. These usually take the form of Union Government officials visiting Zone areas, or meeting with leaders of the Zones or ethnic nationalities.[80] These meetings also serve as a reminder to Zone leaders that they are dependent on the Naypyidaw Government for ongoing support.

The future then raises several questions. The existence of these Zones may rest on the results of the 2014 census, which have only partially been made public. If other ethnic nationalities can fulfil the population requirements as a result of the new census count, then more Zones may be formed in the

[80] See, eg, 'Priority given to self-administered zone/division, state/region for development tasks', *New Light of Myanmar*, 16 August 2012, 10; 'Paddy seeds presented to chairmen of Self-administered Zones/Division', *New Light of Myanmar*, 21 June 2012, 1.

future. It is also possible that existing Zones may be expanded, if the census shows that adjacent townships also have a majority population comprised of that ethnic group. As the existing Zones were only established in 2011, their activities and role must be monitored over a longer period of time in order to understand what function they fulfil and whether this structure can help to facilitate greater participation in governance.

Overall, the case of Myanmar illustrates that authoritarian regimes may include provisions for special recognition of cultural rights for some ethnic groups, as a means of facilitating negotiations and peace deals with such groups. The creation of these rights can therefore be used to legitimise the role of the quasi-civilian government and the function of the Constitution in controlling ethnic rights. Yet the meaning of these rights is dynamic, not static, and it must continue to be assessed over the coming years in order to gauge the impact on the shifting nature of central-local relations in Myanmar more broadly.

FURTHER READING

Burma News International, *Deciphering Myanmar's Peace Process: A Reference Guide 2013*, available at <www.themimu.info/sites/themimu.info/files/documents/Ref%20Doc_DecipheringMyanmar%27sPeaceProcess_BNI_2013.pdf>.

Burma News International, *Deciphering Myanmar's Peace Process: A Reference Guide 2014*, available at <http://mmpeacemonitor.org/images/pdf/deciphering_myanmar_peace_process_2014.pdf>.

M Crouch and T Lindsey (eds), *Law, Society and Transition in Myanmar* (Oxford, Hart Publishing, 2014).

M Crouch, 'Rediscovering "Law" in Myanmar: A Review of Scholarship on the Legal System of Myanmar' (2014) 23(3) *Pacific Rim Law and Policy Review* 543–77.

H Nixon *et al*, *State and Region Governments in Myanmar* (Yangon, The Asia Foundation and MDRI-CESD, 2013), available at <www.theasiafoundation.org>.

J Silverstein, 'Politics in Shan State: The Question of Secession from the Union of Burma' (1958) 18(1) *Journal of Asian Studies* 43.

M Smith, *Burma: Insurgency and the Politics of Ethnicity*, 2nd edn (Bangkok, White Lotus, 1991).

7

The Role of the Central Government and Local Government in Times of Crisis

Japan's Experience After the Great East Japan Earthquake Disaster

SHIGENORI MATSUI

INTRODUCTION

JAPAN IS NOT a federal state, but the autonomy of local government is stipulated in the Constitution. Local government in Japan consists of municipal government (city, town and village) and prefectural government. The division of powers between the central Government and local government has been a very contentious issue, but Japan used to be a highly centralised country. Basically all of the most important powers are held by the central Government, and most of these are delegated to local governments to make sure that they execute them under the supervision of the central Government. Even the power of local government over local matters is heavily regulated by national statutes and is subject to tight control by the central Government. Many commentators have been calling for decentralisation and the granting of more powers to local governments, without, or with less, central supervision.

The Tohoku earthquake, which hit Japan on 11 March 2011, added a new twist to this on-going debate in Japan.[1] Although it is a responsibility of municipal governments to respond to natural disasters, the destruction caused by the Tohoku earthquake was far more wide-ranging, and many municipalities suffered tremendous damage due to the devastating tsunami caused by the earthquake, far beyond their capacity to respond. Rescue,

[1] This chapter is a part of my project on Earthquake, Tsunami, and Nuclear Meltdown: Failure of Law and Politics in Japan after the Tohoku Earthquake.

recovery and reconstruction necessitated a much stronger role for the central Government. Moreover, the normal division of powers between the central Government and local governments turned out to be difficult to maintain in the aftermath of the disaster. However, too much central intervention and central control at times stifled decision-making by local governments, and hindered local residents in accomplishing the reconstruction of their areas.

The nuclear meltdown accident in Fukushima, also caused by the tsunami, raised similar but somewhat different issues. It revealed a critical lack of powers held by the central Government. Simply speaking, the central Government did not have sufficient legal power to exercise during the nuclear crisis. At the same time, the Fukushima meltdown further strengthened the need for careful coordination between the central Government and local governments to carry out rescue, relief and recovery. And the accident revealed the difficulty caused by the need for the central Government to seek consent from local governments in order to build interim storage sites for nuclear waste and to restart the nuclear power plant, thus casting significant doubt on the ability of the central Government to carry out these national tasks.

All these developments cast new light on the division of powers between the central Government and local governments in times of crisis in Japan. This chapter traces these developments and draws some lessons from recent Japanese experience.

LOCAL GOVERNMENT IN JAPAN

Local Government Under the Japanese Constitution

After the Meiji Restoration of 1868, the Japanese Government established a local government system. But this system was highly centralised. Governors and mayors were all appointed by the central Government's Interior Minister.[2] Local government was in reality a local enforcement agency for the central Government. There was felt to be no necessity for local autonomy. Indeed, the Meiji Constitution of 1889, the first modern constitution in Japan, did not contain any provision on local government.

The Japanese Constitution of 1946, adopted after the end of the Pacific War during the occupation and enacted under the strong ideological influence of the United States Constitution, expanded the powers of local government and sought to guarantee some degree of local autonomy. Chapter 8, on 'local self-government', stipulates that '[r]egulations concerning organization and operations of local public entities shall be fixed by law in

[2] Institute for Comparative Studies in Local Governance, Historical Development of Japanese Local Governance, available at <www3.grips.ac.jp/~coslog/test/en/activity/01/05/index.html>.

accordance with the principle of local autonomy'.[3] This provision seeks to guarantee some degree of 'local autonomy' to local government, while granting power to regulate the organisation and operation of local government to the Diet, the national legislature. In turn the Diet passed the Local Government Act of 1947,[4] to set powers and standards in this area.

The Constitution looked to democratic systems with respect to local government, mandating that 'local public entities shall establish assemblies as their deliberative organs, in accordance with law'.[5] Such local assemblies are local legislatures, which may enact local ordinances (by-laws). And the Constitution granted local residents the right to choose their representatives to the local assembly, as well as the head of the local government. Thus, the Constitution stipulates that '[t]he chief executive officers of all local public entities, the members of their assemblies, and such other local officials as may be determined by law shall be elected by direct popular vote within their several communities'.[6]

According to the 1946 Constitution, '[l]ocal public entities shall have the right to manage their property, affairs and administration and to enact their own regulations within law'.[7] This is the only provision in the Constitution on the power of local government and the division of powers between the central Government and local government.[8] This provision indicates that the Diet could provide for limits on the power of local government. And as this chapter explains, this provision triggered an understanding that the power of local government derives from the central Government and must be defined by the Diet, and that local government could only exercise powers granted by the statute.

The Local Government Act

Following these constitutional provisions, the Diet passed the Local Government Act to establish the fundamental organisation, powers and relationship between the central Government and local government. The Act provides that the local public entities referred to in the Constitution are divided into general local governments and special local governments.[9]

[3] Nihonkokukenpō [Constitution of Japan], art 92.

[4] Chihoujichihō [Local Government Act], Law No 67 of 1947.

[5] Nihonkokukenpō [Constitution of Japan], art 93, para 1.

[6] ibid, art 93, para 2.

[7] ibid, art 94.

[8] However, '[a] special law, applicable only to one local public entity, cannot be enacted by the Diet without the consent of the majority of the voters of the local public entity concerned, obtained in accordance with law': ibid, art 95.

[9] Local Government Act, art 1-3, para 1. The special local government comprises a ward, a union of local public entities and the property district: ibid, art 1-3, para 3.

General local governments are further divided into cities, towns, and villages (generally called municipal governments, and differentiated by population) and prefectures.[10] Cities, towns and villages are the basic units of local government,[11] while Japan's 47 prefectures are broader units handling matters beyond the single city, town and village.[12] As of April 2014, there were 790 cities, 745 towns and 183 villages.[13]

Residents cannot form a local government freely. The formation or the organisation of local government must follow all the requirements stipulated in the Local Government Act. Basically, residents need the approval of the Internal Affairs and Communications Minister for everything, including any merger, split or change from town to city. Residents are therefore also unable to structure their local government freely.

The power of local government is somewhat ambiguous. Although the Constitution grants local governments the right to 'manage their property, affairs and administration and to enact their own regulations within law', the precise scope of local power remains unclear. Unlike the United States Constitution, which granted only enumerated powers to the federal Government and left other powers to the States and the people,[14] the Japanese Constitution does not limit the power of the central Government. Thus it is not clear whether there is in fact a limit on the power of the central Government (that is to say, whether there are some powers that must be reserved to the local government and regarding which any interference by the central Government could be unconstitutional). The dominant understanding is that the power of local government derives from the central Government and must be defined by the Diet, and that the local government may only exercise power granted by the Diet. According to the Local Government Act, local government can handle 'local matters' and other matters that are delegated by the statutes or cabinet orders.[15]

Local government may also enact ordinances 'within law'. This means that the local government can enact its own by-laws to regulate local matters. However, this provision also made it clear that local government could not violate statutes passed by the Diet. National law trumps local law. This supremacy of national law, together with virtually unlimited national power, has in practice deprived local government of much of its powers over purely local matters.

[10] ibid, art 1-3, para 2. For instance, in order for a town to become a city, the community must have a population numbering no fewer than 50,000 and satisfy other requirements: ibid, art 8, para 1.

[11] ibid, art 2, para 3.

[12] ibid, art 2, para 5.

[13] Soumusho [Ministry of Internal Affairs and Communications], Shichousonsu no suiihyou [Changes in the Number of Cities, Towns and Villages], available at <www.soumu.go.jp/main_content/000283329.pdf>.

[14] Constitution of the United States, 10th amendment.

[15] Local Government Act, art 2, para 2.

Residents' Participation in Local Government

What is unique about the local government in Japan is its infusion of much active citizen participation. The Japanese Constitution adopted the Westminster model of parliamentary democracy with respect to the central Government. But it adopted a somewhat different system, much like a presidential mechanism, with respect to local government, allowing local residents to elect not only their representatives in local assemblies but also the heads of local government directly. The Local Government Act followed this philosophy and provided for a mechanism to allow local residents to play this considerably more direct role.

Local residents can thus petition for enactment of local ordinances to the local assembly if they have the required number of signatures.[16] If the signature drive attracts the required number of signatures, the head of the local government must convene the local assembly and submit a bill, along with his or her own opinion.[17] The local assembly must thus review the bill endorsed by the signature drive. The assembly is not obliged to pass the bill, but local residents may demand the dissolution of the local assembly with the required number of signatures.[18] If in the following local vote the motion to dissolve the assembly is approved by the majority of participating voters, the local assembly is dissolved.[19] Therefore, rejecting a citizen-initiated bill might carry a risk of losing seats in the local assembly.

Local residents may also call for the dismissal of the heads of local government.[20] If the dismissal is approved by the majority of participating voters then the head is dismissed.[21] A local assembly may also pass a no-confidence motion against the head of local government,[22] in which case the head can either dissolve the local assembly or resign.[23]

The Local Government Act does not assume that the local government will hold a local referendum to decide significant local matters. But the absence of a referendum provision has not prevented some local governments from holding local referenda on pressing local matters. The results of such votes are not binding in law, but they certainly have a kind of de facto power to bind the local government.

[16] ibid, art 74, para 1. The signatures of 2% of all the local voters are required.

[17] ibid, art 74, para 3.

[18] ibid, art 76, para 1. The signatures of one-third of all local voters are required.

[19] ibid, art 78. The local voters could also demand the dismissal of particular assembly members; and if the dismissal is approved in the following vote in the election district, that member would be similarly dismissed: ibid, art 80.

[20] ibid, art 81. The signatures of one-third of all local voters are required.

[21] ibid, art 83. The local voters could similarly demand for the dismissal of vice heads and members of the election commission, audit commission and public safety commission: ibid, art 86. These officials would be dismissed if the three-quarters of the local assembly members, with more than two-thirds being present, approved the dismissal: ibid, art 87.

[22] ibid, art 178, para 1.

[23] ibid, art 178, para 2.

With respect to the central Government, there is no system for petitioning the Diet, the national legislature, for the enactment of a statute, no system for demanding the dissolution of the Diet, and no system for electing or dismissing the Prime Minister as the head of government. There is no system for holding national referenda either. All these methods of active citizen participation in local government mean, therefore, that local government is closer to local residents, and that local residents have a more direct voice within their local government.

The Realities of Local Government

Although the local government is established as 'local self-government' and its autonomy is constitutionally guaranteed, local government in Japan is hardly autonomous and self-governing.[24] With respect to powers of the local government, as we have already seen, it has been assumed that the local governments can exercise powers specifically admitted under the Local Government Act. Few have argued that there are certain local matters that must be handled by the local government and not by the central Government, and that there is a corresponding limit on the power of the central Government to intervene in purely local matters.

Indeed, some matters are exclusively reserved to the central Government, such as national defence or foreign affairs. In addition, before the 1999 attempts at decentralisation, there were many matters left to the central Government, which were nonetheless delegated to the heads of the local governments acting as agents for the central Government, although these heads were elected by the local residents and could be dismissed by them. Since the heads were acting as agents of the central Government, it was assumed that the local assembly could not regulate these activities by local ordinance (by-laws). It was often pointed out that the truly local duties of the heads of local government accounted for roughly only thirty per cent of all their duties, the remainder being the duties delegated from the central Government to heads of the local government by statute.[25]

[24] For local government in Japan, see Council of Local Authorities for International Relations, Local Government in Japan (26 March 2010), available at <www.clair.or.jp/j/forum/series/pdf/j05-e.pdf>; Council of Local Authorities for International Relations, Fact Sheet: An Outline of Local Government in Japan, available at <www.gdrc.org/uem/observatory/logov-japan.pdf> (cited as Fact Sheet).

[25] Chihoubunkensuishin iinkai [Local Decentralisation Promotion Committee], Chuukan houkoku [Interim Report], available at <http://warp.ndl.go.jp/info:ndljp/pid/8313852/www8.cao.go.jp/bunken/bunken-iinkai/middle/> (noting that the jobs delegated to the governors by the central Government occupied 80% of all the permit and approval powers of the governors before 1999 reforms).

This scheme was not popular among local governments or local residents. And it was problematic, because when the heads of local government failed to perform central powers properly, the central Government could institute a suit in the courts to permit relevant ministers of state of the central Government to execute these powers by themselves directly.[26] And until 1991 the central Government could even dismiss the heads of local government if they still failed to exercise central powers properly.

The Government decided to abolish this system of delegation in 1999. Now, these central powers are delegated to local governments themselves and not to the heads of the local government. As a result, it is assumed that a local assembly could regulate these matters by local ordinances, even though they are delegated by the central Government. Moreover, the central Government is no longer allowed to dismiss the heads of local governments. These are significant improvements. Nevertheless, the central Government could still supervise the implementation of delegated powers by the local government,[27] and could initiate a suit to permit the central Government to implement matters directly.[28] Moreover, these central powers, delegated to local government under the supervisory power of the central Government, still occupy the significant part of the duties of local government, accounting for roughly 31 per cent to 36 per cent of local government tasks.[29] The abolition of delegation to the heads of the local government was not accompanied by a significant transfer of powers from the central Government to local government without a degree of central control. Managing family registration, issuing passports, conducting national elections and paying welfare benefits are just some examples of such central Government tasks delegated to local government.

Moreover, the Local Government Act, after the 1999 amendment, introduced a formal system of central supervision of local government even with respect to purely local matters, which existed informally before the 1999 amendment. Every minister of the central Government could ask for information from local governments in order to provide advice or recommendations, or to provide information necessary to the proper handling of local powers.[30] Each minister was also authorised to demand the implementation of necessary measures to correct or improve any failure of prefectural

[26] Local Government Act, art 146 (before 1999 amendment). In some cases, the ministers of state could enforce the delegated authority even without judicial orders.

[27] ibid, art 245-7. Each minister can instruct the prefecture to implement necessary measures if the implementation of delegated powers by the prefecture violates the statute or is grossly improper and harming the public interest.

[28] ibid, art 245-8, paras 1 and 8.

[29] Nana Honma, Shichonsonto ken no yakuwari nitsuite [On the Relationship between Cities, Town and Villages and Prefectures] (7 August 2009), available at <www.pref.aichi.jp/cmsfiles/contents/0000026/26959/shiryou_owari2.pdf>.

[30] Local Government Act, art 245-4, para 1.

governments, if their handling of a matter violated statute or was improper and harmful to the public interest.[31] The prefecture government is in this case mandated to implement the measures as demanded.[32] Thus, education, health care, the collection and disposal of garbage, and other local matters are all regulated by national legislation, and the central Government has powerful authority to control local government.

Local governments can also collect tax revenue under the Local Tax Act.[33] Basically, the tax revenue of prefectures depends upon the tax on business operations, a real-estate acquisition tax and an additional tax on the income of residents.[34] The tax on business operations accounts for the most significant proportion of tax revenue, and thus in general urban prefectures, where many business corporations are clustered, are wealthy, but others not so much so. But it is only the Tokyo Metropolitan Government, where most of the head offices of the major corporations are located, that can sustain its budget through local tax revenue.[35] Other prefectures have to rely on the central Government for redistribution of revenue for their survival. Such redistribution is vital for local governments, since in Japan tax revenue for the central Government far outweighs tax revenue for local governments, whereas the amount of tax spending by local governments far outweighs the amount of tax spending by the central Government.[36] This is largely because much of the work of local government has in fact been delegated by the central Government. Local governments are spending huge amounts of money under the supervision of the central Government. Thus who controls the spending is vitally important.[37]

Many local governments also have to ask for central funding on their building projects, such as highways, bridges, airports and other infrastructure. This dependence upon the central Government forces many local governments to petition for funding during the budget preparation process, and allows powerful politicians within the ruling party to play a power broker role in securing a budget for the benefit of their local constituents. This

[31] ibid, art 245-5, para 1.

[32] ibid, art 245-5, para 5. Each minister can instruct the prefectural governor to demand proper measures from the municipal government if the handling of local matters has violated astatute, or was grossly improper and damaging to the public interest; and each minister can even demand that the municipal government directly implement necessary measures when the matter is urgent: ibid, art 245-5, paras 2 and 4. The prefectural governor can also recommend implementation of necessary measures to the municipal government: ibid, art 245-6.

[33] Chihouzeihō [Local Tax Act], Law No 226 of 1950, art 2.

[34] ibid, art 4, para 2.

[35] Ministry of Internal Affairs and Communications, Heisei 25nendo hutsukouhuzei no kettei nitsuite [On Redistribution of General Tax Money], available at <www.soumu.go.jp/main_content/000269529.pdf>.

[36] Fact Sheet, see n 24.

[37] Ministry of Internal Affairs and Communications, Chihou zaisei hakusho Heisei 24nendo [White Paper on Local Finance 2012], available at <www.soumu.go.jp/menu_seisaku/hakusyo/chihou/24data/index.html>.

dependence also forces many local governments to spend their budget on such big projects after central funding has been allocated. Impressive infrastructure has been built with support from the central Government, but, long after construction, maintenance has been left as a burden for local government. Local governments have had to spend huge amount of local tax money simply to maintain infrastructure after construction, exacerbating miscalculations of possible revenue against maintenance costs. For these and other reasons, many local governments have faced serious financial issues.[38]

As a result, many commentators and heads of local government have argued for decentralisation, calling for the transfer of more power to local government from the central Government without central supervision, and more power to levy local taxes to sustain autonomous self-government[39] The 1999 attempt at decentralisation was a good step forward, but there are many changes to be introduced before more effective decentralisation can be accomplished. It goes without saying that bureaucrats in the central Government were very reluctant to concede further measures of decentralisation. The Tohoku earthquake occurred against this background.

THE GREAT EAST JAPAN EARTHQUAKE DISASTER AND LOCAL GOVERNMENT

The Tohoku Earthquake and its Impact on Local Government

The Tohoku earthquake, which hit the eastern part of Japan on 11 March 2011 with a force of 9.0 on the Richter Scale, left significant casualties and damage in the Tohoku region. Yet the actual casualties and damage from the earthquake itself were vastly outweighed by the losses caused by the tsunami triggered by the earthquake. These were utterly devastating. In total, 15,884 persons died, and a further 2,636 persons were still missing as of 1 February 2014,[40] making it one of the deadliest natural disasters ever to strike Japan. Some 126,458 houses were totally destroyed, and 272, 191 houses were destroyed in part.[41] More than 468,000 persons had to be

[38] The total debt of all local governments reached 142 trillion yen [$1.15 trillion] in 2010, 2.63 times larger than the total sum of general revenue resources: ibid. Only eight cities and towns were actually in the red, but apparently many others are facing financial troubles.

[39] ibid.

[40] Keisatsuchou [National Police Agency], Heisei 23 (2011) nen tohokuchiho taiheiyouoki jishin no higaijoukyo to keisatsusochi [Damages of the 2011 Tohoku Earthquake and the Responses of the Police] (10 June 2013), available at <www.npa.go.jp/archive/keibi/biki/higaijokyo.pdf>.

[41] ibid.

evacuated.[42] The three prefectures of Miyagi, Iwate and Fukushima were most affected, but the damage from the tsunami ranged as far as six prefectures, up to 24,000 hectares.[43] In Japan, we call this the Great East Japan Earthquake Disaster.

Many of the communities of the affected area suffered paralysing loss. Many small local communities lost more than 10 per cent of their population, and more than half of their population had to be evacuated. Many local governments lost a substantial number of their public officials, including their leaders. Substantial areas of these municipalities were wiped out by the tsunami. The city of Rikuzentakata in the Iwate Prefecture, for example, lost almost 1,800 people out of the total population of 23,000. The four-story city hall was almost totally submerged by the tsunami, and 113 city officials died, almost one-third of the total number of local officials. The town of Otsuchi of the Iwate Prefecture lost its mayor as well as roughly 20 per cent of town officials, including most of its high-ranking officials, when the town hall was hit by the tsunami. More than 1,700 people died or were missing out of a population of roughly 15,000. More than 9,000 people had to be evacuated.

Government Responses

Japan is prone to many powerful earthquakes. As a result, perhaps no country has prepared for powerful earthquakes better than Japan. The Fundamental Act on Disaster Countermeasures of 1961 mandated that the central Government should establish a National Disaster Prevention Council and enact a national basic disaster prevention plan.[44] Each prefecture is also mandated to establish a prefectural disaster prevention council and adopt a prefectural disaster prevention plan in accordance with the national plan;[45] and, in turn, each municipal government is mandated to establish a municipal disaster prevention council and adopt a municipal disaster prevention plan.[46] Therefore, each municipal government had already adopted a

[42] Kokudokotsusho [Ministry of Land, Infrastructure, Transportation and Tourism], Heisei 22nendo Kokudokotsuhakusho [White Paper on Land, Infrastructure, Transportation and Tourism 2010], available at <www.mlit.go.jp/hakusyo/mlit/h22/hakusho/h23/html/k1112000.html>.

[43] Nourinsuisansho [Ministry of Agriculture, Forestry and Fisheries], *Higashinihondaishinsai: Nougyou no higaijoukyou* [*Great East Japan Earthquake Disaster: Damages to Agriculture*], available at <www.maff.go.jp/j/pr/aff/1105/spe1_03.html>.

[44] Saigaitaisaku kihonhō [Fundamental Act on Disaster Countermeasures], Law 223 of 1961, art 11, paras 1 and 2.

[45] ibid, art 14, paras 1 and 2.

[46] ibid, art 16, para 1.

municipal disaster prevention plan in case of an earthquake by the time of the Tohoku earthquake.[47]

According to the Disaster Assistance Act of 1947, when certain large-scale natural disasters occur, it is the responsibility of prefectural governors to provide assistance to victims.[48] In general, the affected prefectures must bear the costs of providing assistance,[49] but if the amount of the cost exceeds a certain amount, the central Government is obliged to bear part of it.[50]

Under the Fundamental Act on Disaster Countermeasures, when a disaster occurs, it is the responsibility of the affected municipal government[51] and prefectural government to adopt countermeasures against it.[52] When municipal governments are unable to implement such countermeasures, the governor of the affected prefecture can implement them for the affected municipal government.[53] The governor can also request assistance from other prefectural governments[54] and from the Prime Minister.[55]

On the other hand, when the disaster is 'extremely serious', the Prime Minister can establish an Unusual Disaster Response Headquarters inside the Cabinet Office,[56] appointing one of the ministers of state as director. The Headquarters will coordinate agencies, and instruct the heads of the administrative agencies in the central Government and prefectural governors, as well as the heads of municipal governments.[57] When the disaster is 'extraordinarily serious', the Prime Minister can establish an Extraordinary Emergency Disaster Response Headquarters,[58] with the Prime Minister as director, and the Prime Minister can exercise the same powers of coordination and instruction.[59] It must be emphasised, however, that the powers of the Prime Minister as director of the Extraordinary Emergency Disaster

[47] Taiki Saito, *Disaster Management of Local Government in Japan*, available at <www.uncrd.or.jp/hyogo/hesi/pdf/peru/saito.pdf>.

[48] Saigai kyujohō [Disaster Assistance Act], Law No 108 of 1947, arts 22 and 23 (under the current Act, art 2).

[49] ibid, art 33 (under the current Act, art 18). In order to cover the cost, the prefectures must establish a disaster assistance fund: ibid, art 37 (under the current Act, art 22).

[50] ibid, art 36 (under the current Act, art 21). See Gekijinsaigai ni taishosurutameno tokubetsu no zaiseienjotō nikansuru hōritsu [Act on Special Financial Assistance in order to Respond to Extraordinary Serious Disaster], Law No 150, 1962 (cited as Extraordinary Serious Disaster Act).

[51] Fundamental Act on Disaster Countermeasures, art 62. The head of the affected municipal government could of course request for assistance from other municipal government as well as from the prefecture. Ibid arts 67 and 68.

[52] ibid, art 70. The governor of the prefecture could instruct or request the heads of the municipal government to implement countermeasures, when necessary: ibid, art 72.

[53] ibid, art 73.

[54] ibid, art 74.

[55] ibid, art 74-2.

[56] ibid, arts 24 and 25, para 1.

[57] ibid, art 28, para 2 and art 28-3, para 1.

[58] ibid, art 28-2.

[59] ibid, art 28-6, paras 1 and 2.

Response Headquarters are limited to coordination and instruction. Basically, the Prime Minister can instruct the heads of government agencies, governors or heads of the municipal government, but such instructions are not binding upon the public. The Prime Minister does not have legal power to order the public or to regulate the conducts of the public. In other words, the Prime Minister cannot declare emergency and adopt whatever measures are necessary to cope with the disaster.

In the case of the Tohoku earthquake, of course, the loss and damage far exceeded the capacity of municipal governments, as well as that of the prefectural governments, and the central Government had to step in. Prime Minister Naoto Kan established an Extraordinary Emergency Disaster Response Headquarters immediately after the earthquake. This was the first time this procedure had been used. The Prime Minister ordered the deployment of the Self Defence Force (SDF), and roughly 100,000 SDF personnel, almost half of all active personnel, were mobilised to provide rescue services and assist recovery, together with local police officers, firefighters and rescue crews. The SDF played an important role in rescuing survivors, transporting food and water to evacuees, and removing debris. Rescue and recovery were thus undertaken following intensive central government intervention.

The Implications of Tsunami Relief Work for the Division of Powers Between Central and Local Government

No one doubts that in times of massive natural disaster, the central Government must play a leading role. And the Japanese Government understood that the cost of rescue and recovery, as well as restoration of infrastructure, was far beyond the financial capacity of local and prefectural governments. The cabinet thus designated the disaster resulting from the Tohoku earthquake as an 'extraordinarily serious disaster'[60] under the Extraordinarily Serious Disaster Act of 1962,[61] and decided to cover almost all the costs incurred. As a result, all of the costs of repairs to basic infrastructure and for the disposal of disaster waste were paid by the central Government, to the great relief of local governments.

During a time of crisis, however, the division of powers between the central Government and local government might cause concern as regards the process for undertaking immediate and effective rescue, recovery and assistance activities. For instance, SDF personnel are national public servants supervised by the Ministry of Defence, while police officers are public servants

[60] Higashinihondaishinsai no gekijinsaigai oyobi korenitaishi tekiyousubeki sochi no shitei nikansuru seirei [Cabinet Order on Designation of Great East Japan Earthquake Disaster as Extraordinary Serious Disaster and on Measures to be Applied], Cabinet Order No 60, 2011.

[61] Extraordinary Serious Disaster Act, Law No 150, 1962.

of the prefecture under the central command of the National Police Agency, and firefighters and rescue personnel are all public servants of municipal governments under the supervision of the Ministry of Internal Affairs and Communications. They are all prepared to cooperate in times of emergency and, thankfully, little conflict or disruption seems to have occurred in the aftermath of the Tohoku earthquake.[62] But during the chaotic aftermath of any disaster, there might be issues regarding a lack of coordination among these three levels of government. A well-coordinated rescue and recovery plan for all those levels of government would be essential.

Moreover, a division of powers between the central Government and local government might be difficult to maintain in times of emergency. As a result, some of the powers granted to local government may need to be transferred to the central Government at particular times. For instance, the collection and disposal of ordinary waste is the traditional responsibility of municipal government. But the debris left behind following the earthquake was extraordinary, and many of the municipal governments suffered serious damage to their disposal facilities. The central Government thus initially had to allow the prefectural government to take over the tasks of the municipal governments, and ultimately the central Government itself had to take over those tasks.[63]

Horizontal government relationships were also implicated. Disposal of disaster waste had to rely in part upon other municipal governments that were unaffected by the disaster. However, most of the unaffected municipal governments were unwilling to accept the disposal of tsunami waste from affected municipalities, partly because of their limited capacity to dispose of additional waste and partly because of local residents' fears regarding increased pollution. The Prime Minister had to ask for the voluntary cooperation of other local governments for waste disposal.[64]

It is understandable that it should be municipal (local) governments that are responsible for adopting countermeasures, since municipal governments understand local conditions best. But in times of significant disaster, there

[62] Shoubouchou [Fire and Disaster Management Agency], Higashinihondaishinsai wo humaeta daikibosaigaiji ni okeru shouboudankatsudou no arikata ni kansuru kentoukai houkokusho [Study on the Activities of Firefighters in Times of Massive Disasters in Light of the Great East Japan Earthquake Disaster: Report] (August 2012), available at <www.fdma.go.jp/neuter/topics/houdou/h24/2408/240830_1houdou/01_houkokusyo.pdf>, 14. However, there are some confusions, causing officers of the two organisations to search for survivors in the same area.

[63] Higashinihondaishinsaini yori shoujita saigaihaikibutsu no shori nikansuru tokubetsusochihō [Special Measure Act Concerning Disposal of Disaster Waste Produced by the Great East Japan Earthquake Disaster], Law No 99 of 2011.

[64] Asahi Shimbun (11 February 2012), 'Garekishori, Zenkokujichitaini kyouryokuyousei, Noda shushou' ['Prime minister Noda asks Other Local Government to Help Dispose of Disaster Waste'], available at <www.asahi.com/special/10005/TKY201202100691.html>.

might be good reasons for the central Government to play a leading role and streamline operations. Currently the central Government is able simply to give instructions to local governments. In times of emergency, some kind of extraordinary measures could be adopted by the central Government. However, currently there is no emergency statute authorising the Prime Minister to declare an emergency in affected prefectures and adopt whatever measures are necessary. Consequently, even after the devastation of the Tohoku earthquake, no emergency (in those terms) could be declared, and the Prime Minister could not issue orders to adopt all necessary countermeasures against the disaster. Such a statute might be desirable for the future.

Moreover, the Tohoku earthquake revealed the tremendous burdens local governments may need to shoulder in the aftermath of massive disasters. With so many residents scattered in shelters under the care of other local governments after evacuation, affected local governments experienced tremendous difficulties in providing services to their local residents. Because of the disruption of communication systems and loss of data, for instance, local governments had difficulties finding out who had survived the disaster, or where their residents were staying, and providing services to residents, such as issuing death certificates or certificates of proof of damage, let alone providing food, water and other essentials. Local governments should have adopted plans anticipating all these burdens in the aftermath of the disaster, and should have prepared for such a possibility.

Furthermore, because many affected municipalities lost so many public workers, they were short-staffed during the recovery and reconstruction stages, and they could not perform the necessary functions in a timely enough fashion to satisfy the needs of local residents. They had to rely upon other municipal governments, as well as prefectures, to send public workers to assist with disaster-related tasks.[65] The Japanese Government never anticipated such a loss of manpower in a time of disaster; it never anticipated that the heads of municipal governments, as well as most high-ranking officials, would be unavailable at such a time. Some kind of mechanism should be introduced to counteract such possibilities. In retrospect, local government should have been prepared to seek help from citizen volunteers as well as non-governmental organisations (NGOs) in times of crisis.

[65] Some 56,923 public workers were sent from other local governments to assist affected local governments between 11 March and 1 July 2011: Ministry of Internal Affairs and Communications, *Higashinihondaishinsai niyoru hisaichieno chihoukoumuin no hakenjoukyou* [*Sending Local Public Workers to Affected Local Government after the Great East Japan Earthquake Disaster*] (1 July 2011), available at <www.soumu.go.jp/main_content/000125227.pdf>. Since other local governments do not have extra public workers to spare, this process placed a significant strain on them.

The central Government should have also established a system for assisting affected local governments, not only financially but also by transferring some tasks from local governments to the central Government and providing assistance with personnel.

Reconstruction and Division of Powers Between the Central Government and Local Government

The reconstruction of the Tohoku region has been a daunting task for local governments. They needed to provide temporary housing to evacuees and services to residents; construct permanent public housing for evacuees; rebuild schools, hospitals, roads, bridges and other infrastructure; facilitate group relocation, and promote rezoning and redevelopment in areas wiped out by the tsunami; and come up with plans to promote economic and industrial development.

In order to facilitate the reconstruction of the Tohoku region, the Diet passed the Fundamental Act on Reconstruction followng the Great East Japan Earthquake Disaster of 2011.[66] To implement reconstruction measures, the central Government established the Reconstruction Agency,[67] located in Tokyo. Although local branches of the Agency were set up in the three most affected prefectures of the Tohoku region, there was serious concern whether an agency of the central Government based in Tokyo would be the best body to lead reconstruction in Tohoku.

Moreover, the strong departmentalism of the central Government came to dominate the reconstruction process. In addition to funding restoration of infrastructure, the central Government decided to spend huge amounts of money to facilitate further reconstruction of infrastructure. One of the methods adopted was a reconstruction grant, which was designed to provide funding for reconstruction projects. Affected municipal governments, as well as prefectures, wanted to spend money flexibly and quickly. Thus they wanted the central Government to provide lump-sum funds to local governments without any strings attached. The central Government declined to do so, requiring any funded reconstruction projects to be approved by the relevant agencies of the central Government.

Of course, the departmentalism of the Japanese Government is quite notorious. Each of the government departments has its own agenda and vested interests, and competes with the others for budget increases. In this

[66] Higashinihondaishinsai hukkou kihonhō [Fundamental Act on Reconstruction following the Great East Japan Earthquake Disaster], Law No 76 of 2011.

[67] Hukkocho secchihō [Reconstruction Agency Establishment Act], Law No 125 of 2011.

long-term environment, it was no wonder that none of the departments wanted to lose its grip on the budget for reconstruction.

There has also been serious concern about the ability of local governments to plan and implement appropriate reconstruction projects. For instance, when the mayor of Ishinomaki City in Miyagi Prefecture asked for reconstruction funding for renewal of the city's comics museum, many people were appalled.[68] The comics museum was certainly a symbol of the city, and a plan to renew it, in order to continue attracting tourists, might not be altogether bizarre, but the museum was already being restored with separate assistance from the central Government. The Ishinomaki mayor wanted to upgrade the museum using reconstruction funding to attract further visitors. Was this funding appropriate, when most of the residents were still suffering from the loss of their homes and many were still living in temporary housing? And the infrastructure surrounding the museum had not yet been restored. What was the point of upgrading the museum when the surrounding roads and transportation systems had not been restored? If local governments were allowed to spend reconstruction funding without any strings attached, many central Government officials claimed, they might simply waste the money. In their view, therefore, the central Government had to supervise local governments.

But of course, these concerns were also an excuse for central Government officials in their unwillingness to surrender power to local governments. Many felt that bureaucrats in the central Government also spent huge amounts of money on projects that had only a tenuous connection to reconstruction, and which were a waste of money.[69] The concern with the ability and capacity of the local government to design and implement reconstruction projects remains legitimate, however, especially because many local governments lost substantial number of officials in the tsunami.

When the immediate crisis was over, and when it came to reconstruction, there was a stronger need to allow voluntary and autonomous action by local residents. Such autonomous decision-making would be all the more important because, as we have seen, local residents could actively participate in deciding how to reconstruct their communities. In order to allow local governments to play a stronger role, however, it is imperative that they are supported by being allowed to hire additional public workers and seek

[68] Diamond Online (5 March 2012), Higashinihondaishinsai kara ichinen: Darega hukkouwo korosunoka [One Year After the Great East Japan Earthquake Disaster: Who Kills the Reconstruction?], available at <http://diamond.jp/articles/-/16409>.

[69] For instance, the Ministry of Internal Affairs and Communications spent almost 800 million yen [$8 million] on television programmes about the disaster prepared by one of the subsidiaries of the NHK, a public broadcaster, and the Ministry of Foreign Affairs spent almost 7,200 million yen [$72 million] to invite youngsters from abroad to learn about schools in affected areas: ibid. These are just some examples of spending by the central Government of the reconstruction budget for projects that had only a tenuous relationship to reconstruction.

help from citizen volunteers and NGOs, in addition to receiving help from other local governments.

Delay and Frustration

These issues are all closely related to the division of powers between the central Government and local governments in times of crisis. No one doubts that the central Government should provide far more leadership in response to a natural disaster. But the question still remains as to the proper roles of central and local governments.

More than four years have passed since the earthquake, but the goal of reconstruction of Tohoku is still far from complete. Many residents are still living in temporary housing and waiting for the construction of public housing for disaster victims (reconstruction housing). Group relocation programs, which are designed to allow an entire community to move to a different location, are very slow. The redevelopment of the affected areas is also taking time. Many affected residents are extremely frustrated with these delays. Part of the reason for the delay is the tremendous burden on local governments, including the daunting tasks of group relocation, rezoning and redevelopment, and a shortage of public workers. The Japanese Government has failed to relieve the local governments from these burdens in order to facilitate reconstruction, to relieve their various tasks and to provide extra necessary personnel.

And of course local governments and residents are also frustrated by the procedural requirements established by the central Government in order to seek central approval. In Japan, a decision of the central Government is needed to do almost anything. Preparing for approval, submission of necessary documents, and necessity to persuade officials in the central Government are indeed very intimidating and frustrating.

Local government and residents are also frustrated because they have not been able to decide for themselves how to reconstruct their communities. Even though residents have an opportunity to participate in the decision-making process in local government, the ultimate decision always rests with the central Government, and neither local government nor residents have any significant say in the end result.

Of course, fundamental policies for reconstruction need to be established at the national level. It is surely necessary for the central Government to ensure that local communities will be rebuilt to secure, as much as possible, against future disasters, and to assure that the economy of affected communities would be improved. However, it is imperative for local residents to have an opportunity to decide these issues autonomously for themselves, or at least to participate in decision-making, within a framework established by the central Government. The Japanese Government should have left ultimate decisions on reconstruction to local governments.

THE NUCLEAR MELTDOWN IN FUKUSHIMA AND LOCAL GOVERNMENT

The Nuclear Meltdown in Fukushima

The Tohoku earthquake and tsunami brought another significant disaster to Japan: the nuclear meltdown in Fukushima. The powerful tsunami surged into the Fukushima No 1 Nuclear Power-plant, operated by the Tokyo Electric Power Company (TEPCO), swamping the tsunami barrier. As a result, even though all the reactors were automatically shut down due to the earthquake, and backup generators automatically started to supply power, all of these generators, as well as the fuel tanks, were submerged and knocked out. The nuclear power plant thus lost its ability to circulate the cooling water to cool the nuclear rods in the reactor as well as in the cooling-fuel pool. Without circulating cooling water, nuclear rods were gradually overheated. Heat will evaporate the covering water, and the nuclear fuel rods, exposed out of water, began to melt down. The meltdown produced hydrogen and the subsequent hydrogen blast destroyed the facilities, and radioactive materials were spread into the air.[70]

The nuclear power-plant accident in Fukushima raised very interesting issues regarding the relationship between the central Government and local government. First, the accident revealed that there was a critical lack of legal power in the central Government to respond to such a serious nuclear accident. Secondly, the accident revealed the necessity for far better coordination between central and local government in preparation for such emergencies. Thirdly, the accident necessitated the central Government's seeking consent from local government before building an interim storage site for nuclear waste and restarting the nuclear power plants, casting doubt on the appropriateness of requiring consent from local government before the central Government was able to carry out national tasks.

Critical Lack of Power in the Central Government

The Fukushima accident revealed that there is a critical lack of power in the central Government, and that the division of powers between central and local government could prevent attempts by the central Government to respond to a nuclear disaster and emergency.

[70] IAEA, Report of Japanese Government to IAEA Ministerial Conference on Nuclear Safety—Accident at TEPCO's Fukushima Nuclear Power Stations (7 June 2011), available at <www.iaea.org/newscenter/focus/fukushima/japan-report/>.

Informed of the serious situation in Fukushima, Prime Minister Naoto Kan declared a 'nuclear emergency'[71] in accordance with the Nuclear Disaster Special Measures Act of 1999, and established the Headquarters for Responding to Nuclear Disaster.[72] The Prime Minister could then instruct governors and heads of municipal governments in the specified areas on matters relating to evacuation or implementation of other nuclear emergency measures.[73]

It is a primary responsibility of the operator of the nuclear reactor, in this case the TEPCO, to respond to a nuclear emergency.[74] Nevertheless, the Prime Minster actively intervened in the decisions to respond, attempting to micromanage the response. But the scope of the power of the Prime Minister to respond to the nuclear disaster is unclear and there was a question whether all the conduct of the Prime Minister could be legally justified. At the time of the accident, under the Nuclear Regulatory Act of 1957, the Economy, Trade and Industry Minister did have legal authority to order the power company to take necessary measures,[75] but the Prime Minister only has the general power to supervise the head of the department, in this case the Economy, Trade and Industry Minister. With respect to serious nuclear accidents such as one that occurred in Fukushima, the Prime Minister should have been granted the power to issue an order directly to the power company, rather than simply to issue instructions to the agency head, in this case the Economy, Trade and Industry Minister, or the governor, in this case, the Fukushima governor. In other words, central power should be delineated more clearly, and should more clearly rest with the Prime Minister.

Moreover, in order to supply water to cool down the overheated nuclear rods, the TEPCO workers did all they could. The Prime Minister ordered the SDF to spray water from above, using helicopters, but this was ineffective. The Prime Minister then decided to request the cooperation of municipal government firefighters, to use their fire engines to supply water directly to the nuclear facilities. This was accomplished through a request by the Fire and Disaster Management Agency to the heads of the municipal governments, as well as to governors of the neighbouring prefectures, such as the governor of the Tokyo Metropolitan Government, to send firefighters to Fukushima and engage in the supply of water. This request was inevitable, since it is the responsibility of the municipal government to maintain fire

[71] Genshiryoku saigai taisaku tokubetsu sochihō [Nuclear Disaster Special Measures Act], Law No 156 of 1999, art 15, para 2.

[72] ibid, art 16, para 1.

[73] ibid, art 15, para 3.

[74] ibid, art 3.

[75] Kakugenryoubusshitsu, kakunenryoubusshitsu oyobi genshiro no kisei nikansuru hōritsu [Nuclear Regulatory Act], Law No 166 of 1957, art 43-3-23 (after the 2012 amendment, the power to order appropriate measures to the power company was granted to the newly created Nuclear Regulatory Authority).

departments and rescue departments, and neither the Prime Minister nor the head of the Fire and Disaster Management Agency has the power to directly order local firefighters to come to the rescue. The Constitution does not contain any provision on emergencies, and there is no emergency legislation in Japan authorising the granting of exceptional powers to the Prime Minister or the central Government to take emergency measures (beyond legislation adopted for specific disasters, as in this case). As a result, the central Government could only ask for help from the local government.

In times of emergency, it might be difficult to maintain the division of powers between the central Government and local governments, and it might be better to enact emergency legislation, to allow the Prime Minister to order all public officials, including local government officials, to carry out necessary measures to contain the disaster. Moreover, the central Government might be better off vesting legal power to respond to such a nuclear emergency in itself, rather than simply being able to order TEPCO (or other entities) to adopt necessary countermeasures. Serious nuclear accidents may be better handled as a matter of national concern, to be taken care of primarily by and through central government power, not as a matter to be dealt with by power companies.

Evacuation and the Necessity for Coordination

Informed of the nuclear accident at the Fukushima plant, the Prime Minister ordered the evacuation of all local residents living close to the powerplant.[76] The evacuation order was actually an instruction from the Prime Minister as the director of the Headquarters for Responding to Nuclear Disaster, directed to the Governor of Fukushima Prefecture, to evacuate the residents. Neither the central Government nor the prefectural governor has any legal power to order mandatory evacuation. The Governor of Fukushima Prefecture instructed the heads of the municipal governments to evacuate their local residents. Since the instruction did not have legal power and was not binding upon the public, a considerable number of local residents remained in areas from which they had been instructed to evacuate. There was little the Prime Minister or Fukushima Governor could do if these local residents refused to obey the evacuation instruction. This is another clear example of the critical lack of power in the central Government to respond to a nuclear disaster.

Under the current Fundamental Act on Disaster Countermeasures, it is the head of a municipal government who has power to declare certain

[76] Chief Cabinet Secretary's Press Release (11 March 2011), available at <www.kantei.go.jp/jp/tyoukanpress/201103/11_p4.html>.

areas as 'hazardous areas' in order to prohibit entry and force evacuation.[77] Violators of such an order can be punished. No one else has power to force evacuation or prohibit entry into a dangerous area other than the head of the municipal government. Apparently, however, heads of municipal governments near the Fukushima power-plant did not declare the areas close to the power-plant as hazardous areas, and it was the Prime Minister, as director of the Nuclear Disaster Headquarters, who instructed the Governor of Fukushima Prefecture to ask for evacuation. Areas around the Fukushima plant were declared hazardous areas only later, when the Prime Minister finally agreed on this declaration.[78] It is indeed strange that the Prime Minister does not have legal power to order evacuation to protect the lives of citizens even in times of emergency, and that the head of the municipal government who has a legal power exercises this power based only upon an 'instruction' from the Prime Minister.

Moreover, the Prime Minister's evacuation instruction was issued without sufficient consultation with the Governor of Fukushima and heads of the relevant municipal governments. In addition, the areas from which evacuation was ordered were quickly expanded, but such expansion was undertaken without consultation with affected local governments. The Fukushima Governor had to decide where to take all these evacuees and how to transport them. The local residents were thus simply told to evacuate, without knowing where they would be going or for how long, causing significant confusion and chaos.

In times of emergency, apparently, more broad-based powers need to be granted to the Prime Minister or the central Government. However, the Prime Minister or the central Government could not enforce emergency measures without sufficient local coordination. There might be no time for consultation before issuing an evacuation instruction. But in order to implement the evacuation order effectively, some kinds of preparation and consultation with affected local governments might be necessary. At the very least, preparations for evacuation should have been made in advance.

On the other hand, there was concern whether the evacuation instruction was issued to everyone at risk. Indeed, it turned out that some of the communities north of the power-plant showed high radiation exposure due to the direction of the wind, but the local residents were not immediately told of those risks. Although they were eventually instructed to evacuate by the Prime Minister, local governments should play a more active role in protecting the safety of their local residents. Simply relying on the central

[77] Fundamental Act on Disaster Countermeasures, art 63, para 1.

[78] Chief Cabinet Secretary's Press Release (21 April 2011), available at <www.kantei.go.jp/jp/tyoukanpress/201104/21_a.html>.

Government is clearly not sufficient.[79] Preparation for evacuation requires granting local government a certain autonomous initiative to act.

Is it Appropriate to Require Consent from Local Government?

The aftermath of the nuclear power-plant meltdown accident in Fukushima required the central Government to seek cooperation from the local governments, raising a question as to the appropriateness of demanding such consent from local governments.

First, the accident produced a huge quantity of agricultural products contaminated with radioactive materials, which were prohibited from being marketed. Moreover, the accident necessitated a wide-ranging decontamination of the environment in the vicinity of the power-plant. All the contaminated products, soils, leaves and other matter had to be collected and disposed of as nuclear waste. The central Government was forced to find interim storage sites for this contaminated waste. Unfortunately for the central Government, but understandably, no one wanted such sites to be built nearby. As a result, the Prime Minister had no choice but to request the cooperation of the Governor of Fukushima Prefecture and the heads of several municipal governments close to the Fukushima power-plant, to allow the construction of the interim storage sites. The difficulty of getting the latter consent has prevented environmental contamination operations. Moreover, even if the consent for building interim storage sites were to be obtained, there is practically no hope of getting consent for building final disposal sites. This consent is all the more important for the central Government before the decommissioning of the nuclear reactors gets underway. The practical necessity of getting consent from local government would be a major obstacle to a future decontamination operation, as well as to the destruction and disposal of nuclear rods and reactors from the Fukushima power-plant.

Secondly, all the nuclear reactors were automatically shut down due to the earthquake. In order to restart them, the consent of the affected local government is required due to safety agreements with the local government.

[79] The Ministry of Education, Culture, Sports, Science and Technology (MEXT) has developed a system to predict the spread of radiation called System for Prediction of Environment Emergency Dose Information (SPEEDI) and the simulation data showed the likelihood of radiation exposure in some communities outside of the areas where evacuation was instructed, but the central government did not disclose this data when it issued an evacuation instruction. Yomiuri Shimbun (12 June, 2012), SPEEDI kouhyouokurewa tekitou: Monkashouhoukokusho [MEXT Report Concluded that the Delay in Disclosing the SPEEDI Data Was Appropriate], available at <www.yomiuri.co.jp/politics/news/20120612-OYT1T00212.htm>. Perhaps, the local community should have set up its own radiation measurement system to protect its residents.

These safety agreements were not mandated by statute or regulations, they were informal agreements between the power company and the municipal government in order to dispel concerns about the safety of the nuclear plant. Given the renewed concern as to the safety of nuclear power, all the heads of the municipal governments became reluctant to give consent. As a result, it became extremely difficult for the central Government to restart the reactors after the Tohoku earthquake. Since the plant's nuclear power provided a significant percentage of Japan's power generation, the country suddenly faced the prospect of not generating enough power to sustain industrial as well as household demand.

Since it is primarily local residents who have the most acute interest in the safety of the nuclear power-plant, it is understandable that they must have the right to voice their opinions. But it is at least controversial whether local residents should be granted the right to refuse consent, thus preventing the enforcement of national policy, including the disposal of nuclear waste and the restarting of the nuclear power-plant.

LESSONS LEARNED

The Japanese people learned significant lessons from these very difficult experiences. The central Government decided to amend the Fundamental Act on Disaster Countermeasures to improve preparations for future earthquakes.[80] It decided to revise the national disaster prevention plan after the Great East Japan Earthquake Disaster to reflect these lessons, and mandated that each prefecture and municipal government should revise its disaster prevention plans in accordance with the revised national plan.[81]

Believing that the nuclear power-plant accident in Fukushima was caused by the absence of an independent regulatory agency and the consistent failure of the power company and the central Government to require more demanding safety standards, the Japanese Government also revised the Nuclear Regulatory Act to establish the Nuclear Regulatory Authority in the Ministry of Environment, to regulate the safety of nuclear power-plants and impose more demanding safety standards.[82] The central Government also required the establishment of more realistic evacuation plans for local governments close to nuclear power-plants.

[80] Saigaitaisaku kihonhō no ichibuwo kaiseisuru hōritsu [Act to Amend the Part of the Fundamental Act on Disaster Countermeasures], Law No 41 of 2012; Saigaitaisaku kihonhōtō no ichibuwo kaiseisuru hōritsu [Act to Amend the Part of the Fundamental Act on Disaster Countermeasures and Others], Law No 54 of 2013.

[81] World Bank, *Disaster Management Plans*, available at <http://wbi.worldbank.org/wbi/Data/wbi/wbicms/files/drupal-acquia/wbi/drm_kn2-2.pdf>.

[82] Genshiryoku kiseiiinkai secchihō [Act to Establish the Nuclear Regulatory Authority], Law No 47 of 2012.

However, no significant changes were initiated to alter the relationship between the central Government and local governments. There is still no statute authorising the Prime Minister or the central Government to take over the tasks of local government in times of emergency. Reconstruction is not left to the autonomous decision of local governments. Support for affected local governments remains insufficient. Even in times of nuclear emergency, the Prime Minister and the central Government do not have legal power to take appropriate measures to contain the crisis. Even though coordination between the central Government and local governments for the preparation of evacuation was advanced after the disaster, it remains unclear whether coordination will really work the next time such a disaster occurs. The central Government continues to experience major challenges in constructing the interim storage sites for nuclear waste, and in securing consent from the relevant local governments to restart the nuclear power-plant.

So far, no consensus has yet been reached on the proper relationship between the central Government and the local government, and there is no serious attempt to reconsider the proper relationship between the central Government and the local government on these disaster issues.

CONCLUSION

The Tohoku earthquake and the subsequent tsunami raised significant constitutional issues as regards the division of powers between the central Government and local governments. These issues added a new dimension to the long-standing debate over decentralisation. The earthquake and tsunami showed the clear necessity for allowing a more active role to the central Government in times of emergency, but at the same time it also indicated the necessity for granting some autonomy to local governments after such crises, along with the need to provide assistance to affected local governments. The nuclear meltdown in Fukushima further revealed the critical lack of power in the central Government in times of nuclear emergency, and the necessity for coordination between the central Government and local governments in preparation for a nuclear emergency, but at the same time also revealed doubts as to the appropriateness of requiring the consent of the local government for the central Government to carry out national tasks. The Japanese people must consider these issues in preparing for the next massive earthquake. And similar issues might be implicated in other countries as well in times of national emergency. In this sense, the Japanese experience provides valuable lessons for other countries.

FURTHER READING

J Kingston, ed, *Natural Disaster and Nuclear Crisis in Japan* (New York, Routledge 2012).

R Samuels, *3.11: Disaster and Change in Japan* (Ithaca, NY, Cornell University Press, 2013).

S Matsui, *The Constitution of Japan: A Contextual Analysis* (Oxford, Hart Publishing, 2010).

M Muramatsu (translated by B Scheiner & J White), *Local Power in the Japanese State* (Berkeley, CA, University of California Press, 1997).

8

Local Democracy in a Multi-layered Constitutional System: Malaysian Local Government Reconsidered

ANDREW HARDING

INTRODUCTION

THIS CHAPTER EXPLORES the possibility of elected local self-government in a complex constitutional system with the following features: Malaysia has a federal structure, a Westminster-type democratic Constitution embracing constitutional monarchy, with an ethnically divided society under an authoritarian state evolving, seemingly, into a two-party system following closely fought general elections in 2008 and 2013. The key question, one that implicates a number of Malaysian constitutional issues as well as the politics of local power, is whether or how local self-government might function in circumstances where political polarisation offers two diametrically opposed notions of local government.

The first notion, held by the ruling *Barisan Nasional* coalition, which has been in power since independence of the Federation of Malaya in 1957 and through the formation of Malaysia in 1963, is that the political polarisation that reigns in Malaysia requires a structure in which inter-ethnic coalition constructed along the lines of consociationalism imposes authoritarian government. Here, in the view of the *Barisan Nasional* coalition, local self-government would merely undermine the imposed solution by offering further possibilities for fragmentation going beyond even those offered by federalism. Local government elections would pour more fuel on the fires of political polarisation. Malaysia does not need politically, and cannot sustain financially, three levels of elections, and citizens can look to State governments to ensure provision of local services via the appointment of competent local councillors. This has been the theory and the practical situation over most of Malaysia's last half century, during which the *Barisan Nasional* has been the dominant political force. Federalism has resulted in a high degree of centralisation due to the *Barisan Nasional*'s occupying government for most of the time at the state level, or all of the time in some States.

The second notion is that local self-government represents a significant opportunity for the exercise of autonomy that can help to lower the tensions of contestation over big prizes at the national level, empowering communities irrespective of ethnic composition, and also empowering fragile communities such as small indigenous groups living in the same area, for example in Sabah and Sarawak, which have never had elected local government authorities. This view holds democratic participation to be more important than saving costs, and that the reinstatement of local government elections is a priority as an aspect of political reform. This is the position espoused by the opposition *Pakatan Rakayat* coalition, which has held power in two States, Penang and Selangor, since 2008, and in another (Kelantan) since 1990; *Pakatan Rakayat* has also held power recently in Perak (2008–09) and Kedah (2008–13).

If one looks at the government of the State of Penang, a small City-State where local government started more than 200 years ago, and which has been under *Pakatan Rakayat* rule since 2008, evidence may be seen of local autonomy galvanising impressive development and local pride. It is not surprising that Penang has been one State attempting to return to local government elections as part of a reform package.[1]

Yet the issue of local government elections, which is the focus of this chapter, is complicated by a number of factors. The most important of these is that, typically, federalism itself offers an opportunity for local autonomy of precisely the kind envisaged under the second notion of local government outlined above, as it has done in Penang, for example. Indeed in Malaysia since 2008, opposition control over State governments has become a highly significant political development; moreover, local government is a State function, and therefore in principle State governments can, if they choose, devolve autonomy even further down to local authorities, within the limits of State powers under the Constitution. We shall see, however, that in practice this has not yet occurred. In addition there are real questions about whether in a country the size of Malaysia, three levels of government are really sustainable in the administrative and fiscal senses. Elections are an expensive item, and there would have to be acceptance that political differences should not lead to administrative chaos when clearly all three levels of government have to work together. Another issue would be whether introducing local government elections would be viable in the vast territories of Sabah and Sarawak, the two Borneo States, where the ills of urbanisation are less of an issue than the fragility of rural communities, and where there have not been local government elections in the past, unlike in Peninsular or West Malaysia.

[1] T Yeoh, *States of Reform: Governing Selangor and Penang* (Penang, Penang Institute, 2012).

The importance of this issue in the context of central-local relations in Asia is that, while authoritarian government has been the norm in post-war Asia, the progress towards constitutional government that we see across most of the region raises new issues for central-local relations. This is apparent in the other chapters of this book. Can local communities take responsibility for their own local issues without arousing the Leviathan of authoritarian government? Would a reinvigoration of local government via local government elections represent a significant shift in implementing democracy? This issue is especially acute in Malaysia at the present juncture, in which a new state, articulated at several levels by democratic aspirations, struggles to emerge from the shadow of an old state bent on maintaining the authoritarianism which it considers has served the country well for more than half a century.[2] This divide is apparent in very many areas other than local self-government; and yet local self-government offers experimentation with real practical solutions going beyond rhetorical warfare. Perhaps acute polarisation is indeed best overcome by getting opposing parties to work on practical issues where their objectives are not very much different. This might be particularly true of local government—after all, it is hard to find even determined political opponents disagreeing about the desirability of sensitive spatial planning, good drainage, conscientious enforcement of building codes or effective garbage disposal.

HISTORICAL AND CONSTITUTIONAL BACKGROUND

Before the colonial period local chiefs exercised great power, on which the power of the Ruler (the *Rajah*, nowadays styled 'Sultan') relied. Jurisdiction was defined by allegiance rather than by function or territoriality. Malaysian local government along its present lines can be traced back to the British occupation of Penang, which later formed, with Malacca and Singapore, the Straits Settlements (1826–1946; and a Crown colony from 1867). In 1801, a Committee of Assessors was established in Penang to supervise urban development. Local government elections can be traced back as far as 1857, when the Georgetown Municipal Commission in Penang was elected; these elections were abolished in 1913.[3] Local authorities were established gradually in the Straits Settlements, and later in the Malay States, but only as and when it appeared necessary in a particular urban setting, rural areas remaining entirely under State jurisdiction in the Malay States. As independence

[2] A Harding, *The Malaysian Constitution: A Contextual Analysis* (Oxford, Hart Publishing, 2012).

[3] The history of local government elections in Penang is neatly set out in the submissions of counsel for the Penang government (and accepted in full by the Federal Court) in *Government of the State of Penang & Anor v Government of Malaysia & Anor* [2014] 7 *Current Law Journal* 861, 868 ff.

loomed after 1945, experimentation with democracy was undertaken at the level of urban local government, as was done in many other locations of decolonisation across the British Empire. By the time the Federation of Malaya became independent in 1957, there were no fewer than 289 local authorities in Malaya, major city councils being elected on a general franchise. These elections were held first in Georgetown, Penang (1951) then in Kuala Lumpur (1952), followed by other cities. In 1960, with the passing of the Local Government Elections Act, responsibility for local government elections passed from State governments to the Election Commission.

Two major changes have been made to local government since independence in 1957.[4] First, in 1965, in the midst of Indonesia's '*konfrontasi*', or confrontation against the creation of Malaysia in 1963, Malaysian local government elections were suspended as an emergency measure under the Emergency (Suspension of Local Government Elections) Regulations 1965, and have not been reinstated since then.[5] At the same time, a Royal Commission of Inquiry on Local Authorities was established (the *Nahappen Report* after its chairman), which in 1968 recommended continuing local elections and reducing the number of local authorities. Unfortunately the proposed reforms were overtaken by the episode of 13 May 1969; serious inter-ethnic rioting following general election results prompted a reorientation of state priorities in favour of intensified authoritarianism.[6] A development-orientated state emerged, in which power was increasingly centralised in Kuala Lumpur: there was no room here for autonomy at any level, let alone through local self-government. In 1971 the Development Administration Unit (DAU) of the Prime Minister's Department rejected the *Nahappan Report*'s recommendation for reinstating local elections, arguing that elected local government, which facilitated the domination of the haves over the have-nots, provided for 'over-democratised over-government at the local level', and was no longer consonant with the objectives of the redefined state under which resources were to be devoted to development, democracy taking a subordinate position.[7]

The passing of the main statute, the Local Government Act 1976, was the second major reform, designed to implement the other main recommendation of the *Nahappan Report*. The 1976 Act (preceded by the Local Government (Temporary Provisions) Act 1973) regularised local authorities in Peninsular Malaya, which had grown in number from 289 in 1957

[4] For the reforms of the 1970s, see MW Norris, *Local Government in Peninsular Malaysia* (Farnborough, Gower, 1980).

[5] The Local Government (Temporary Provisions) Act 1973 abolished all elected local authorities and gave the power to appoint local authorities to the State governments; see now Local Government Act 1976, s 15; and see P Tennant, 'The Decline of Elective Local Government in Malaysia' (1973) 13 *Asian Survey* 347.

[6] Harding, above n 2, chs 1, 2.

[7] J Saravanamuttu, 'Act of Betrayal: The Snuffing Out of Local Democracy in Malaysia', *Aliran Monthly* 2000, available at <http://aliran.com/archives/monthly/2000/04h.html>.

to an even more unwieldy 373, in five different categories, by 1973. With implementation of this legislation during 1973–88, and an equivalent exercise in Sabah and Sarawak (which joined the Federation in 1963), the total number of local authorities in the whole of Malaysia was eventually reduced to 138 and the categories to three: municipal councils, city councils and district councils. At present there are 151 local authorities, of which 39 are municipal councils and 12 are city councils, the latter being led by a *Datuk Bandar* (mayor).[8]

The suspension of local government elections was followed by their abolition: despite assurances that they would be reinstated, section 15 of the Local Government Act 1976 stated that all provisions relating to local government elections ceased to have effect. Oddly, the Local Government Elections Act 1960 was not repealed and remains in force, subject to section 15. When two State governments asked the Election Commission to hold local government elections in their States in 2010, the Commission replied that this was impossible in view of section 15, and in view of Article 95A of the Constitution, which gives the National Local Government Council (NLGC) power to formulate policy for local government nationally. In the Election Commission's view, permission would be required from the NLGC before local government elections could be held. This seems incorrect. The constitutional position is disputed, but once it is clear that State governments have the power to hold local government elections, then any policy decided by the NLGC would be subject to the exercise of that power. In other words, State governments could hold local government elections irrespective of any NLGC policy, as it is the law, not policy, that governs.

LOCAL GOVERNMENT IN CONTEMPORARY MALAYSIA

Currently more than two-thirds of Malaysians live in urban areas, and these correspond to Malaysia's 'local government areas', that is, those areas that have local authorities as defined by the Local Government Act. Rural areas are under the authority of district councils, which are still administered with respect to local functions by the colonial system of District Officers, who are appointed by, and are responsible to, either the State government or the federal Government, depending on the State in which the authority lies. The District Officers are Presidents of the district councils, which are advised by various committees of specialists. The districts have never had representative local government; indeed they are not even regarded as being part of the system of local government as such under the Local Government Act. Nonetheless, they perform the same functions as municipal and city councils.

[8] For full information on these, see <www.lawyerment.com/guide/gov/Local_Authorities/>.

Local government is the lowest level of Malaysia's multi-layered system of government, employing only 7 per cent of public employees. The public sector as a whole is, however, bloated, with 4.68 per cent of all employees being in the public service, compared, for example, with Singapore's 1.4 per cent. This is not denied but rather defended by the Government, which sees the public service as a provider of jobs.[9] Nonetheless, local government functions, such as development control, public housing, parks and public places, and control of public nuisances, are an extremely important aspect of urban living and the environment. Citizens are demanding more and better local government services.[10]

Local councils consist of between eight and 24 persons, and are appointed by the State governments from amongst prominent citizens resident in the locality.[11] They therefore tend to reflect the interests of the party or coalition in power at the State level. With regard to Kuala Lumpur itself, since it is a Federal Territory, the *Datuk Bandar* is appointed by the Federal Government for a period of five years, and the *Dewan Bandar Kuala Lumpur* (Kuala Lumpur City Council) is placed under the Prime Minister's Department.[12] The NLGC, comprising federal and State appointees and set up under Article 95A of the Constitution, coordinates policy for the 'promotion, development and control of local government' and the administration of local government law. This does not apply to Sabah or Sarawak, which nonetheless send observers to NLGC meetings.

Local authorities derive their revenue from rents, fees for services and licences (about 32 per cent); from State governments and the federal Government by fiscal transfers, for example for road maintenance or development projects (about 17 per cent); and from local taxation in the form of property assessments or the equivalent (about 51 per cent). Fiscal transfers in the form of equalisation grants are made to local authorities by the federal Government, but in general, according to statistics of the Ministry of Housing and Local Government, these represent only about 10 per cent of the shortfall in revenue against local authorities' assessed needs.[13] Local authorities are also empowered to borrow money from State governments and the federal Government, and from financial institutions.

[9] 'Putrajaya defends bloated civil service, says providing jobs', *Malay Mail Online*, 18 November 2013, available at <www.themalaymailonline.com/malaysia/article/putrajaya-defends-bloated-civil-service-says-providing-jobs>.

[10] Hazman Shah Abdullah and Maniam Kalianan, 'From customer satisfaction to citizen satisfaction: Rethinking local government service delivery in Malaysia' (2008) 4(11) *Asian Social Science* 87; Goh Ban Lee, 'The demise of local government elections and urban politics' in M Puthucheary and Norani Othman (eds), *Elections and Democracy in Malaysia* (Bangi, UKM Press, 2005).

[11] Local Government Act 1976, ss 3, 13.

[12] Federal Capital Act 1960, rev 1970, ss 4, 7.

[13] UNESCAP, 'Country Paper: Malaysia', in *Local Government in Asia and the Pacific: A Comparative Study* (Bangkok, United Nations Economic and Social Commission for Asia and the Pacific, 1999).

The result of the lack of adequate resourcing has been an understandable emphasis on maintaining services rather than on development and response to changing needs. Little has been done to improve the provision of services at similar or lower cost by privatising local government services.[14] There is consequently a deficit in effective enforcement of relevant laws, authorities seemingly unable in many ways to utilise their powers in full. One particular but eminently solveable problem is that, since local government employees do not form part of the public service as such but are simply employees of the local authority in question, they cannot be transferred to other local authorities. Thus meritorious employees can get stuck at middle levels of promotion for years, there being few opportunities for advancement, and may leave the service for positions with better prospects elsewhere; mediocre employees, on the other hand, tend to remain where they are.[15] Given the bloated public sector, little imagination is required to see how local government could be invigorated by increased numbers and increased professionalism of local government employees.

Another problem with the local government system is its secrecy. In February 2006, even a federal minister was moved to call local-government authorities 'secret societies' because of

> the lack of transparency and accountability, highlighted by public concern over mismanagement, wastage of public funds on overseas junkets under the pretext of study tours, approvals for deforestation of land causing untold damage to the environment, lack of enforcement, bribery and corruption in local townships.[16]

Even though the meetings of local authorities are open to public scrutiny, they have the option to make the minutes secret. Committee meetings are even more inaccessible, because there is a presumption of secrecy.[17] A study of public participation in the preparation of Petaling Jaya's Structure Plan in 1996 revealed that even during a process of statutory public consultation, so little information was actually released that it was difficult for the public to produce strong and constructive criticism.[18] The lack of a substantive legal right to demand information and the existence of laws that actually limit access to information are serious concerns in the local government, and

[14] Ahmad Tory Hussain and Malike Brahim, 'Administrative Modernisation in the Malaysian Local Government: A Study in Promoting Efficiency, Effectiveness and Productivity' (2006) 14(1) *Pertanika Journal of Social Sciences and Humanities* 51.

[15] UNESCAP, above n 14.

[16] Cited in PG Lim, 'Elected Government Should be Considered Again by Malaysia', *City Mayor Politics*, 20 February 2006, available at <www.citymayors.com/politics/malaysia_locdem.html>.

[17] LGA, ss 23, 27.

[18] AJ Harding and Azmi Sharom, 'Access to Environmental Justice in Malaysia (Kuala Lumpur)' in AJ Harding (ed), *Access to Environmental Justice: A Comparative Study* (Leiden, Martinus Nijhoff, 2007) ch 5; see also Ainul Jaria Maidin, 'Access to public participation in the land planning and environmental decision-making process in Malaysia' (2011) 1(3) *International Journal of Humanities and Social Sciences* 148.

indeed other, contexts. Reform of planning law is also an important issue, and it is local authorities that are responsible for development control.[19]

Without either elections or access to information regarding local authority decision-making, it is extremely difficult for members of the public to determine whether local authorities are acting in the public interest. Since many urban concerns (particularly public nuisances and planning issues, but also the provision of environmental services) are under the control of local government, the State governments' attitude towards local government becomes an important factor. The absence of electoral or any form of accountability, and the general fiscal weakness of local authorities, indicate that the State governments have generally regarded local authorities as minor instruments of policy rather than as the dynamic and autonomous development agencies they could be. This assumption is now challenged by the new politics of popular participation, in which Malaysian citizens have increasingly demanded the rights of citizenship—the vote, free expression and control over their own affairs.[20] It is for this reason that the issue of local government elections is answered by the opposed views set out at the start of this chapter.

The current position, namely the malaise of local government, is disappointing when it is considered that the suspension of local elections was implemented initially only because of the Indonesian confrontation with Malaysia in 1964–65: the Royal Commission had actually recommended not only the retention of local government elections, but also their extension to all (that is rural as well as urban) local government areas.

In view of enormous changes socially, economically and politically since the 1960s, one would have thought the case for reinstatement of local government elections to be overwhelming; and indeed the case for restoring them has never actually fallen silent. The urban electorate is now highly educated and cosmopolitan. It is also highly critical of the federal Government, which may explain the reluctance at the federal level to return to elected local government. The experience of local democracy even in the 1950s and 1960s indicates that control of local authorities would probably tend to fall to opposition parties, whose support tends to be concentrated in urban areas, which, as we have seen, are local government areas under the Local Government Act 1976.[21]

It seems that government has not considered that local politics might act as a safety valve, releasing tension in national politics. The prevailing discourse

[19] A Harding, 'Planning, environment and development: A comparison of planning law in Malaysia and England' (2003) 5(4) *Environmental Law Review* 231.

[20] See, eg, the Bersih movement for free and fair elections, at <www.bersih.org/>.

[21] Eg, in the 1962 local council elections in Perak, an opposition party, PPP, won 57% of the votes and 112 of the 150 seats contested in the Kinta District, even though the *Barisan Nasional* had won the federal election by a large margin: see Saravanamuttu, above n 8.

seems to be that it would intensify this tension,[22] and yet it is hard to see why—the opportunity to control State governments has not had this effect. In any event, the lack of accountability ensuing from the lack of elections is significant. For example, even now, most local authorities do not produce annual public financial accounts or activity reports. The conclusion of Tennant as long ago as 1973, that 'elective local government was a late colonial intrusion which did not flourish in the Malaysian political system',[23] seems as apposite now as it was 40 years ago; but perhaps not for much longer.

Now that, following the 2008 elections, some States are controlled by opposition parties, those States wish to reinstate local elections; since the Local Government Act 1976 abolished local government elections, the only recourse, other than raising the issue with the NLGC with a view to national legislation, is to have the law clarified in favour of State power to implement local government elections, or to find a way round the law. These possibilities are discussed in the next section. Interestingly enough, a study in 2000 indicated that 72 per cent of voters favoured a return to elected local authorities.[24] There is therefore much political capital to be gained from furthering this issue.

THE PROSPECTS FOR RESTORING LOCAL GOVERNMENT ELECTIONS

What, then, are the prospects for restoring local government elections?

If the politics of local government elections are not a sufficient disincentive for those seeking to restore them, the legalities make matters even more problematic. Do State governments actually have the power to reintroduce them?

The difficulty, as we have seen, is that federal statute law prohibits local government elections being held. But the matter is not so simple. Does the federal parliament have the power to prohibit them completely? Does this prohibition not cut against the autonomy of States and their powers over local government, which are secured by the Constitution? This issue was tested in a case brought to the Federal Court by the Penang government and a Penang resident, and decided in August 2014.[25]

In an attempt to hold local government elections in Penang, the State government secured the enactment by the State Legislative Assembly of the Local Government Elections (Penang Island and Province Wellesley) Enactment 2012.[26] It asked the Court for declarations that would have in effect

[22] 'Local polls may lead to May 13, Hadi warns DAP', *Malaysiakini*, 23 January 2015.
[23] Tennant, above n 6, 365.
[24] ibid.
[25] Above, n 4.
[26] Enactment 17, w.e.f. 28 March 2013.

compelled the National Elections Commission to hold elections in Penang under the 2012 Enactment. The State government argued that the federal parliament had no power to abolish local government elections under the Local Government Act 1976, which abolition had been effected by section 15 of that Act, since this was a State function under the Constitution. The 2012 Enactment was passed following the exemption of two local government areas, comprising the whole of the State of Penang, from the operation of section 15, and on this basis the State government had (unsuccessfully) petitioned the National Election Commission to conduct local government elections in the two areas in question. The exemption was based on section 1(4) of the Local Government Act 1976, which allows a State government to exempt 'any area within any local authority area' from the operation of any provision of the Act.

The Federal Court held that the 2012 Enactment was constitutionally invalid as being contrary to federal law (the Local Government Act 1976).[27] The State government had also not consulted the NLGC before legislating on local government (construed by the Court as including local government elections), as required by the federal Constitution.[28] The Court set some store by the fact that the federal Constitution, at Article 76(4), allows the federal parliament to legislate with respect to any matter falling under the State List 'for the purpose of securing uniformity of law and policy', and that the NLGC had taken a policy decision to abolish local government elections; the exemption of local government areas by the State government 'would be contrary to the national policy of suspending local government elections'.[29] The decision leaves the issues not finally nor satisfactorily resolved.

First, the exemption of the two local government areas is certainly contrary to national policy as paid down by the NLGC, but it is not explained by the Federal Court why 'policy' should in law have an overriding effect with respect to an executive decision apparently made under a power explicitly granted to the State government by the Local Government Act itself. The 2012 Enactment could only be contrary to the 1976 Act if the exemption of the two local government areas were invalid.

Secondly, while it is true that the State government should have consulted the NLGC, it seems clear that the latter would have rejected a proposal to pass legislation allowing the holding of local government elections. If this result were now achieved with regard to another proposal following the Court's decision, what would be constitutional position be? Would the requirement of consultation have been complied with, or would the consent of the NLGC in effect be required before further action could be taken.

[27] Federal Constitution, art 75.
[28] Art 95A.
[29] Above, n 4, at 880.

Thirdly, the Court left undecided the question whether, as the federal Government argued, an exemption could include the *whole (as opposed to part)* of a local government area, or the whole of two areas comprising the entire jurisdiction of the State. On the analogy of emergency laws, one would imagine it irresistible that 'any area' could include all areas, rendering a total exemption of the State from the prohibition of local elections quite possible in law.

At the time of writing, it remains unclear how this issue will be resolved. The immediate response of the Penang government was that the decision would be respected, and the only solution would be a change in the federal Government. However, in order to hold local government elections, the cooperation of the Election Commission would be required. The Commission considers, reasonably, that it is not empowered to grant such cooperation without a change in the law. Such change is unlikely to occur without a complete change of national policy. One might conclude here that this issue remains unresolved, but is ultimately a test not just of the possibility of local self-government, but also of the existence of State autonomy. The issue of local government elections speaks to the nature of democracy, as well as to the nature of the federal structure.

As academic Dr Goh Ban Lee has written:

> Generally, the decision to hold local government elections should not be a matter of decisions by lawyers and judges. In a democratic society, the peoples' right to vote for their representatives even in the third tier of government, should be the intrinsic right of taxpayers.[30]

Indeed, the Penang resident who joined the State government's petition in the case just discussed, based his position squarely on the right to vote, his point being that councillors spend revenues raised at the local government level but are not accountable in any way to the electorate. This point did not succeed in law, given that the right to vote under the federal Constitution (Article 119) relates only to the federal and State legislatures; but politically it amounts to a convincing argument: 'No taxation without representation.'

One view of this, not necessarily endorsed by the State government of Selangor but expressed in a paper prepared for that government by authors who include prominent legal practitioner Andrew Khoo, holds that elections can be held anyway, irrespective of the legalities we have discussed.[31] This view may well have been decisively refuted by the Federal Court. The argument proceeds in this way. The State government has power to appoint

[30] Goh Ban Lee, 'Push for local elections', *The Sun Daily*, 30 December 2013, available at <www.thesundaily.my/news/917265>.

[31] A Khoo, Wong Chin Huat and Maria Chin Abdullah, *An advocacy paper: Bring back local government elections*, Coalition for Good Governance, commissioned by the Selangor State Government, June 2009, available at <http://empowermalaysia.org/pdf/resources(research)/Bring%20Back%20Local%20Government%20Elections.pdf>.

members of local authorities. As with other statutory powers, there is nothing to prevent the State government from consulting the people in what is carefully termed a 'people-oriented selection process'. What better way to do this than by asking registered voters to express their preferences via an election-like process, using electoral rolls and wards already in place? Attractive as this argument seems, it perhaps falls at the point where existing electoral apparatus and processes are proposed to be used, because statute law, as we have seen, gives this task to the Election Commission. This probably means that the State government would be acting unlawfully, not by consulting the people, but by using the apparatus of an election to do so.

Nonetheless, some steps in this general direction have been made, on the assumption, it seems, that what is not clearly or expressly prohibited in law is permissible. In Perak, briefly under *Pakatan Rakayat* control in 2008–09, 817 Malay village heads were elected—only to be sacked immediately following a change of the State government to *Barisan Nasional* control in 2009. In Selangor, elections were held in 2011 for the heads of three Chinese model villages. The State government also proposed the election of 30 per cent of local councillors in 2011. This was not carried through, but the State government, in retiring 50 per cent of existing councillors, has reserved 30 per cent of the positions for women and 25 per cent for non-governmental organisations (NGOs), also placing a two-term limit on councillors.[32] In Penang, mock local government elections were held at Penang Forum 3, a public forum, in which 10 candidates were chosen; but the State government appointed only two of these candidates to local government authorities. In the same State, elections were held for mosque committee members in 2013, a form of local democracy that was also adopted by Selangor in 2009, which also extended the process to *surau* (prayer hall) committees.[33] An NGO even seized the initiative in public accountability of local authorities by inventing a mobile phone application as part of its 'MyCleanCity' program, designed to help citizens report local problems.[34]

However, during 2014 the Selangor State government was consumed by a constitutional crisis, caused by a split in the main ruling party in Selangor (PKR).[35] This resulted in the replacement of the *Menteri Besar*

[32] 'Move to retire 50% of Selangor's local councillors', *The Malaysian Reserve*, 25 July 2013, available at <http://themalaysianreserve.com/main/news/corporate-malaysia/4231-move-to-retire-50-of-selangors-local-councillors>. Currently councillors are appointed from lists provided by parties and NGOs. The two-term limit is criticised on the basis that since terms are only two years long, good councillors cannot be retained: Goh Ban Lee, 'Pick councillors on time', *The Sun Daily*, 24 February 2014, available at <www.thesundaily.my/node/242257>.

[33] Yeoh, above n 1, at 14.

[34] 'MyCleanCity app will only work if local councils embrace change, says columnist', *The Malaysian Insider*, 10 January 2015.

[35] 'Selangor MB crisis: Palace sends out letter appointing Azmin', *The Star*, 22 September 2014, available at <www.thestar.com.my/News/Nation/2014/09/22/Selangor-MB-crisis-palace-sends-out-lettter-appointing-azmin/>.

(Chief Minister), which has at least set back the process of democratising local government, or else caused its abandonment. Faced with the possibility of a strong *Barisan Nasional* challenge in that State, it seems likely that the *Pakatan Rakayat* government will not wish to provide an opportunity for the *Barisan Nasional* to restrict its powers by winning local elections.

CONCLUSION

This chapter focuses on debates on and the possible future of local government elections in Malaysia, rather than on more general questions of central-local relations relating to federal issues. Clearly, however, federal issues are implicated in these debates. There is a palpable sense that in many ways Malaysian society itself is outgrowing the authoritarian state, and is impatient for more transparency, more accountability, more participation, and more efficiency and effectiveness in the delivery of services by government at all levels. The issue of local government elections, as has been argued and illustrated here, cannot be separated from the political polarisation that has been apparent since 1997 and has grown significantly since the general election of 2008. An agreed and principled position on a return to local government elections seems impossible when the governing *Barisan Nasional* is completely against them and the *Pakatan Rakyat* is completely for them. It may well be argued that one should be sceptical about this issue, and that both positions, for and against local government elections, suit the political interests of those holding them. For now the *Pakatan Rakyat* can expect to gain in local government elections, whereas the *Barisan Nasional* can expect to lose. But this calculation also entails that the entrenched positions indicated here may change over time. For example, resistance to local government elections may ultimately work to the disadvantage of the *Barisan Nasional*, given that most Malaysians apparently favour a return to such elections; and the *Pakatan Rakyat* faces the prospect of elected local councillors, who will not by any means all support it politically, opposing measures of the State governments under *Pakatan Rakyat* control.

We cannot predict what the attitude of voters will be in the long term, and whether they would reward the *Pakatan Rakyat* for its democratic reforms or simply use local government elections as a basis to make further demands. We also cannot tell whether a return to local government elections would take place across the whole of Malaysia, or only in *Pakatan Rakyat*-controlled States. Political polarisation may not militate in favour of the kind of administrative cooperation between governments at different levels that is required to improve services, although the federal Government appears to have no significant administrative difficulties cohabiting with opposition-controlled State governments. Experimentation with cohabitation between the federal Government and State governments in different hands seems indeed an inevitable pre-condition to moving to a third level of elected government.

The larger lesson to be drawn from all this is that local democracy appears to be an event on the horizon, irrespective of the legalities of reintroducing local government elections. Citizens seem determined to seize back power by demanding accountability and transparency, by demanding to be able to vote for their councillors and by, where necessary, protesting in large numbers against undemocratic electoral practices, as with the Bersih protests for free and fair elections that took place in 2007 and 2011. In the context of local democracy this inevitably means that even without, or pending, a return to local government elections, new ways are being found to consult the public, and to respond to their needs and their views. An example of this is the renovation of two heritage-site markets in Penang in 2011–12. The Malaysian Heritage Trust was engaged by the local authority to consult the public and vendors in vernacular language, to ascertain their views on the development and preservation of the markets. The report they produced was acted upon by the State government, and the consultation is widely seen as a model for future public consultations.[36]

Thus the redefinition of central-local relations in Malaysia seems inevitably to be leading towards a more open and more democratic form of constitutional ordering, in which local self-government will play a new and potentially creative role, as State government is already doing at a higher level. Ultimately, the issue of local government elections is a test of the reality of federalism within a structure that has been seen until recently either as quasi-federal, or as representing a highly centralised form of federalism.

FURTHER READING

A Harding, *The Malaysian Constitution: A Contextual Analysis* (Oxford, Hart Publishing, 2012).

Ahmad Tory Hussain, *Kerajaan Tempatan: Teori dan Peranan di Malaysia* (Kuala Lumpur, Dewan Bahasa dan Pustaka, 1997) (in Bahasa Melayu).

MW Norris, *Local Government in Peninsular Malaysia* (Farnborough, Gower, 1980).

T Yeoh, *States of Reform: Governing Selangor and Penang* (Penang, Penang Institute, 2012).

[36] 'On the pulse of market folk surveys to gauge what the community wants to see', *The Star*, 19 March 2011, available at <www.thestar.com.my/story/?file=%2F2011%2F3%2F19%2Fnorth%2F8300260&sec=north>.

Index

www.ingramcontent.com/pod-product-compliance
Lightning Source LLC
LaVergne TN
LVHW022038200926
848481LV00003B/715

9781509921072